16.20

THE PIANO MAKERS

DAVID WAINWRIGHT

The Piano Makers

HUTCHINSON OF LONDON

HUTCHINSON & CO (Publishers) LTD
3 Fitzroy Square, London W1

London Melbourne Sydney Auckland
Wellington Johannesburg Cape Town
and agencies throughout the world

First published 1975
© Piano Publicity Association Ltd 1975

For E.H.
con amore

Set in Monotype Baskerville
Printed in Great Britain by The Anchor Press Ltd
and bound by Wm Brendon & Son Ltd
both of Tiptree, Essex

ISBN 0 09 122950 2

Contents

	Preface	11
	Acknowledgements	13
1	The First Experiments	15
2	Selling the Idea	40
3	The Virtuoso Arrives	60
4	The Domestic Instrument	83
5	The Exhibited Definition	96
6	A Foreign Threat	119
7	Survival of the Fittest	140
8	Challenge of Electronics	153
9	Post-war Rationalization	163
10	A New Confidence	168
	Bibliography	182
	Discography	183
	Index	185

List of Illustrations

'The Singing Mouse', an etching by George Cruikshank, 1847.
Peter Jackson Collection. Page 59

Between pages 48 and 49

1 'Piano e forte' by Bartolomeo Cristofori of Florence. Metropolitan Museum of Art, New York
2 John Broadwood (1732–1812). John Broadwood and Sons Limited
3 Cipriani Potter (1792–1871). Royal Academy of Music
4, 5 William Crotch (1775–1847). Royal Academy of Music
6 William Sterndale Bennett (1816–1875). Royal Academy of Music
7 Square piano forte by Johann Christoph Zumpe, London, 1767. Victoria and Albert Museum
8 Square piano forte by George Astor and Company, London, 1790. Robert Morley and Company
9 Burkat Shudi the harpischord maker and his family, about 1744. John Broadwood and Sons Limited
10 Square piano forte by Clementi and Company, London, 1810. Robert Morley and Company
11 Square piano forte by John Broadwood and Sons, London, 1820. Robert Morley and Company
12 Grand pianoforte by Erard of Paris, about 1810. Robert Morley and Company
13 Grand forte piano by John Broadwood and Sons, London, 1815. Robert Morley and Company
14 Grand forte piano by Clementi and Company, London, about 1815. Robert Morley and Company
15 Piccolo upright piano by Wornum and Wilkinson, London, 1818. Robert Morley and Company

16 Grand pianoforte by William Stodart, London, 1835. Robert Morley and Company

17 Pocket grand piano by Robert Wornum, London, 1840. Robert Morley and Company

18 Design for an upright piano in the Gothic style. Victoria and Albert Museum and Michael I. Wilson

19 Upright grand piano by Henry Morley, London, 1850. Robert Morley and Company

Between pages 80 and 81

20 Upright piano by Lambert of London, 1851. British Piano Museum and Frank W. Holland, F.I.M.I.T.

21 Plan of the original Steinway overstrung grand. Steinway and Company

22 The down-striking Robert Wornum grand, 1868–9. Victoria and Albert Museum and Michael I. Wilson

23 The Priestly three-foot-high upright. Victoria and Albert Museum

24 An inlaid upright of the 1860s by Collard and Collard. Victoria and Albert Museum

25 The 'Empress Eugénie' Bosendorfer grand piano. Piano Publicity Association

26 Detail of the 'Empress Eugénie' grand. Piano Publicity Association

27 The Byzantine Broadwood grand, designed in 1878. The Victoria and Albert Museum and Michael I. Wilson

28 Giraffe piano by Van der Hoef, Amsterdam, about 1810

29 Three types of case for the upright piano of the early twentieth century. John Broadwood and Sons Limited

30 Broadwood grand designed by Edwin Lutyens, 1901. John Broadwood and Sons Limited

31 Jacob Blüthner with his British agents W. J. Whelpdale and W. M. Y. Maxwell, about 1890. Whelpdale, Maxwell and Codd Limited

32 Arthur M. Whelpdale, head of Whelpdale and Maxwell. Whelpdale, Maxwell and Codd Limited

33 Ignacy Jan Paderewski (1860–1941). Steinway and Company

Between pages 112 and 113

34 The Broadwood solid-tyre delivery lorry. John Broadwood and Sons Limited

35 Preparing aircraft fuselages for despatch from the Broadwood piano factory during the 1914–18 war. John Broadwood and Sons Limited

36–42 A selection of photographs from the Broadwood album, showing the Broadwood factory, 1903. John Broadwood and Sons Limited

43–45 Apprentices at the London County Council piano course at Bethnal Street, about 1910. Greater London Council

46 Preparing to cast the iron frame of a grand piano at the Booth and Brookes foundry. *Maldon and Burnham Standard*

47 The finished cast frame of a grand piano. *Maldon and Burnham Standard*

48–55 Eight stages in the manufacture of a modern piano. Piano Publicity Association

56 The Knight upright piano

Between pages 144 and 145

57 'The piano thumpers' – a sing-song round the family piano, about 1908. Radio Times Hulton Picture Library

58 The Steinway Duo-Art reproducing piano of the 1920s. Steinway and Company

59 Mantovani playing the Eavestaff Minipiano, 1935. W. G. Eavestaff and Sons

60 The Eavestaff Minigrand, 1935. W. G. Eavestaff and Sons

61 The Kemble overstrung 'Minx', 1936. The Kemble Piano Company

62 The Kemble 'Olympia', about 1936. The Kemble Piano Company

63 The Kemble modern 'Cubist' upright, 1936. The Kemble Piano Company

64 A contemporary newspaper advertisement for the Challen 'baby grand' of the 1930s. Piano Publicity Association

65–71 Fifteen representative pianos made by the principal British manufacturers. Piano Publicity Association

72 Michael Kemble, co-founder of Kemble and Company

73 Victor Jacobs, co-founder of Kemble and Company

74 Denzil Jacobs, chairman of Kemble and Company

75 Robert Kemble, director of Kemble and Company

76 Jack Codd, of Whelpdale, Maxwell and Codd

77 Captain Evelyn Broadwood MC, chairman of John Broadwood and Sons.

78 William Danemann, founder of W. Danemann and Company
79 Edgar and Tom Danemann, directors of W. Danemann and Company and sons of the founder, with the new generation in the company, Jacqui and Timothy Danemann.
80 William Shepherd Watts, director of Monington and Weston
81 Bernard Watts, director of Monington and Weston
82 John Morley, director of Robert Morley and Company
83 Alfred Knight, o.b.e., founder of the Knight Piano Company
84 William Evans, c.b.e., creator of the successful Challen baby grand
85 H. Tom Hicks, of Henry Hicks and Company
86 Frederick Saffell, chairman of Barratt and Robinson
87 Gerald Brasted, m.b.e., of Brasted Brothers and W. G. Eavestaff and Sons
88 Douglas Brasted, of Brasted Brothers and W. G. Eavestaff and Sons
89 Stanley Murdoch, of Murdoch and Murdoch
90 Richard Grover with his son David Grover and the portrait of his father Douglas Grover, founder of the Bentley Piano Company
91 Herbert Lowry, director of George Rogers and Son
92 Ivan Zender, director of Sydney Zender

Preface

A musical instrument is a tribute to its maker, as well as an illumination of the interpreter who plays upon it. The piano is a construction in which skill and craftsmanship march together with technology. This book is about the craftsmen who have made and are still making pianos; how this instrument came to be created and developed; and how it has survived the emergence of more modern forms of domestic and public entertainment to sustain its present popularity.

The idea of this book came from the Piano Publicity Association. This volume owes any virtue it may possess to Stanley Murdoch, whose great experience of piano making in Britain has been generously placed at my disposal.

The piano industry in Britain, as this book records, has endured misfortune as well as success. But today the piano makers are busy, and for that reason I record my thanks to those who gave up their time to answer my questions – particularly Gerald Brasted, Captain Evelyn Broadwood, M.C., Stuart Broadwood, Jack Codd, Richard Grover, M.B.E., J.P., H. Tom Hicks, Denzil Jacobs, Alfred Knight, O.B.E., Douglas Morley, John Morley, Frederick Saffell, John H. Steinway, Leonard Squibb, and Mrs Sylvia York.

Acknowledgements

For permission to quote I am grateful to the following, with apologies for any omissions: the Chappell Piano Company Limited for *The Chappell Story* by Carlene Mair; Henry Marcy Collard, Esq., for *A Short History of a Great House – Collard and Collard*, by Edward Lamburn; Michael Freedland for *Irving Berlin* (W. H. Allen); Arthur Loesser, Simon and Schuster Inc. and Victor Gollancz Limited for *Men, Women and Pianos* by Arthur Loesser; Madame Irena Sydow and William Heinemann Limited for *The Selected Correspondence of Fryderyk Chopin* by B. E. Sydow, translated and edited by Arthur Hedley (William Heinemann); Ivor Newton, C.B.E., for *At the Piano – Ivor Newton* (Hamish Hamilton); Oxford University Press for *Walford Davies* by H. C. Colles; Patrick Piggott and Faber and Faber Limited for *John Field*; Mrs Gilbert Russell and Faber and Faber Limited for *The Harpsichord and Clavichord* by Raymond Russell; John H. Steinway for *People and Pianos* by Theodore E. Steinway; and the Victoria and Albert Museum and Michael I. Wilson for 'The Case of the Victorian Piano', an article in the *Victoria and Albert Museum Year Book*, 1972.

Much useful information on the later period was cheerfully excavated for me by Mrs Elizabeth Stevenson; and David Rule loyally pursued the piano makers through many dusty directories. I am also grateful for information, anecdotes and assistance to Sir Anthony Lewis, C. F. Colt, Ivor Newton, C.B.E., James Toone, Fred Turner, David Rodrick, and Michael I. Wilson.

The London Library has, as always, been a fruitful source. Finally, I thank Mrs Mary Baxter for her patience and kindness during the composition of these variations upon a theme.

London 1974   D.W.

I

The First Experiments

In 1780 when William Gardiner of Leicester was ten years old his mother bought him 'a piano-forte, not much bigger than two writing-desks put together'. It was therefore a small instrument, not more than three feet long, and a rarity: Gardiner believed that there were only two or three of them in that town at the time. The only keyboard instruments used for concerts were the chamber organ or harpsichord. At home, the delicate clavichord was the favourite.

When the infant prodigy William Crotch visited Leicester in 1782 he was taken to the Gardiners' house where 'being then not more than five years old, he played upon the piano-forte as he sat upon his mother's knee'. The instrument was, like the clavichord, too soft and quiet for the concert-hall: Crotch played the organ and violin at his public concerts.

The Gardiners were enthusiastic amateur musicians. The father, a wealthy hosiery manufacturer, played the 'cello and flute. On Sundays 'everyone that had a voice, and could lend a hand with hautboy, bassoon or flute repaired to the singing-loft of the church', where the orchestra was still battling for survival against the newly installed organ (the Snetzler organ was put into St Martin's Church, Leicester, in 1774). Young William's boyish ear was also attracted to the military bands that marched through the streets, with their clarinets and drums.

Having been given a pianoforte, because his parents were outraged by the inaccuracy of his violin practising, William had to teach himself to play it. 'As we had no masters in Leicester, I was obliged to hammer by myself, and bad as it was, I might call it celestial music compared to my fiddling.' The piano was 'esteemed a good one, made by John Pohlman, I suppose in Germany, and before any were made in England'.

William Gardiner wrote his memoirs later in life. His idea that his first pianoforte was made in Germany was probably wrong, for by 1780 the German-born Johannes Pohlmann had been settled in London for twenty years and had been making his pianos in England for most of that time.

Gardiner's life spanned the development of the piano. In middle age he summed up its influence. 'The invention of the piano-forte has formed a most important era in the musical art,' he wrote. 'No instrument has contributed so much to the improvement of science, or so much displayed the beauties of taste and expression.' In one man's lifetime the piano had developed from a rare toy to become a principal instrument, fit both for the concert-hall and the drawing-room.

The young prodigy pianist William Crotch survived his boyhood exposure on concert-tours round the country as 'the English Mozart'. The son of a Norwich carpenter, he must in fact have been six or seven when Gardiner heard him play in Leicester (it was the custom in that century of prodigies to take a year or two off their ages to impress the public). At eleven he was pupil-assistant to the organist of King's and Trinity Colleges, Cambridge, and at fifteen organist of Christ Church, Oxford. At twenty-two he became Professor of Music in the University, and subsequently first Principal of the Royal Academy of Music, London. Two portraits of him, when young, hang in the Duke's Hall at the Academy (see plates 4 and 5).

One shows him at about the age of three, a winsome chubby child in a white dress and blue sash, seated at a two-manual organ console. In the second picture he is eight or nine, auburn hair flowing romantically. He is dressed in a coffee-coloured suit with a broad lace collar, and his face is understandably hard, knowing and adult. But unlike many other prodigies he enjoyed a long and successful life, composing a quantity of predominantly church music and dying much respected at the age of seventy-two.

For centuries men have found pleasure in making musical sounds. Even the most primitive tribes devised instruments using some or all of the three basic principles – percussion, wind or string. The simple drum sending messages across tracts of jungle was known

to the earliest men. The wind principle, the vibration of a column
of air inside a pipe, could have been discovered by a hunter
making a blowpipe. The vibration of a tautened string is the most
complex, since there must be several factors in its control. How to
regulate the tautness of the string. How to add resonance to the
sound by stretching the string across a soundboard. Finally, how
to make the string vibrate, by plucking with a finger or plectrum
(the guitar, harpsichord or harp), by stroking with a bow (the
violin family), or by hitting with a hammer (the dulcimer and
piano).

As early as 2650 B.C. the Chinese had devised an instrument
with fifty silk strings strung across a box five feet long. In 582 B.C.
Pythagoras used a monochord – a single-string guitar – for experiments into the mathematical relationships of musical sounds.
About A.D. 100 Guido of Arezzo is said to have invented the
movable bridge, which produced more correct intonation. All
these instruments were plucked by hand.

The keyboard was devised as a method of giving greater control
over that most mechanical of early instruments, the organ. An
organ with two manuals (keyboards) existed at Winchester
Cathedral in the tenth century A.D.; but as this instrument had
forty stops and required three men to 'play' it, the keys were
probably more like levers than the keys of a modern manual. The
first keyboards seem to have consisted of plain keys only (the
white notes). Then, as music matured from the 'Modes' and a
need was felt to provide an intermediary note between A and B,
a small half-key was built in at the back of the keyboard (B flat).
Later four more intermediary notes were added (the black notes),
until by about 1450 the keyboard was established approximately
as we know it.

A keyboard stringed instrument called a Clavicytherium is
known to have been made in Italy about 1300, and later improved
by Germans who were thinking their way towards a hammer
action. The original version was evidently a small harp placed
horizontally, and plucked by quill plectra. The refined version,
with metal strings instead of catgut, used a simple type of hammer
action: the depressed key rose to touch the string with a brass
pin or tangent. From the addition of the key (the 'clavis') the
instrument became known as the clavichord. A strip of cloth was

threaded between the strings to damp or silence each note as the tangent fell from it.

In spite of its quiet tone the clavichord was capable of expression, and for five centuries remained a favourite chamber keyboard instrument. Mozart's clavichord, which he took with him on his travels and on which he composed some of his operas, is still to be seen in his birthplace in Salzburg.

However, the tone of the clavichord was too muted for it to become anything more than a solo instrument for the pleasure of the performer. It had many of the mechanical characteristics of the piano – soundboard, metal strings, the hammer action to vibrate the strings, and a damping system. But it was overshadowed by the more powerful harpsichord.

Makers were drawn to the plucking action rather than the hammer action, and experimented with various methods of achieving the most satisfactory sound. While the layout of the strings in a harp-shape, like an elongated grand piano, seems to have been set by the mid-fifteenth century, experiments were still being conducted into different types of action. A treatise written about that time by the physician to the Duke of Burgundy, Henri Arnault, describes four types of harpsichord action.

The oblong case also had its adherents. In Venice in 1503 Giovanni Spinnetti produced a four-octave instrument with an oblong case in which the strings were plucked by a quill, and then damped by a small piece of cloth attached to the jack which was raised by pressure on the key. The spinet (known in England as the virginals) became the most popular domestic instrument.

Queen Elizabeth I played the virginals. However, the name did not derive from the 'virgin queen', for the Privy Purse expenses of her father King Henry VIII contain references to 'a payer of virginalls'. Some say the name comes from the instrument's use in convents, for accompanying hymns to the Virgin. Evidently the Queen's musicality was inherited, for there are references to 'clavycords' in the account books of her grandfather King Henry VII in the early 1500s.

In that century there were nearly twenty makers of keyboard instruments in England, most of them in London. Italy was the musical leader of Europe, and Italian instruments seem to have been the most fashionable. In the Victoria and Albert Museum,

London, there is an Italian spinet of cypress wood, elaborately decorated and bearing the royal arms. This 4½-octave instrument, very like others made in Italy by Benedetto Floriani in the 1570s has traditionally been known as 'Queen Elizabeth's Virginals'.

She was not immune from the coyness that amateur musicians sometimes affect. Sir James Melville, envoy from her half-sister Mary Queen of Scots, was questioned by Queen Elizabeth about Mary.

She asked what kind of exercises she used. I answered . . . that sometimes she recreated herself in playing upon the lute and virginals. She asked if she played well. I said, reasonably for a Queen. That same day after dinner my Lord of Hunsdean drew me to a quiet gallery, that I might hear some music, (but he said that he durst not avow it) where I might hear the Queen play upon the virginals. After I had hearkened awhile, I took by the tapestry that hung before the door, I entred within the chamber, and stood a pretty space hearing her play excellently well.

But she left off immediately, so soon as she turned her about and saw me. She appeared to be surprised to see me and came forward, seeming to strike me with her hand; alledging she used not to play before men, but when she was solitary, to shun melancholy. She asked how I came there. I answered, As I was walking with my Lord of Hunsdean, as we passed by the chamber door, I heard such melody as ravished me, whereby I was drawn in ere I knew how . . . She enquired whether my Queen or she played best. In that I found myself obliged to give her the praise.

However diplomatic Melville may have felt obliged to be on that occasion, it is probable that Queen Elizabeth did indeed play well. When in after years Dr Burney examined her Virginal Book he found it full of complicated music by Byrd, Tallis, Farnaby and Bull that he said no master in Europe would undertake to play without a month's practice.

The small virginals or spinet continued in popularity for domestic use. Half a century later Samuel Pepys bought one, in 1668 from Charles Haward of Aldgate Street.

Up betimes, and by coach towards White Hall, and took Aldgate Street in my way, and there called upon one Haward, that makes virginalls, and did there like of a little espinette, and will have him finish it for me: for I had a mind to a small harpsichon, but this takes up less room, and will do my business as to finding out of chords, and I am well pleased that I have found it.

Three months later the spinet was delivered: Pepys paid £5 for it.

The Hawards and the Hitchcocks were the most prolific makers of virginals, spinets and harpsichords in the late seventeenth and early eighteenth centuries in England, and a number of their instruments survive. At Knole Park, Sevenoaks, there is a single manual harpsichord built by John Haward in 1622: from the construction it seems to have had three sets of strings, one set tuned differently from the other two (either in octaves, or fourths or fifths). Charles Haward, forty years later, made a variety of keyboard instruments in Aldgate apart from spinets such as the one he sold to Pepys.

The Hitchcock family (John, Thomas I and Thomas II) were among the makers who further developed the harpsichord, producing double-manual instruments, adding extra keys and jacks, refining the actions and eventually incorporating different stops to vary the sound. Two common stops were the lute, with a second set of jacks to pluck the string near the nut, producing a hard bright tone; and the harp or buff stop, to bring up a set of felt pads against the string, producing a muted effect.

Another maker in early eighteenth-century London was Hermann Tabel, who produced harpsichords at his house in Oxendon Street 'over against the Black Horse in Piccadily'. He is said to have been a Fleming who served his apprenticeship in the famous Ruckers workshop in Antwerp before coming to London. But though he may well have invented one notable feature of the large eighteenth-century English harpsichord, the upper manual eight-foot common to both manuals, and thus may have set the pattern for the successful double-manual harpsichords of that century, he is significant for another reason. Two of his apprentices were Burkat Shudi and Jacob Kirckman. Between them they became the best-known harpsichord makers of the eighteenth century in England; and Shudi's business was ultimately to be the foundation of the first commercial production of what is recognizably the modern pianoforte.

The changes and additions made to the harpsichord in the seventeenth and eighteenth centuries reflected the basically unsatisfactory character of that instrument in the ears of many composers. In the preface to his first book of Harpsichord Pieces, published in 1713, François Couperin wrote:

The Harpsichord is perfect as to its compass, and brilliant in itself, but as it is impossible to swell out or diminish the volume of its sound I shall always feel grateful to any who, by the exercise of infinite art supported by fine taste, contrives to render this instrument capable of expression.

Some have read this as a plea for sensitive touch in playing the harpsichord as it then existed. Others have seen in it an appeal for technical improvements that would make the instrument itself capable of expression. In either case, Couperin was certainly aware that technical innovations were being made at that time in France, Germany and Italy.

Throughout history there are plenty of accounts of men who nearly made some great intellectual breakthrough but who, by failing to visualize the final mental link in a chain of reason, or through the discouragement of their contemporaries, just fell short of the vital discovery, the development of a theory into its practical application. Many musicians in the sixteenth and seventeenth centuries recognized the limitations of the harpsichord and clavichord. A number realized that longer strings and stronger cases would be required to give the harpsichord power, and that hammers would be needed to vibrate the strings rather than the traditional plucking action. Nearly all the experimenters were makers of harpsichords and so it was natural that they based their innovations on the keyboard instrument with which they were familiar.

One did not. He was Pantaleon Hebenstreit. A German, he observed the dulcimer, then as now a basic instrument in German peasant music. The dulcimer is trapezium-shaped, not unlike the more familiar hand-plucked zither; the strings are stretched across a soundbox with two holes, and are hit by two hammers held by the performer, like a xylophone. Hebenstreit constructed an enormous dulcimer, nine feet long. He provided it with a double soundboard and 186 strings, and a keyboard controlling double-sided hammers covered with leather, one side of which was hard and the other soft, enabling the performer to play soft (piano) or loud (forte).

This extraordinary instrument and its inventor toured Europe, and when in 1705 it was played before Louis XIV of France he named it the Pantaleon. On his return to Dresden, Hebenstreit taught pupils to play the Pantaleon. But its almost insurmountable difficulty, together with the cost of construction and maintenance, discouraged all potential patrons: the Pantaleon was too complicated, too difficult and too expensive, and when Dr Burney visited Dresden a few years later he could find only the wreck of the great invention that had once captivated musical Europe.

If the Pantaleon died out with its inventor, it must have confirmed other makers who were experimenting with hammer actions that they were on the right lines, since many who heard the Pantaleon commented favourably on the satisfying effect of its sustained harmonics and resonant bass. In Italy, France and Germany harpsichord makers worked to perfect a hammer action.

The most successful was developed in Florence during the first decade of the eighteenth century by Bartolomeo Cristofori (1655–1731), keeper of musical instruments to Prince Ferdinand dei Medici. Cristofori replaced the harpsichord jacks with hammers, and invented an escapement system to enable the key to damp the string as it sprang back to its home position. In 1709 Cristofori had already made three of these instruments, and they deeply impressed a writer from Rome, Scipione Maffei, when he visited Prince Ferdinand in Florence to seek his patronage for a literary journal.

A professional journalist was thus fortunately at hand to write and publish an account of Cristofori's *Gravicembalo col piano e forte.* Maffei wrote of these instruments:

They have all succeeded to perfection. The production of more or less sound depends upon the force the player uses in pressing upon the keys, by regulating which not only are the *piano* and the *forte* heard, but also the degrees of tone, as in the violoncello . . . Instead of the jacks that produced sound by quills there is a little row of hammers that strike the string from below, the tops of which are covered with leather. Every hammer has the end inserted into a circular butt, that renders it movable; these butts are partially embedded and strung together in a receiver. Near the butt, and under the stem of the hammer, there is a projecting part or support that, receiving the blow from beneath, raises the hammer and causes it to strike the string with whatever degree of force is given by the hand of the performer; hence the sound produced can be greater or less, at the pleasure of the player.

With the publication of Maffei's enthusiastic report, many instrument makers, both professional and amateur, made haste to copy this discovery – aided by Maffei's publication of a drawing of the action.

The problem that Cristofori had successfully overcome was simply the way in which a single movement of the key could enable two distinct events to happen in sequence: first, the sounding of the string, and secondly its damping or silencing. This had been achieved in the clavichord by the strip of cloth that effectively stopped a string vibrating the moment the metal tangent was taken away from the string by lifting the finger from the key. But this would only work on an instrument as small-scale and delicate as the clavichord with its fine light stringing.

On hand-plucked instruments the player must damp the string by putting his finger on it after it has vibrated. There are two distinct movements. On the harpsichord, damping was achieved by mounting a small piece of cloth at the top of each jack (the vertical piece of wood holding the quill or leather plectrum). As the harpsichord key is depressed, the jack flies upward, plucking the string as it passes. When the key is released the weighted jack drops back and the cloth or felt at its peak comes down to silence the string.

An instrument to be struck by hammers from below the strings posed the problem of how to damp the strings as the keys were released and the hammers fell away. Cristofori worked out his solution from both the harpsichord and the clavichord. In essence he removed the strip of cloth from the clavichord, replacing it with a series of small cloth pads each linked to a single key, and pressed up to the strings by secondary jacks pivoting on levers. When the key was depressed, the damper was lowered from the string, enabling it to vibrate when struck. Simultaneously, another set of jacks actuated by the same levers threw up a small leather-covered hammer to strike the string from beneath. When the key was released, the damper pad was again lifted against the string to silence it.

The action was a great deal more complicated than the harpsichord or clavichord action, but vastly simpler and less cumbersome than the Pantaleon. It did everything that Maffei claimed for it: in particular, it enabled performers to play softly or loudly, within the limited power of the strings and the hammers. But Cristofori's action met opposition because the feel of the keyboard was wholly different from anything musicians had hitherto played (a reaction familiar to any pianist who encounters a harpsichord action for the first time). The main disadvantage of Cristofori's action was that it took a fraction of a second for each key to complete its double movement of first striking the string and then damping it: so there were complaints from harpsichordists who tried fast runs on it that the keys tended to be unresponsive and to stick.

But the Maffei report circulated widely, and in an age that was fascinated by mechanical toys of many kinds a number of people began to experiment along similar lines.

In 1711 Father Wood, an English monk living in Rome, built a pianoforte apparently based on Cristofori's design. He sold it to Samuel Crisp, a friend of Dr Johnson, and he brought it to London and eventually sold it for 100 guineas to Fulke Greville. The first 'pianoforte' to be heard in London, it caused a considerable sensation among musicians. But while it was effective in slow and resonant music (the Dead March in 'Saul' is said to have sounded well on it, particularly as such a piece could hardly be performed on the harpsichord) the action was sluggish.

Nevertheless other London makers tried to copy it, among them Rutgerus Plenius, but without real success. The difference in touch was too much for most players to achieve satisfactorily and they went back to the harpsichord. It was typical of Plenius to make the attempt, for his inventive turn of mind was constantly creating new instruments: in 1741 he had some success with the Lyrichord, a hurdy-gurdy with keys. This was played by means of a keyboard and treadle, the treadle turning a circular bow that vibrated the string when a key pressed it forward against the barrel.

Meanwhile Cristofori went on improving his *gravicembalo*, and is said to have made about twenty of them (an average of one a year) before his death in 1731. The later ones had a much stronger case to withstand the tension of the heavier strings. There was also an improved escapement device or check, so that the damper was fixed to the back end of the key itself instead of the pivoting lever, thus giving a swifter and more accurate damping effect.

Two other important experiments took place within a year or two of Cristofori's achievement. One was in Paris and the other in Dresden. In Paris, Marius submitted three types of hammer action to the Academy of Sciences in 1716, though it does not seem that any actual instrument was built on these principles.

In Dresden an eighteen-year-old pupil of the School of the Holy Cross heard the Pantaleon and, realizing its potential, invented two 'piano' actions – one with hammers below the string, one with hammers above. In 1717 this young man, Christoph Gottlieb Schroeter, persuaded a cousin who was a journeyman cabinet maker to produce a working prototype, and it was demonstrated to the court of the King of Saxony.

It was:

a double model on a long and narrow little box, which had an overall length of four feet and was six inches wide. In front and rear it had three keys. At one place the stroke upon the strings came from below, but at the other, it came from above. Both kinds were as easy to play as an ordinary clavichord. On each of the models loud or soft sounds could be brought forth in differing degrees.

The court does not seem to have been impressed by Schroeter's invention, but he was to remark bitterly in later years that other people were – that considerable band of instrument makers who adapted an action very like this for the first pianos made in Germany, whereupon the action became known as the German action.

But if young Schroeter had a good idea, it was in the workshop of Gottfried Silbermann that the idea was put into practice. Silbermann came from a family of organ builders and was himself well known as an organ builder and maker of clavichords. He lived at Freiberg, twenty-five miles from Dresden, and he contracted with Hebenstreit to maintain the original highly complicated Pantaleon. From time to time he was officially commissioned to make copies, and from time to time he made them unofficially. To prevent this infringement of his rights as an inventor, Hebenstreit obtained an injunction from the King of Saxony.

Silbermann was a renowned practical joker, evidently a lively fellow well liked by his friends. One of his friends, Koenig, translated Maffei's description of Cristofori's piano action into German. So with that to hand, and the original Pantaleon frequently in his workshop, Silberman was not short of stimuli to attempt making pianofortes on his own account. The first ones had a heavy and hard touch. Silbermann demonstrated one to Johann Sebastian Bach when the famous Leipzig musical director visited Dresden in 1736: the composer was unenthusiastic. The piano touch was certainly strange, and Bach was then over fifty and in no need of new means of self-expression.

Bach's second son, Carl Philipp Emanuel, showed more interest. He had bought a Silbermann clavichord and kept in touch with its maker. As clavier player to King Frederick of Prussia, C. P. E. Bach was better prepared to be interested in novelties. He took a Silbermann piano to Potsdam, and Frederick the Great was indeed fascinated by it – he ordered several, half a dozen or more.

By this time Silbermann (or his pupil Andreas Stein, who was later to make pianofortes for Mozart in Augsburg) had improved the action so that the hammer pivoted on a lever forming a V-shape with the key, the hammer facing the performer and the damper falling on the string from above. This gave a brisker action and a brittle tone.

Another of Silbermann's inventive pupils was C. E. Friederici, who moved fifty miles west of Freiberg to Gera, where in 1745 he built a vertical grand piano – perhaps the first 'upright'. But his contemporaries and his master Silbermann held to the traditional flat position of the strings.

When Johann Sebastian Bach visited the court at Potsdam in 1747 the King immediately showed off his new toy. This time Bach liked it better. By that time it was a better instrument than he had seen a decade earlier, and his approval may have been more than courtly discretion. According to a contemporary account:

Toward evening, at about the time that the customary chamber music in the Royal apartments usually commences, His Majesty was notified that Music Director Bach had reached Potsdam. His Highness straightway gave the command to have him come in; upon his entrance (His Majesty) went to the so-called Forte and Piano and without any preparation deigned, in His own exalted Person, to play a theme for Music Director Bach, which the latter was to work out into a fugue. This was accomplished so successfully by the aforesaid Music Director than not only was His Majesty pleased to express His own gracious approval, but all those present were moved to astonishment.

With this seal of royal and musical approbation upon it, the Silbermann 'Forte and Piano' was soon in great demand and the workmen were kept busy. Among them were Johannes Zumpe and the young Dutchman, Americus Backers. Musicians were fascinated by this square box, not unlike a clavichord to look at, but with the capability of making sounds with expression and a greater resonance than keyboard instruments had hitherto possessed.

One of these new 'square pianofortes' was bought in 1755 at Hamburg by the Rev. William Mason, a young Cambridge graduate newly ordained and travelling in Europe. He wrote to his friend Thomas Gray, the poet and amateur harpsichordist: 'Oh, Mr Gray! I bought at Hamburg such a pianoforte, and so cheap!' From his description this was a combined harpsichord and pianoforte. Mr Mason was an enthusiast, a gregarious and sociable man. He talked and wrote about his new discovery to such an extent that many people in England came to associate it, at least for a time, with him; and so the Cristofori technical developments as adopted by Silbermann, Zumpe and Pohlmann in Saxony became known here as 'Mason's action'. There is no evidence, however, that he personally made any improvements to it.

Nevertheless it was due to the enthusiastic propaganda of such amateurs as Mason that the work of the 'German piano makers' became known and admired in London, then rapidly gaining ground as one of the musical centres of Europe. Thus it was that when, by an accident of history, the piano makers of Saxony were unable to carry on in their own country, it was to London that they looked for employment.

In September 1756 the Prussian army under Frederick the Great marched into Saxony to begin what is now known as the Seven Years War. As the soldiers of Prussia, Austria, France and Russia battled to and fro across the country the fortunes of Gottfried Silbermann and his musical instrument workshop wilted and died. Communications and transport were disrupted, the potential patrons at court and among the nobility turned to music more martial than that of the pianoforte.

The Dutch workman Americus Backers was among the first to leave Freiberg, no doubt because he was a 'foreigner' in Saxony. He came to London. In 1760 more of his fellow-workmen, Silbermann's apprentices and pupils, followed him. There were a dozen of them in all, and they became known as the 'twelve apostles'. Among them were Johannes Zumpe and Johannes Pohlmann.

There were two leading makers of harpsichords in London in 1760. Both, ironically, had come to London from western Europe as young men, and both were apprenticed to the harpsichord maker Hermann Tabel in Oxendon Street. They were Burkat Shudi and Jacob Kirckman.

The elder was born Burkhardt Tschudi at Schwanden, near Glarus, Switzerland. His uncle was a joiner and on his arrival in London in 1718 at the age of sixteen the youth began an apprenticeship with Tabel. He must have set up on his own soon after completing his indentures, for a harpsichord survives dated 1729 with his name on it. By that time he had simplified his name to Shudi. Ten years later he was living in Meard Street, off Dean Street, Soho. In 1742 he moved round the corner to Great Poultney Street. Most of Shudi's harpsichords were of two types, both derived from Tabel's instruments – a single manual, and a double manual. Both types were of five octaves, some with lute and harp stops.

Clearly contacts were maintained with Europe, for in 1765 Shudi made a harpsichord for King Frederick of Prussia. The arrival of the pianoforte stirred Shudi to further exertions to devise a method of making the harpsichord sound 'soft and loud': in 1769 he patented a mechanism called the 'Venetian swell'. This consisted of an inner lid to the harpsichord containing shutters that could be opened and closed with a pedal, like an organ swell.

Jacob Kirckman, the other leading harpsichord maker in London, came from near Strasbourg and like Shudi served his apprenticeship with Tabel, whose foreman he became. It seems probable that when Tabel died in the late 1730s, Kirckman inherited his business, which he moved to 'the corner of Pulteney Court in Cambridge Street, over against Silver Street, near Golden Square'. In 1738 he married Tabel's widow.

These businesses were known throughout Europe, and their products were very highly regarded. They were expensive. A single-manual Shudi harpsichord cost between thirty-five and forty guineas in the 1770s, or fifty guineas with the 'Venetian swell'. A double-manual harpsichord with swell cost about eighty guineas. But these were products of high craftsmanship, as is illustrated by the estimate[1] that Shudi's output between 1729 to 1793 was no more than 1155 harpsichords – which would mean no more than eighteen a year.

When Johannes Zumpe came to Shudi's workshop in 1760 he brought with him the secret of the Cristofori piano action, as refined and improved by Silbermann. Zumpe had designed a simple pianoforte, and soon he began to manufacture it in London, taking premises in Hanover Square. His small oblong boxes immediately became fashionable. As they were a novelty he was able to sell them at £50 each, even though they were much cheaper and simpler to manufacture than the harpsichord. Soon Zumpe was unable to make enough 'square pianofortes' to satisfy the demand, and his compatriot and fellow 'apostle' Johannes Pohlmann also began to make them. Some of Pohlmann's instruments were slightly more complicated, with hand stops and a pedal 'swell'. It was one of the simpler Pohlmanns, 'not much bigger than two writing-desks put together', that young William Gardiner was given by his mother in Leicester in 1780.

These first English pianofortes were capable of expression, but they were no challenge to the harpsichord for concert work in their early years. Looking back with the hindsight of fifty years, Gardiner recalled that 'the wretched little piano-fortes of that day had no pretension to be introduced into a concert-room'.

But they sold. The first recorded advertisement for a piano in Britain is in 1763, when in the list of musical instrument makers

1. Raymond Russell: *The Harpsichord and Clavichord* (Faber, 1973).

in *Mortimer's Directory* is Frederic Neubaur (perhaps another 'apostle') who announces that he is selling 'harpsichords, piano-fortes, lyrichords, and claffichords'.

Soon enough they began to appear in public. On 15 May 1767 in London a certain Miss Brickler sang a song in an *entr'acte* of the *Beggar's Opera* 'accompanied by Mr Dibdin on a new instrument called the Piano Forte'.

That might have been done as a novelty. But soon the piano achieved a greater authority when the Queen's music master played one at a public concert. The music master was Johann Christian Bach, the youngest son of the great Johann Sebastian. He had arrived in London to conduct the Italian opera, then highly fashionable. He came to London from Italy, where he had been a successful opera conductor as well as organist of Milan Cathedral. It was natural that as music master to the German-born Queen Charlotte, wife of George III, J. C. Bach should use the new 'German' piano. On 2 June 1768, at one of a series of concerts given by Bach with two other visiting German musicians, Friedrich Abel (viol-da-gamba) and Johann Christian Fischer (oboe), Bach played on a Zumpe pianoforte the first known piano solo in a concert in Britain, at the Thatched House, St James's.

The effect of the popularity of the pianoforte upon the manu-facturers of harpsichords may be imagined. Shudi produced his 'Venetian swell', but it was no real answer. However, he had already taken into his business the man who was to revolutionize it.

In 1761, the year after Zumpe and Pohlmann arrived in London from Saxony and began to lay the foundations for the success of the little 'square pianoforte', Burkat Shudi took into his employment a skilled Scottish cabinet maker. He was twenty-nine, and had come to London to seek his fortune, leaving his home in the Berwickshire town of Cockburnspath at the foot of the Lammermuir Hills. His name was John Broadwood.

Broadwood proved to be an efficient craftsman, a forward-looking manager and a hard-driving businessman. In 1769 he became Shudi's son-in-law on his marriage to the harpsichord-maker's daughter Barbara: soon afterwards he was made a partner in the business. When the old man retired in 1771 (he died two years later) the firm became Shudi & Broadwood, run by John Broadwood and Burkat Shudi the younger. But by that time the Scot was the genius behind the business and soon afterwards the title was changed to John Broadwood and Sons, as it remains to this day.

When John Broadwood retired in 1811 he had transformed a small and distinguished harpsichord workshop into a large and no less famous factory making excellent pianos and exporting them all over Europe, a leader in improvement and innovation. Just how successful Broadwood was in the introduction of factory methods is demonstrated by the production figures. Shudi had made fewer than twenty harpsichords a year. Between 1782 and 1802 John Broadwood and Sons made 7000 square pianos and 1000 grand pianos, an average of 400 a year.

Broadwood came late to the piano business. His first decade with Shudi were years of study and experiment, while the rival makers, Zumpe and Pohlmann, shared the market (both amateur and professional) between them. Thomas Gray was by now playing a Zumpe piano in his Cambridge rooms: Pohlmann made a piano for the composer Gluck.

It was in 1771, the year that Shudi retired, that Broadwood launched his first square pianoforte. It was well made, and sold well in an established market. It followed the designs of Zumpe and Pohlmann, using the 'over damper'. But Broadwood was not satisfied with this action. Nor were his contemporaries, and they searched for improvements.

The Dutchman Americus Backers was still in London. Having been a fellow-pupil of Zumpe in Silbermann's workshop at Freiberg, he could trace the development of the piano action directly back to the original Cristofori invention; few men can have known more about the various developments that had taken place over half a century. Backers and Broadwood, assisted by a bright young apprentice, Robert Stodart, perfected an action that included a check on the descending hammer. One failing of the earlier pianos had been that the hammer could sometimes bounce back and hit a note for the second time. This made the touch of the keyboard stodgy and unreliable. The check ensured greater clarity of touch. The Backers/Broadwood/Stodart action, first described in a patent for a combined piano and harpsichord designed by Robert Stodart in 1777, came to be known as the

'English Grand Action' and was the most notable refinement of piano construction.

While the English makers were working on the perfection of the piano action, the German makers were tackling another problem of the new instrument – the weakness of the case in relation to the tension exacted by the strings. Earlier keyboard instruments had used thin strings. The hammers of the piano put more strain on the strings, and through them on the case itself, particularly the wrest-plank (the piece of wood in which were embedded the wrest-pins or tuning-pins) and the soundboard.

Wolfgang Amadeus Mozart examined the various pianos then being made and in 1777 wrote home to his father Leopold about the instruments being made in Augsburg by Andreas Stein, another former Silbermann pupil.

I begin, in describing different pianos, with those of Stein. His are better and more commodious. In passages that require vigorous play I can lift the finger or leave it on the note, for the sound is not prolonged beyond the instant in which it is heard; it never shivers, nor does it ever fail to sound, as in other pianos.

It is true that Stein never lets a piano go under three hundred florins, but one cannot sufficiently repay the trouble and zeal he employs; his instruments have one quality found in them, and, above all, they have the escape movement, without which it is almost impossible that a piano can render a well-articulated sound. The hammers fall again as soon as they have touched the string, whether the finger be left on the key or not.

When Stein has finished a piano he plays all kinds of passages upon it, and never quits it until it is capable of anything, for he labours not for pecuniary interest, but for his love of the art. He frequently says: 'Were I not myself a passionate amateur in music, my patience would long ago have failed me; but I like an instrument that assists the musician, and serves for a long time.' His pianos, in fact, are very lasting.

Stein warrants the solidity of his sounding-boards. When he has completed one, he exposes it to the air, rain, sun and snow – in a word, to every atmosphere – that it may split; then, by means of slips firmly glued in, he closes the crevices. When a sounding-board has been thus prepared it may be regarded as safe against all accidents.

Mozart also praised the 'pedals', which Stein placed as flaps beneath the keyboard. Previously a damping effect had been achieved by means of pull-knobs placed, as were the harpsichord's stop-controls, above or beside the keyboard where they required the player to lift a hand from the keys to manipulate them.

It was Broadwood who in 1783 provided the piano with a foot-pedal that could lift the bank of dampers and hold them up as long as the pedal was depressed – the origin of the sustaining pedal. He also added the second pedal to soften the sound by pressing a cloth pad against the strings. The hammers were by now no longer simple leather pads, but were covered with felt.

Broadwood then became concerned about the layout of the piano. He questioned whether the strings were the best length, whether the hammers struck them at the most effective point, whether the wrest-pins should be at the front, the side, or the back of the case. He was not alone in this: all over Europe instrument makers were experimenting with every possible permutation of shapes and stringing, producing square pianos, harp-shaped pianos, flat pianos and upright pianos.

But Broadwood went further than most of his contemporaries. In 1788 he went to two experts in physical science – a Signor Cavallo and Dr Gray of the British Museum, to get technical advice on tension and string length. The result of this was that he divided the belly-bridge – the bridge on the soundboard that governs the sounding-length of a string, like the bridge on a violin – so shortening the bass strings. He found that the best point at which the hammer could strike the string was about one-ninth of the way along its vibrating length; shortening the bass strings enabled him to string the instrument so that most strings would be struck at this point. Apparently no instrument maker had previously considered this problem scientifically, and as soon as Broadwood's discovery was put into practice it was copied by virtually every other manufacturer.

By thus obtaining surer control over the notes at the top and bottom of the keyboard Broadwood was able to extend the piano's range, first by adding half an octave of extra notes in the treble, and then another half octave in the bass, until by the 1790s he was producing a standard six-octave piano. He also took the wrest-pins off the soundboard, mounting them on a wrest-plank at the back of the case. He then added a second soundboard beneath the first, to give greater resonance.

By this time the English pianoforte had virtually superseded the harpsichord. Innovations such as those introduced by Broadwood had given it sufficient carrying-power for it to enter the concert-hall in triumph. Haydn and Mozart were writing for it. Infant prodigies were being produced to demonstrate their skill on it.

Johann Nepomuk Hummel was brought to London as a boy of thirteen in 1791. A pupil of Mozart, he enjoyed a great success both as a pianist and composer. William Gardiner of Leicester met him in June 1791 at a dinner-party given by the music publisher James Longman. Gardiner believed that the boy 'came from Vienna to have the honour of turning over the book for Mr Bates, who conducted the grand performances in Westminster Abbey [of Handel oratorios]'. He did do that, no doubt as an exercise in public relations, but the purpose of his visit was more prosaic: his father wanted to launch him in the musical world of London as the young Mozart had been launched thirty years earlier.

The effort was successful. The boy played the piano at the 'best' dinner-parties (Gardiner, that June evening in 1791 at Longmans, 'heard him play a beautiful sonata he had just published dedicated to the Queen, in which he introduced the then popular air of the "Ploughboy" with inimitable variations . . . As a youth, he was the most surprising performer that had ever visited this country, except the young Mozart'). Hummel also gave public concerts: on 5 May 1792 he played a Mozart piano concerto at the Hanover Square Rooms. He also played a Haydn piano sonata, and with the disarming clarity of boyhood was less thrilled by the applause than by the fact that the composer, who was in the audience, tipped him a guinea. Haydn later became his teacher, and Hummel succeeded him as musical director to the Esterhazy family. He became one of the first and greatest teachers of the piano, and wrote a noteworthy and widely used treatise on the art of piano-playing.

The outbreak of the French Revolution and the subsequent disorder of life in Paris drew a number of instrument makers and musicians to London. One of them was Sebastian Erard, then in his thirties and building his reputation as a harpsichord and piano maker. He had been born in Strasbourg, but went to Paris

as a boy and became apprenticed to a harpsichord maker. However, his enthusiasm ran away with him and he was sacked for
being 'too inquisitive'. He soon found other patrons. In 1772, at
the age of twenty, he built his first square piano (probably a copy
of an English Zumpe), obtained more orders for it, and set up his
own business.

During his time in London he evidently used his enquiring
mind to the full, and on his return to Paris in 1796 began to
produce excellent pianos and harps incorporating the latest
English innovations.

Another Parisian favourite in London at that period was Jan
Ladislav Dussek, probably the first of the bravura concert
pianists. Then in his thirties, he was called 'le beau Dussek'
because of his good looks – and is said to have been the first
pianist to play with his right side to the audience, since that
gave them the pleasure of his profile. He enjoyed great popularity:
Broadwood supplied him with a piano for his concerts.

This was the beginning of the keen marketing sense that was
to expand the Broadwood business. Whenever a popular virtuoso
came to London, Broadwood used to send along a piano. As a
simple device of sales promotion, it was infallible.

Dussek, however, became tired with success. A popular pianist
and composer for the piano, in Percy Scholes' words 'he took too
little exercise, became stout, found motion tiresome, took to lying
in bed, felt bored, drank, and died'.

By 1793 the harpsichord was becoming extinct. Broadwood
made his last harpsichord in that year, and soon afterwards wrote
to a customer who, ordering a piano, wanted to trade in a harpsichord in part-exchange that nothing could be given for harpsichords because there was no sale for them.

On 4 June 1793 Broadwood sent a harpsichord to St James's
Palace as they did annually for the performance of the King's
birthday ode. The harpsichord was used in rehearsal, but the
director of the King's band called for a pianoforte for the actual
performance. The harpsichord was banished and never used
again. It was a symbol of the piano's arrival in the musical
establishment.

When in 1796 Don Manuel de Godoy, the favourite of Queen
Maria Louisa of Spain, wanted to give his lady a rich and remark-

able present he ordered a Broadwood pianoforte. As it was to be made regardless of cost, Broadwood commissioned Thomas Sheraton, the leading cabinet maker of the day, to design the case. Sheraton, who was evidently unfamiliar with the grand piano, produced a design in satinwood richly ornamented with medallions by Wedgwood and Tassie, but ignoring the pedals – perhaps considering them a part of the piano mechanism with which a cabinet maker need have no concern.

The order was taken on 8 February 1796 from 'the Prince of the Peace' (a title bestowed on Godoy for concluding the Treaty of Basle between Spain and France), 'Le Comte de Mopox el de Jarnico, at Grenier's Hotel, Jermyn Street'. The pianoforte was shipped on 22 June, and the description in the Broadwood books, together with a copy of the invoice, give an indication of the method of packing and despatch in those days. ('Taylor' was a miniaturist who exhibited at the Royal Academy; perhaps the Queen did not care for such a constant reminder of her Prince, for the medallion was later removed).

Mopox,
A G.P.F. addl. keys [a Grand Piano Forte with additional keys] from C to C in sattinwood case superbly ornamented. A cover of green striped leather and stockings for the legs. A Green baize Cover and two quires of silver paper in two very strong deal cases, the frame in one and case in ye other marked C.D.S.C. No 1 and 2. Delivered at the Bull, Porters Galley Key for the Esperanza, Belotte, Bilbao.

The invoice indicates the extravagant cost of the instrument:

The Count Mopox Grenier's Hotel. Dr. –	
A Grand Pianoforte 6 octaves C to C, in sattinwood case ornamented with different woods with water gilt mouldings and Wedgwood's and Tassie's medallions, etc. The Prince of Peace's arms chased and gilt in burnished gold rich carved frame, etc.	£223 13 0
The Prince's portrait in front by Taylor	10 10 0
A Cover of green striped Leather and stockings for the legs	9 9 0
A Green baize Cover	1 7 0
A Deal case very stout for the Instr.	5 10 0
A do. do. frame	5 7 0

Strings, forks, etc.	I	I o
Cartage to the Key	o	7 6
	£257	4 6

The popularity of the pianoforte meant the popularity of music that exploited the particular characteristics of the piano. The music of Bach went out of fashion because (as Gardiner wrote)

from the features of his compositions, it is evident they were the product of the harpsichord, an instrument of very limited powers, the boldest effects of which were exhibited in trills, and by sprinkling the chords in arpeggio.

The early sonatas of Haydn also bear marks of the influence of this instrument, and possess nothing of the expression of his later works. On the introduction of the piano-forte, this unmeaning style was abandoned for one more bold and flowing. This instrument has been the means of developing the sublimest ideas of the composer, and the delicacy of its touch has enabled him to give the lightest shades as well as the boldest strokes of musical expression.

Carl Philipp Emanuel Bach was among the first composers to exploit the 'singing' tone of the piano. In 1773 Clementi's Sonata Opus 2 is said to have been the first piece of music composed specifically for the piano rather than the harpsichord.

Haydn's later piano sonatas were widely popular, but it was Mozart who, with his piano concertos, set the piano into its modern concert context, both as a composer and a performer. Then in 1795 Beethoven wrote his first piano concerto.

The new pianoforte, and the new music written for it, meant a great increase in the quantity of music publishing. The presence of an expressive keyboard instrument in the home led to the production of a vast quantity of 'arrangements' for piano of operas, symphonies and songs.

Music publishing changed in character with the emergence of the piano. In Leipzig in 1755 Immanuel Breitkopf devised a method of printing notes from movable type. It formed the basis of the Breitkopf and Hartel music publishing business (they were Beethoven's publishers) and was taken up throughout London.

In London, the James Longman who gave a dinner-party for the boy prodigy Hummel founded his music publishing business under the sign of the Harp and Crown at 26 Cheapside in the 1760s. He was joined in 1771 by a man named Lukey, and then in 1778 Francis Broderip became Longman's partner and the name of the firm was changed to Longman and Broderip. The firm sold musical instruments also, marked with their own name although they seem to have been manufactured elsewhere and sold under 'own name' contract, an arrangement that was to be usual in the music business for many years. At Cheapside they sold organs, pianos, harpsichords, and spinets as well as 'Glove-Horns, Sticcado-Pastorals, Pipes and Tabors, Upright Harpsichords "with curious newly-invented swell", and Portable Clavicens "agreeable for travelling with, they may be carried or even performed on in a coach" '. They had a music publishing shop at 26 Haymarket, and their catalogue for 1789 lists 1664 different items of which the greater number are for pianoforte or harpsichord.

The Longman and Broderip harpsichords, says Raymond Russell, are of the same design as those of Shudi and Kirckman. They may perhaps have come from those famous workshops, Longman and Broderip may have sponsored piano manufacture even if they did not themselves make pianos: a patent for the English Double Action was taken out in 1786 by one John Geib, described as a workman employed by Longman and Broderip.

However, the sheer unmanageable size of the publishing list, allied perhaps to extravagant socializing in the cause of business, drove the firm into bankruptcy in 1795.

But ambitious young men were attracted to London as the centre of a flourishing industry in musical instrument manufacture. In about 1778 Georg Astor, then about eighteen years old and the son of a Mannheim merchant, came to London and took employment with a flute maker. He asked his younger brother Johann Jacob Astor to come and join him, and together they set up a business making flutes.

Their business prospered and they began to make other instruments, including pianos. In 1783 the younger brother set out for America with a consignment of flutes for sale. Legend has it that he was crossing America to visit another Astor brother in Baltimore when he got into conversation with a stranger who advised him to invest his money in furs. He did, took them back to London and made a large profit.

Ten years later John Jacob Astor had settled in New York, and was importing square pianos from his brother George Astor's shop in Wych Street, Drury Lane (very handsome they were: see Plate 8). He was also buying furs and property, which became the foundation of the Astor fortune.

The six-octave pianoforte was now an accepted instrument, having taken over from the harpsichord and extended the range of expression of which a keyboard instrument was capable, both in the home and on the concert platform. Its first notable executants had come forward and had begun to create the cult of the soloist. Composers of genius had started to explore the strange balance, the love-hate relationship that could be exploited between pianoforte and orchestra.

The age of classical conformity was dead. The age of individualism and romantic self-expression had dawned, with the pianoforte as its instrument.

2

Selling the Idea

On his tomb in Westminster Abbey is the legend: 'Muzio Clementi, Musician – Father of the Pianoforte'. It is almost true, for in his many-sided dedication to the piano as maker, brilliant soloist, teacher, composer, salesman and roving ambassador, Clementi became the first and probably the greatest propagandist the instrument has ever known.

He was born in Rome in 1752, the son of a silversmith. His father encouraged his musical gifts: by the age of seven he had learnt harmony and at eleven was appointed organist of a Rome church. When he was fourteen one of several large-scale Masses he had composed was performed publicly to considerable acclaim. Then, when Clementi was fifteen, he was discovered by a rich Englishman on the Grand Tour. Peter Beckford was a Member of Parliament, a cousin of that eccentric William Beckford of Fonthill (who, incidentally, had been taught the piano by the young Mozart when he was five), author of *Vathek*.

Peter Beckford was a civilized all-rounder in the age of elegance, a man of education, style, and evident perception. It was said that he would 'bag a fox in Greek, find a hare in Latin, inspect his kennels in Italian, and direct the economy of his stables in exquisite French'. Clearly the young Clementi was already, at fifteen, a youth of considerable musical promise, and Peter Beckford proposed to see that it was fulfilled.

Some financial arrangement was made between Beckford and Clementi's father – Beckford referred to his protégé later as 'the celebrated Clementi, whom I bought from his father for seven years'. But the facts of the case are less harsh than that sentence would suggest, and in the historical context greatly to Beckford's credit. In that age of prodigies it would not have been surprising if the fifteen-year-old Clementi had been launched on the London musical scene of 1767, a world ever eager for fresh youngsters over whom to pour adulation.

Instead, Beckford brought Clementi back to his country home, Steepleton House, Iwerne. There for three years, in the quiet of the wooded Dorset countryside between Blandford and Cranborne Chase, the young Clementi was given a broad general and musical education, and taught English. He was kept firmly away from the predatory public. Then, from the age of eighteen, he was brought up to London from time to time to give concerts on the new pianoforte. In 1773, newly emerged from his strange 'apprenticeship', he produced his first piano sonatas which were published by Longman. Fully armed, Clementi leapt straight into the forefront of London musical activity. At twenty-five he was conductor of the Italian opera in London, then at the height of its popularity. He began to earn a reputation as a teacher of the piano, and was soon on terms of familiarity with all the leading musicians living in or visiting London.

In 1781 he went on a concert tour of Europe, taking his English pianos with him. He gave recitals in Paris, Strasbourg, Munich and Vienna. There he met and became friendly with Haydn, and at the invitation of the Emperor Joseph II undertook a 'challenge match' with Mozart, competing to improvise on themes provided by the Emperor.

Back in London in 1785 he began to consider the pattern of his future. He was still writing piano music, and also producing exercises, tutors, and the famous collection of studies 'Gradus ad Parnassum'. He decided that it would be in his interest to have a financial stake in the firm that was publishing all this, and he became a partner in Longman and Broderip. His reputation was now that of the leading executant of the day (the French called him *le Pape des musiciens*), and also the best teacher, who could attract the most promising pupils. Among them were Jean Baptiste Cramer (son of the King's musical director Wilhelm Cramer) and Johann Nepomuk Hummel (who was sent to Clementi by Mozart for a year).

It was towards the end of Hummel's year with Clementi that a new pupil arrived in London. He was John Field, and his father paid the extraordinary sum of 100 guineas to apprentice the boy to Clementi, an amount equivalent to about £2000 today. Within a few months the boy was giving public concerts in London billed as 'Master Field, the talented ten-year-old pupil of Clementi'. Joseph Haydn heard him play at a concert in May 1794 and noted in his diary that he 'plays the pianoforte extremely well'.

He was then, in fact, twelve years old (impresarios were still trimming the years from youthful prodigies like gardeners taking off buds to make flowers bloom the brighter). Field was born in Dublin in July 1782, and at the age of nine was being promoted on the concert platform there by the leading music teacher in that city, Tommaso Giordani. His début was on 24 March 1792 at the Rotunda Assembly Rooms when the programme included 'Madam Krumpholtz's difficult pedal harp concerto performed on the Grand Piano Forte by Master Field'. The local paper reported that it was 'really an astonishing performance by such a child, and had a precision and execution far beyond what could have been expected'. In advertisements for a second concert he was described as 'the Much-Admired Master Field, a youth of eight years' (he was ten at the time).

At this point his parents, evidently deciding that the boy had reached the top of the tree in Dublin, determined to bring him to London. The family took ship for England, coming to London where John Field was apprenticed to Clementi. The sum paid for his articles was extraordinary because Robert Field, the father, was only a theatre violinist and 100 guineas must have represented a great amount of money to him.

Clementi was sufficiently impressed with the boy to launch him into public concerts in his first summer in London. Then Field was taken out of the public view for four years. Clementi was busy with a new interest – making and selling pianos. At what point he went into the business of manufacture is unknown. But by the 1790s his pupils were expected, in return for lessons from the great man and the musical and social cachet of association with him, to pay for their keep by acting as salesmen-demonstrators, playing Clementi pianos to prospective customers. No doubt it was commercially advantageous to have the pianos demonstrated by youngsters, like Cramer and Field, who were already virtuosi in their own right and capable of making the

still temperamental piano sound magnificent. There is no record
of the feelings of customers when they found, at home, that they
could not make their pianos sound as Cramer and Field did.

No doubt some enrolled for lessons with Clementi. For the
master now had most aspects of an expanding business brilliantly
under his control. He played the piano better than anyone else
at public concerts. That encouraged the fashionable to buy
pianos from him, and as a further encouragement they would
hear their instrument played by Cramer or Field. Then Clementi
would sell them his piano tutors and piano music. Each aspect of
the business fertilized the rest. He was as superlative a businessman
as he was a musician.

Then in 1795 the music publishing and instrument retailing
firm of Longman and Broderip went bankrupt. Within a few
months Clementi had gathered a group of associates round him,
and the new name above 26 Cheapside became Clementi and
Company. At first the partnership was that of Clementi, Banger,
Hyde, Collard and Davies. One by one the other partners dropped
out – probably Clementi bought them out – until within a year
or two the partners were Clementi and Collard.

Clementi was the salesman, the contact-man, the cultivated
genius on intimate terms with every leading composer and
executant in Europe, and every court and rich patron. Frederick
William Collard was the piano maker, the craftsman, the man
who ran the London office and workshop.

He had come up to London from Wiveliscombe in Somerset
with a few shillings in his pocket, an ambitious young carpenter.
He had found that he was skilful at making piano soundboards
and was soon in demand as a 'belly-maker'. Clementi addressed
him, and his fellow-workmen, in the tones of a kindly uncle:

Now, young Collard, you have a good pair of ears, see that the tone is
pure and true; and you, young Davies, a delicate set of digits, see that
the touch is light and responsive.

Between them Clementi and Collard created an organization to
rival Broadwood.

Across the English Channel, Napoleon, as First Consul, was
formulating his plan to demolish English sea-power and trade by
means of a blockade. That scarcely seems to have troubled the

international world of musicians, which managed to maintain friendship and business intercourse across political frontiers as it generally has done.

In 1801 an alliance of Russia and the states of Northern Europe against Britain in a 'League of Armed Neutrality' crumbled, first when Czar Paul of Russia was strangled in a palace revolution, secondly when Nelson shattered the Danish fleet at the Battle of Copenhagen. Towards the end of the year – some months before the Peace of Amiens was concluded in March 1802 – Clementi was planning an extensive sales trip across Europe. His contact in Paris was Ignaz Pleyel.

Pleyel had settled in Paris as a music publisher in the late 1790s (he later became one of the most distinguished of French piano makers). He had been born in 1757 at Rupperstahl, near Vienna, the twenty-fourth child of the village schoolmaster. His mother died at his birth and his father, marrying again, had a second family of fourteen children. Young Ignaz came to the attention of a wealthy Hungarian nobleman, Count Erloedy, who sent him to study with Haydn whose favourite pupil he became. By the 1780s he was organist and choirmaster of Strasbourg Cathedral, but as a German was obliged to give up the post in the years following the French Revolution.

It may thus have been an act of generosity on Clementi's part, as well as shrewd business, to offer Pleyel the French publishing rights of a quantity of music Clementi was publishing in London, including three sonatas by John Field.

William Gardiner of Leicester (who dined with everyone in the musical world) dined with Clementi in the summer of 1802.

The peace [of Amiens] had brought many foreigners to England and I sat down at [Clementi's] table with French, Spanish, Germans, Italians, Russians, Turks and Arabs, and with every one of these Clementi held a conversation, generally in their own language . . . While we were at table a young gentleman named Field, an *élève* of Mr Clementi, sat down to the pianoforte and gratified the company by playing one of Bach's fugues, in which by force of touch he maintained a clear distinction in the four different parts.

Muzio Clementi and his protégé John Field crossed the Channel that autumn and were the guests of Ignaz Pleyel in Paris. While

Clementi conducted publishing business with Pleyel, Field showed off the English pianos. They travelled on to Vienna, where they were the guests of the publisher Artaria.

And there they had a rip-roaring row. The strain between Clementi, rich, successful, smooth and socializing, and his twenty-year-old pupil Field, awkward, morose, his smouldering Irish temperament still immature, must have been building up for some time. It is clear that Clementi intended to 'plant' his prize pupil in Vienna, still the heart of musical Europe, as the agent to boost the sales of Clementi and Company, to sell Clementi pianos and Clementi music. Incidentally, he could take lessons with Beethoven's teacher, Albrechtsberger, the great expert in counterpoint, who lived in Vienna.

On the eve of Clementi's departure for St Petersburg, Field rebelled. He would not stay in Vienna. He would come on to St Petersburg too.

Clementi was not accustomed to having his carefully laid plans disrupted in this way. The journey between Vienna and St Petersburg must have been sulphurous. In St Petersburg, then the Russian capital (where Clementi's contact was the publisher Faversear), Field was put to demonstrating pianos in the warehouse. The German violinist and composer Louis Spohr, then a young man, remembered

The figure of the pale overgrown youth whom I have never seen since . . . When Field, who had outgrown his clothes, placed himself at the piano, stretched out his arms over the keyboard so that the sleeves shrunk up nearly to his elbows, his whole figure appeared awkward and stiff to the highest degree; but as soon as his touching instrumentation began, everything else was forgotten, and one became all ear.

Spohr also visited Clementi and Field at their hotel, the Hôtel de Paris, and came upon them with their arms up to the elbow in soapsuds, doing the weekly wash. Clementi said that the St Petersburg washerwomen were much too expensive, and anyway ruined his clothes. Field was still in disgrace and when Clementi was out teaching rich pupils, or negotiating publishing business, he allowed the young Field very little money.

It is said that he met in the market a footman from an aristocratic house, who befriended him and used to take him back and give him meals in the kitchen. One night, when Clementi took Field to play at that house, the footman opened the door to them and made desperate efforts to dissuade Field from walking into the drawing-room. But as the time came for Clementi to move on, he negotiated another of his little arrangements. He had been teaching the daughter of Prince Demidov, and one evening took Field to play there for an evening party. The moody Irishman was an immediate success; he was taken up by the aristocracy, commissioned to give lessons to their daughters, and launched into the world of musical patronage.

One of his patrons was General Marklovsky, who ordered 'a grand pianoforte (with additional keys)' from Clementi, who wrote back to London warning the workshop to 'be most particular, for the General minds no expense, and is a warm, good fellow'. Another of Field's pupils was the future composer Glinka. Field stayed in Russia (he was referred to in London as 'Russian Field'), and moved to Moscow where he married a Frenchwoman. As a composer he was the creator of the Nocturne, later taken up by Chopin, and an edition of Field's Nocturnes was published with an enthusiastic preface by Liszt. Of him is told the classic story of the meeting of two famous pianists (though it must be said that it has been attributed to the meeting of various pairs of virtuosi pianists ever since).

When Johann Nepomuk Hummel visited Moscow in 1822 he went to visit Field, who was then famous as pianist and composer. Hummel disguised himself modestly as 'a German businessman with an interest in music'. Field, interrupted in a lesson, somewhat gracelessly played a piece and then invited his visitor to do so. Hummel played with such bravura and attack that Field leapt up exclaiming 'Either you are the devil or you are Hummel!'

Having divested himself of the young Field, Clementi was free to continue his sales trip. It was not without incident, mainly because the whole of Europe was still caught up in the turmoil of Napoleon's wars. It says much for Clementi's confidence in Collard in London that he could make his way across the continent, sending back orders for pianos and music to London, assured that sooner or later they would be fulfilled. A letter might take a month to arrive, a consignment of pianos many months, but the demand was there and the customers were prepared to wait.

He wrote from Dresden in 1803:

I left St Petersburg five weeks ago and should have left earlier had not Mars deranged all my plans. I came via Riga, Danzig, Königsberg, and over land to Berlin, and from there to here where at last I am at anchor on the Elbe.

He did business in Dresden through Baron Ball,

who is become my friend and who is a Banker to the Emperor. I cultivate his friendship, first for his good qualities and then because he may become very useful to our house.

He did: he ordered a Clementi grand piano. So did the Customs official who cleared Clementi's luggage, and so did the interpreter whom Clementi engaged for business discussions. The interpreter, Clementi records with pardonable pride in his salesmanship, owned two pianos already. But he was still capitalizing on his contacts in Russia.

Hoeke is in Moscow what Faversear [the publisher] is in Petersburg, and I believe, by what he said, he may become a very considerable correspondent. Hoeke said he would send for a small quantity [of pianos] at first, but afterwards by the dozen, for in Moscow they want instruments extremely, and the people in general are much richer than in the Capital. Pray send good stuff, and let every wood be well seasoned.

When he ordered pianos, Clementi reminded his London office to send music as well.

Send also complete copies of my works with this so that they might with study become both masters and lovers of the instrument – and Evangelists for the Art.

Moving on to Leipzig, he was swiftly in negotiation with the leading music publishers and retailers Breitkopf and Hartel – selling them English pianos (against all the odds, for they seemed very expensive in Germany in contrast to the locally produced pianos with the lighter 'German action').

He (Hartel) has a great assortment of P. Fortes of various makers, principally from Vienna; but on my recommendation he would wish to make a trial of ours, of which I gave him the *lowest* prices, that seemed to him *high* enough! In short the *price*, the heaviness, and the *depth of touch* are the general objections throughout Germany to English P. Fortes; but especially the *first* (the money) sticks most confoundedly in their gizzard. Poor devils!

Collard sent a piano to Clementi in Berlin, and the Master was not pleased.

The touch is both a lazy and lousy one – tho' 'tis thrummed on night and day, it is as disobedient as ever. Some radical fault. Remember a light, well-repeating touch is a grand article in Germany. Pray mind what you send me – I dare not show this one as a bait, for the tone likewise is far from tempting – being as dry as my purse . . .

Having been away from the workshop for so long, Clementi began to wonder (as salesmen will) whether he should be back at the works checking on quality control.

The Prince [Prince Louis] was lately here, and immediately paid me the *first* visit, which I (politely) soon returned. He played a couple of hours to me, for which I gave him only three dishes of tea. He said he had three gr. P. Fortes of ours, the first of which was much the best; concluding our manufacture to have considerably suffered *by my absence*, and as the devil would have it, he had some plea to confirm his assertion, as poor Lauska's instrument happened to be in my house (till his return) whose tone and touch – but no more on that *sore* subject – we will not *renovare dolorem* [renew the grief].

Clementi's offer to let Hartel have pianos at 'the lowest prices' was not solely inspired by the commerce in pianos. It was bait to catch a bigger fish – the British publishing rights in the works of the greatest composer then writing for the piano.

With regard to Beethoven I have laid a still better plan than before, to possess all his MSS, for as he is *well*, I say he is *well* with Hartel, I have engaged with this last that he shall contract for all the former's compositions in MS for the future; and whatever (reasonable) price he shall pay him, I'll go halves with him for the copyright in the British Dominions. And by contracting for all, Hartel is sure we shall possess his works at a tolerably easy rate, for he is otherwise very exorbitant.

1. 'Piano e forte' by Bartolomeo Cristofori of Florence. This model, the improved type built about 1720, is in the Metropolitan Museum of Art, New York, and is the earliest known piano to survive

2. *Above*, John Broadwood (1732–1812), foremost of the early British piano makers

3. *Opposite*, Cipriani Potter (1792–1871). Pianist, who repaired Beethoven's Broadwood grand, and subsequently gave the first performances in London of Beethoven's piano concertos

4, 5. William Crotch (1775–1847). The son of a Norwich carpenter, he toured Britain as an infant prodigy playing piano, organ and violin. He later became Principal of the Royal Academy of Music, where these portraits hang

6. William Sterndale Bennett (1816–1875). An acclaimed pianist in his youth, he became principal of the Royal Academy of Music, Professor of Music at Cambridge and conductor of the Philharmonic Society of London

7. *Opposite, top,* square piano forte by Johann Christoph Zumpe, London, 1767

8. *Bottom,* square piano forte by George Astor and Company, London, 1790

9.   Burkat Shudi the harpsichord maker and his family. This picture of Broadwood's master was painted about 1744 and was fitted into the panelling of the front parlour of Shudi's house in Pulteney Street, Soho. The harpsichord he is tuning is said to be the one he made for Frederick the Great

10. *Opposite, top*, square piano forte by Clementi and Company, London, 1810

11. *Bottom*, square piano forte by John Broadwood and Sons, London, 1820

12. *Right*, grand piano forte by Erard of Paris, about 1810. This model with four pedals is similar to the one made for Napoleon

13. Grand forte piano by John Broadwood and Sons, London, 1815. This is the same model as the one Broadwoods supplied to Beethoven

14.   Grand forte piano by Clementi and Company, London, about 1815. This instrument shows the harpsichord 'jack-rail' still in use

15.   *Opposite*, piccolo upright piano by Wornum and Wilkinson, London, 1818

16. Grand pianoforte by William Stodart, London, 1835. The metal tubes were introduced by Stodarts to strengthen the frame

17. Pocket grand piano by Robert Wornum, London, 1840

18. *Opposite*, design for an upright piano in the Gothic style, from F. M. and M. A. Nicholson's *The Practical Cabinet Maker, Upholsterer and Complete Decorator*, 1826

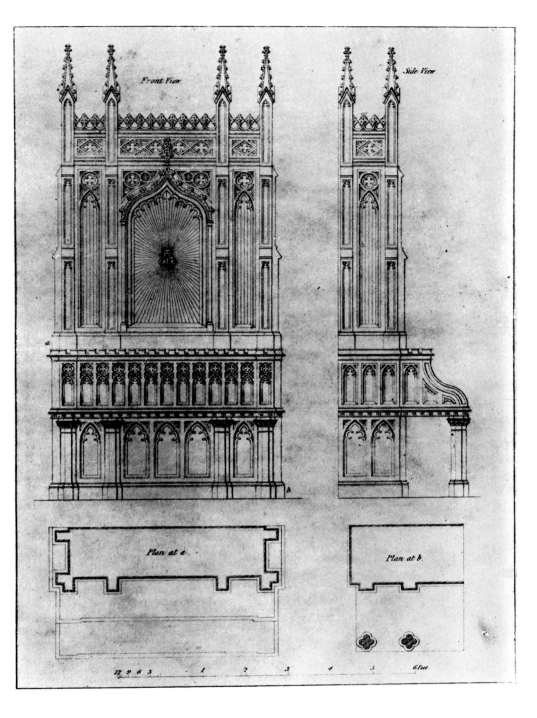

Front View.

Side View.

Plan at a.

Plan at b.

12 9 6 3   1   2   3   4   5   6 Feet

19. Upright grand piano by Henry Morley, London, 1850, with pleated cloth front

Berlin held Clementi for some months during 1804–5, for he was courting and marrying a young lady, Caroline. A year later he wrote back to London ordering a piano for 'the little Cupid who is daily and nightly expected . . . apropos, make haste with the Gr. P. Forte, for no doubt he'll want to play as soon as he is born – or I'll cut him off with a shilling, for a bastard ("Oh fie! for shame!" says Mrs Collard).' The cheerfulness was tragically short-lived. Caroline died in childbirth. Clementi gave the piano to her parents.

Soon he was moving on again. In the summer of 1806 he was back in St Petersburg, once more capitalizing on his name and popularity to 'place' pupils, as he had done with Field.

The two pupils I took with me from Berlin have met with much success in this country, and I have advised them to make hay while the sun shines. Therefore they stay. I have procured them plenty of scholars, and as they will now and then want instruments to sell, I have persuaded them to send for ours on their own account, and to encourage them I have promised to furnish them with £50 each grand (good plain mahogany). Their names are Klengel and Berger, two very honest industrious young men as ever lived. They make it a joint concern, to avoid all dispute.

Send them by the 1st opportunity six grand and two square patent, with pedal. The small, you'll charge as low as you can. But pray, pray, pray now let me entreat you to pick out as excellent in tone and touch as you possibly can, from which you may in future expect great orders, for they'll push like the devil; as they love and want money. Rather don't hurry in the choice; and keep them sometime in a very warm room, in order to discover whether the wood won't warp, or any other mischief don't ensue.

The letter demonstrates the businesslike attitude of Clementi towards his music business – and towards his pupils. If they recognized that music was a means to prosperity, then they could be on to a good thing. The last quotation no doubt demonstrates one reason for Clementi's irritation with the wild Irishman John Field, who was not prepared to be interested in business.

Has Field sent you the Concerto, the Quintette, and *something more*, as I had agreed with him, for his Grand Piano? If not pray write (by Faversear [the St Petersburg publisher]) to him. He is a lazy dog. I'll endeavour to write to him too.

In the spring of 1807 Clementi was back in Vienna, delicately cultivating a difficult but highly important contact. Soon he was able to write back to London:

By a little management, and without committing myself I have made at last a conquest of that *haughty beauty* Beethoven; who first began at public places to grin and coquet with me, which of course I took care not to discourage; then slid into familiar chat, till meeting him by chance one day in the street – 'Where do you lodge?' says he, 'I have not seen you this *long* while!' Upon which I gave him my address. Two days later I find on my table his card, brought by himself, from the maid's description of his lovely form. This will do, thought I. Three days after that, he calls again, and finds me at home. Conceive then the mutual ecstasy of such a meeting!

I took pretty good care to improve it to our house's advantage. Thereafter as soon as decency would allow, after praising very handsomely some of his compositions, 'Are you engaged with any publisher in London?' 'No,' says he. 'Suppose then, you prefer *me*.' 'With all my heart.' 'Done.' 'What have you ready?' 'I'll bring you a list.'

In short, I agreed with him to take in MS three Quartetts, a Symphony, an Overture, a Concerto for the Violin which is beautiful, and which, at my request, he will adopt for the Pianoforte with and without additional keys; and a Concerto for the Pianoforte. For all of which we are to pay him two hundred Pounds Sterling . . .

The Symphony (No. 4) and Overture (Coriolanus) are wonderfully fine – so that I think I have made a good bargain. Today the courier sets off for London via Russia.

The courier was obliged to take that round-about route because war was once again raging throughout Europe. If Clementi had wanted to get home, it would have been a difficult journey – for it could hardly have been achieved on land, and he was a poor sailor.

When shall I see you again? Shall I be obliged to venture my life on a long sea voyage? I fear neither wind or wave, but I am miserably ill the whole time at sea.

Still in Vienna towards the end of 1807, he received the gloomy news that the company's piano factory in Tottenham Court Road had been burnt down on 20 March 1807. The loss, including completed instruments, was estimated at £40,000, and insurance only accounted for £15,000. But such was the prosperity of the company and Clementi's personal wealth that this did not prove a crippling blow.

The war and the disruption of communications caused a number of embarrassing problems; perhaps because of the disastrous fire there was difficulty in transferring Beethoven's payment from London to Vienna and it was nearly two and a half years before he got his money. Clementi claimed that he could not come home until he had settled honourably with Beethoven. Once this was done, he returned to London in 1810, where he married again. Having spent a decade as a businessman and salesman, he dedicated himself to composition – having ensured that his works were published simultaneously by Clementi & Co in London, by Pleyel in Paris and by Breitkopf and Hartel in Leipzig. He was at the centre of musical life in London for another fifteen years, conducting concerts from the piano for the Philharmonic Society which he helped to found. He spent the winter of 1820 in Leipzig, greatly honoured: he was publicly presented with a vase for 'his invaluable contribution to contemporary music'.

London's musical world gave a public dinner in his honour in 1827.

One of his successors as a leading London pianist, Ignaz Moscheles, has left an account of the moving occasion when the old man, then seventy-five, played for his friends for the last time.

Ninety of us sat down to dinner. When the cloth was removed we had speeches, toasts and music. Of course a wish was expressed and rapturously applauded, that Clementi, the father of pianoforte playing, should be heard on this occasion, and thus prove his right to the title. Clementi rose from his chair; Smart, Cramer and I led him to the instrument.

The excitement was great, the whole party eagerly listening. Clementi had not been heard for years. He extemporised on a theme of Handel, and completely carried us away by his fine playing. His eyes gleamed with youthful fire; those of many of his hearers were dimmed with tears of emotion. Amidst shouts of applause, and the heartiest congratulations, he resumed his seat.

Clementi's pianoforte playing when he was young [adds Moscheles] was famed for its exquisite legato, pearliness of touch in rapid passages, and unerring certainty of execution. Even now the remains of these qualities were recognised and admired, but what chiefly delighted his audience was the charm and freshness of his modulations in improvisation.

Clementi retired to a somewhat lonely and isolated old age at Evesham where, one of his children remembered:

My father took little interest in us . . . When in the house, he spent his whole time in his study which was always locked against intruders; sparsely furnished with a simple iron bedstead, his grand piano, of course, and one or two simple chairs and a table. The walls were covered by bookcases from floor to ceiling, containing a beautiful library of the best editions. When, occasionally, I was allowed a brief entrance to the room, I found him sitting at his instrument, his fingers wonderfully active at the keyboard, and on the music rest before him a book – not of music – but of the plays of Euripides or Sophocles.

There in 1832, returning perhaps in spirit to the discoveries of those youthful years in Dorset when music and scholarship were his companions, set apart from the bustle of business and the cheers of the crowd, at the age of eighty Muzio Clementi died.

After the disastrous fire at the Clementi piano factory in Tottenham Court Road in 1807, it was the firm's principal rivals who came to their aid. Broadwoods helped Fred Collard to fulfil outstanding orders for Clementi pianos; and the workmen at Broadwoods collected enough money among themselves to re-equip all the Collard workmen who had lost the tools of their trade. Piano-making was a competitive business. But craftsmen were companionable men, and Broadwoods were now the world's leading piano makers in both quantity and acknowledged quality, and could afford to be generous. John Broadwood was seventy-five in 1807, the grand old man of the piano business. His elder son, James Shudi Broadwood, had become a partner in 1795 and by taking into partnership a younger son, Thomas Broadwood, the firm in 1807 became John Broadwood and Sons.

Old John Broadwood was a cabinet maker by trade, a craftsman in wood. His pianos were naturally wood-cased: there was no other material. His employment of Thomas Sheraton, the leading cabinet maker of the day, as a designer of piano-cases was no accident. Wood remained the heart and secret of a piano, the source of its resonance, the main feature that distinguished it from the now obsolescent harpsichord.

Mozart had recognized Stein's genius in weathering soundboards so that they did not split or crack. Clementi had written home to Collard instructing him to see that the soundboard wood was properly seasoned. Wood was a craftsman's material. As yet, metal was not. Metal might be used for a piano's strings and tuning-pins, but the old piano makers were wary of losing the resonance that (they believed) only wood could ensure, if they introduced more metal into the piano frame.

When a firm is leading in its market, and its products are eagerly sought by a wide public, there is a temptation for its directors to be sceptical of change and novelty. This is particularly so when the firm's historic rivals have been forced to copy. With the ending of the harpsichord market, Broadwood had the pleasure of seeing the son of Shudi's old rival, Joseph Kirkman, follow him into manufacturing pianos at the close of the century in which Kirkmans had been leaders in harpsichord-making.[1]

Similarly Schoene, assistant to Zumpe in his square pianoforte business and inheritor of it at Hanover Square, had by this time followed Broadwood and was manufacturing grand pianos.

Broadwoods were prospering in 1807, and were to continue to do so. Apart from the Royal Household, they supplied pianos to the Duke of Wellington and to Admiral Lord Nelson. By 1802 they were exporting pianos in quantity to Charleston, where they had three agents, one of whom was selling pianos to the value of more than £500 a year. In December 1802, Broadwoods had to write in response to an order from Glasgow that there would be some delay in completing it because 'from the great demand, we have sold every thing we had prepared for sale in the summer'.

Production was now on such a scale that in February 1804 they ordered from a Mons. Lieber 400 lb of steel wire in four gauges, pointing out that 'we use a greater quantity of music

1. The Kirkmans did well, and continued to make fine pianos throughout the nineteenth century. When in 1896 the last of the male line died, the remaining female descendant handed the company over to Collard and Collard at cost, on the understanding that the traditions of the company should be maintained. That understanding was honoured until, in difficult commercial conditions forty years later, Collards themselves went out of business.

wire than any other manufacturer in this Kingdom and we think it will answer your purpose to send us the best.'

The piano was a fashionable instrument, and an eager public was keen to exchange older instruments for it. Harpsichords were distinctly unfashionable: 'The harpsichord we cannot allow anything for, as owing to their almost total disuse, they are unsaleable.' Some customers were not entirely sure what they were buying. A lady in Ipswich enquired what the advantage was in a 'pedal' on a small piano. Broadwoods wrote: 'The pedal mentioned is to take off the dampers like the right hand pedal of the Grand Pianoforte.'

Others were not satisfied with the instrument when they received it. One customer wrote asking for 'a softer pedal'.

It has never been thought necessary [replied Broadwoods] as the beauty of the instrument, which has caused it to supersede both the organ and the harpsichord, has been thought to consist in the means it affords the player of modulating its tones from piano to forte by the delicacy of touch, which is to be acquired by a little practice.

Inevitably some customers were casual in payment; and at least one took his piano across the Atlantic before it was paid for:

To Mr Edmond Phelps, Trinidad, an account for £76 15s 0d.
Sir, Above we have sent our Account which you must know is right, and beg the favour of a remittance to the Account by return of Packet – else, as we cannot think ourselves well used by your departure without thinking to give us any intimation notwithstanding the length of time you were in London previous, we shall put into the hand of a friend high in the Law in Trinidad. We hope, however, you will prevent us, by doing justice to, Sir, your most obedient servants, John Broadwood and Son.

To another customer, an Army colonel who was similarly defaulting on payment, they wrote warning that unless the money was sent they would feel it necessary to write to his mother. Now and again, however, they had to resort to a final demand: 'To Dr. Baker of Derby. If you don't pay in a few days, you will be arrested.'

But the Industrial Revolution was in full flood. Old John Broadwood adopted some of the new methods of production, including a form of assembly-line that enabled the firm to make pianos in unprecedented quantity.

The nineteenth century was to be the Age of Iron. As the piano keyboard was extended from five octaves to six with 'additional keys', new and greater stresses were placed on the piano-case. wooden bracing could scarcely sustain them. But it is not surprising that men such as Broadwood, whose lifelong experience was in fashioning wood, should have hesitated long before prejudicing the piano's tone (as they must have thought would happen) by introducing metal into the case.

In Paris, the Erard brothers had no such inhibitions. Under Napoleon's patronage they were working in a country only recently emerged from chaos, a country with a new political system and a passion for change.

Sebastian Erard had been a harpsichord maker under the old regime. He had arrived in Paris as a sixteen-year-old, and a few years later discovered the English Zumpe square pianofortes. Under the patronage of the Duchess de Villeroi, he began to build square pianos of the English design in 1776 (the fashion was spreading: a year earlier, Johann Behrend made the first square piano in Philadelphia). Erard was so successful that he summoned his brother Jean-Baptiste from Strasbourg to join him in business. The two of them prospered so well, indeed, that the Paris lutenists petitioned King Louis XVI to have the business shut down. The King, noting that the French-made pianos were proving more popular in Paris than the English imports, gave Erard permission to continue.

At the time of the Revolution, Erard thought it discreet to come to London, leaving his brother to run the Paris business. Meanwhile a confiscation of musical instruments from the great houses of Paris took place, and the records[1] of the man in charge, Antonio Bartolomeo Bruni, give a picture of the predominance of Erard's square pianos in the Paris of the 1790s – and also the popularity of imports from England in the preceding years.

Of the 127 keyboard instruments confiscated, 63 were harpsichords and 64 pianofortes. Of the pianos, 20 were French-made, and 12 were by Erard. Most of the remaining 44 were English; of the 29 whose names were listed, 16 were by Zumpe or Schoene,

1. Quoted in *Men, Women and Pianos* by Arthur Loesser (London: Gollancz).

and most of the remainder by Pohlmann, Beck, Adam Berger and Longman and Broderip.

While in London, Sebastian Erard made an intensive study of the English piano-manufacturing business and also opened a shop in Great Marlborough Street. Soon after returning to Paris, Erard produced his first grand piano using the English action; and by 1802 his Paris factory was organized on the pattern of Broadwoods, with the workmen assigned to particular jobs on a production-line basis. Erard did not limit his interest to the piano alone. He perfected the double-action for the harp, which enabled it to be played in any key.

Erard was evidently fascinated by the industrial age and by the technical challenges it posed. In the decade from 1800 to 1810 Erards were probably making a greater variety of pianos than most comparable manufacturers. Thus in 1801 they made a piano for Napoleon with the (now old-fashioned) Vienna action, and with five pedals – not only the *una corda* and sustaining pedals, but also a bassoon, a celeste, and a 'Janizary music' pedal which brought into play drums and a triangle. Napoleon, it is said, played it himself, and no doubt enjoyed fighting over his battles on it.

Substantial quantities of 'Turkish' or 'Battle' music were written at the time; some saw the piano as the natural successor to the eighteenth-century mechanical toy.

Such extravaganzas were not uncommon. While Broadwood and Clementi in London had worked out a successful 'standard' for grand and square pianos, selling at a reasonable price that made them accessible to the well-to-do citizen, other makers were still experimenting with ways of making the new instruments make strange and exotic sounds.

Most of Sebastian Erard's inventions were intensely practical. About 1808 he began to add to his grand pianos the 'agraffe', fixed behind the wrest-plank. Each string passes through a perforation in its agraffe after being wound round the tuning-pin, and the metal plate defines the sounding-length of the string precisely. It also helps to sustain the tension of the string under the hammer-blows, and it proved such an advance that it has since been adopted for all pianos.

In about the same year Erard also began work on his 'repetition action', a system of holding the hammer near the string after hitting the note, as long as the key is depressed. Previously in the English action the hammer was allowed to fall back to its resting-place, and when a note was repeated the hammer had to travel its full distance. The Erard repetition action made the playing of rapid repeated notes more practicable and efficient, and was an aid to the bravura piano performances of the nineteenth-century pianists. These were two of the innovations that took Erard pianos into the lead on the concert platform.

As grand pianos became larger and more powerful, the distance in performance between the grand and its smaller cousin the square piano became more obvious and pronounced. The magisterial tone of the grand piano with its six octaves, sparkling treble and resonant bass made the square piano with its four and a half or five octaves seem undesirably restricting. The makers began to look for ways of obtaining the 'grand' sound in a smaller space.

The parallels between the piano and the harp attracted people to the idea of putting strings, frame and sounding-board on their side, in an 'upright' position. This happened at the very beginning of piano manufacture, when in 1745 C. E. Friederici of Gera, a pupil of Silbermann, made an upright piano. But he, like his contemporaries, went on to make square pianos.

Once the horizontal grand piano had come into favour, makers looked again at the upright shape. In 1795 William Stodart – a young relative of that Robert Stodart who had been one of Broadwood's best apprentices, and later a leading piano maker on his own account – took out a patent for an 'upright grand'. This was simply a grand piano turned through ninety degrees and mounted on a stand at right-angles to the keyboard. This meant that the instruments were eight or nine feet tall. Sometimes they were hidden in the shape of a bookcase or cupboard, shelves filling the empty space at the tail (or, in this case, the top) of the instrument. These early uprights were dangerously top-heavy, especially when the fronts were covered with mirror-doors, as one was when made for the Prince of Wales (later King George IV).

Other makers formed a deliberate feature out of the shape, turning the top of the upright into a pyramid, or into the pillared curve of an imitation harp. The latter design became known as the 'Giraffe' – there is an example of it, made by van der Hoef of Amsterdam in 1810, in the Victoria and Albert Museum, London (see plate 28).

In 1798 William Southwell of Dublin put a square piano on its side to produce a small upright and gave it the name of the 'cabinet' piano – a name that outlived the instrument. The first real uprights were those produced by Matthias Muller in Vienna, and John Isaac Hawkins in Philadelphia.

Muller's piano, produced in 1800, was called the Ditanklasis, and is remarkable in that the 'harp' of the piano was placed with its tail on the floor and the bass at the top, with a clever adjustment of the action by which the hammers struck approximately at the middle of the strings.

In 1800 John Isaac Hawkins, an English piano maker working in Philadelphia, produced an upright piano that was only four feet seven inches high, and had two other remarkable features. The soundboard and strings were suspended within an all-metal frame; and coiled wire was used (perhaps for the first time) for the bass strings. The design was patented in England by the inventor's father, Isaac Hawkins, and either produced or sold at Dalby Terrace, City Road. The coiled bass strings gave a resonance that allowed the length to be shortened, and thus the height of the piano reduced.

This interesting design did not apparently affect the sales of the established makers. Perhaps in spite of its pointers to future developments, the stark combination of wood and metal was unappealing to both piano makers and the public. Perhaps it was that Hawkins added a curious device – the keyboard folded up into the frame, and the instrument was specifically advertised as being useful for ships' cabins and confined spaces.

The conventional wisdom was that the bass strings must be full length; and uprights had been given a bad name by the fact that the first ones, by perforating the soundboard to fit the action, produced a weaker construction.

In 1802 Thomas Loud of London patented an upright that was six feet three inches high. But significantly for future developments, he suggested – seemingly as an afterthought rather than a practical proposition – that if a more portable piano were required, the bass strings might be fixed from top left to bottom right of the case, which would allow the bass strings their full length in a height (for his patented piano) of only five feet two inches. This 'oblique stringing' was to be the basis of upright piano construction, but the rationality of it seems to have been slow to dawn on the piano makers – no doubt because grands and squares were still selling in commercial quantity.

One maker was more convinced of the prospects for the upright. He was Robert Wornum, who went into partnership with George Wilkinson in Oxford Street in 1810. In the next year he patented an upright with an improved double English action; but in 1812 the Wornum and Wilkinson factory was burnt to the ground. Undaunted, Wornum started up again a year later at 42 Wigmore Street, describing himself as 'Upright and Horizontal Pianoforte Maker'. This suggests a deliberate choice of priorities, and possibly a determination to exploit one section of the trade left undeveloped by Broadwood and Clementi. But it was a further twelve years before Wornum patented his 'tape-check' upright action, the basic mechanism for subsequent uprights, at first known as 'piccolo' or 'cottage' pianos.

Musical mice were a phenomenon of early Victorian London. This one, drawn by George Cruikshank in 1847 when it was exhibited at Palmer's Hair Cutting Rooms in the Strand, evidently not only boasted a voice 'whose notes resemble those of a bird in spring' but also played an early Victorian cottage piano

3
The Virtuoso Arrives

In the early nineteenth century musicians depended for a live-lihood, as they had done throughout the previous century, on the patronage of a comparatively small number of rich and fashion-able people. Musical organization revolved about the church and the court – though in Europe a 'court' might be no larger than the great house of some affluent aristocrat. The idea of orchestral concerts in a hall holding thousands, commonplace today, would have seemed very surprising in the eighteenth century.

Orchestras were then chamber orchestras of fifteen to twenty players, and the music was written to conform with the available instruments and musicians. In London, the arrival of Handel and J. C. Bach gave new stimulus to the performance of music, though concerts given before a subscribing audience whose numbers were strictly limited could hardly be called 'public'.

Bach, with C. F. Abel, formed such a society – the Academy of Antient Music – in the 1760s, and for nearly fifty years the 'Antient Concerts' at the Hanover Square Rooms were the focal point of London music-making. From 1775 they were directed by John Peter Salomon, the German-born violinist. Haydn attended them when he was in London, and it was at one of the Antient Concerts at the Hanover Square Rooms, in 1792, that he heard the twelve-year-old Hummel make his London début as a pianist. But the Antient Concerts had only 400 subscribing members, and the Hanover Square Rooms could hold only around 600.

The musical world tended to be introspective, and youngsters were encouraged: when Haydn conducted six of his symphonies at the Antient Concerts in 1791 (Salomon had commissioned them) the tympanist was the fifteen-year-old George Smart,

then deputy organist of the Chapel Royal, St James's, and a
piano pupil of J. B. Cramer.

Smart's career illustrates the character of London music in
1813. In that year he was appointed conductor of the Royal
Opera House, Covent Garden, and also conductor of the season
of oratorios given at the Theatre Royal, Drury Lane, during Lent.
He was also one of the organists of the Chapel Royal (and organist
for many royal funerals and coronations at Westminster Abbey).

A contemporary wrote:

The advance of music in popular favour had not then attained to
anything approaching the dimensions it has now assumed. The
patronage bestowed upon it was, in a measure, merely partial, and
emanated rather from the rich and prosperous than from the multitude.
The performance of Handel's oratorios during the season of Lent
attracted some attention; but until Sir George Smart was entrusted
with the direction, they met with little consideration . . . During the
thirteen years that he filled the arduous post of conductor at Drury
Lane and Covent Garden, contending against the frivolities of one
set of patrons and the requirements of another, as well as against a
large amount of public indifference, he yet managed to assert the
claims of the higher works of musical science . . . Even so early as the
year 1814 he contrived to introduce Beethoven's *Mount of Olives*. He
also brought out at the same theatre in 1815 that master's celebrated
Battle Symphony. Although the former work failed to obtain the general
appreciation to which the genius of Beethoven was entitled, it yet
marked a period in the advancement of musical taste.

This was the Regency, the age of fashion, when even the
Battle of Waterloo could be preceded by a great Ball. Despite the
war, London was full of European musicians. Evidently they
felt the need to extend the scope of music-making. At the beginning of 1813 Johann Baptist Cramer, P. A. Corri and W. Dance
invited various professional musicians to meet them on Sunday
24 January to discuss a plan to establish a society of professional
musicians meeting together regularly to give concerts.

Cramer, Clementi's star pupil, was now at the height of his
fame as a London pianist, teacher and composer. Philip Anthony
Corri was also a composer, a member of a prolific Italian family
whose father Domenico Corri had opened a music shop at 67
Dean Street, Soho, in 1790. Philip's sister Sophia married the

fashionable pianist Jan Ladislaw Dussek, and Domenico Corri went into partnership with him at 28 Haymarket as Corri, Dussek and Company.

William Dance was probably the leading orchestral player of the time. A grandson of George Dance the architect, he was a violinist and a focal point of London music. The invitation to professional musicians was sent out from his house, 17 Manchester Street.

The group met at 124 New Bond Street, in rooms above Samuel Chappell's music publishing business. The business had moved there just two years earlier. On Wednesday 23 January 1811 the *Morning Chronicle* contained this advertisement:

Chappell & Co beg leave to acquaint the nobility and gentry that they have taken the extensive premises lately occupied by Goulding & Co, 124 New Bond Street, and have laid in a complete assortment of music of the best authors, ancient and modern, as well as a variety of instruments, consisting of Grand and square Piano-fortes, Harps &c. for sale or hire.

Johann Baptist Cramer, former prodigy, son of George III's musical director, had now at the age of forty settled in London as pianist, composer and teacher. He had emulated Clementi also by going into business, taking a partnership with Sam Chappell and Francis Tatton Latour, another notable teacher. One of the first works published by Chappell had been Cramer's *Studies for the Pianoforte*; and Chappell advertised that all the pianos in his showrooms were 'personally selected by Messrs Cramer and Latour'.

The Broadwoods greeted the emergence of rival piano makers with distinct wariness. A letter to J. B. Cramer in the Broadwood letter-books of the period demonstrates this. Their relations with P. A. Corri were even worse, as the following letter (dated 16 November 1809) indicates:

P. A. Corri, 36 Newman Street.
We have received your letter containing the very prejudiced statements of the case you have thought proper to lay before several truly respectable gentlemen. It would ill become us to notice your most insulting and ungentlemanly insinuations. And the purpose of this is

to recommend you not to subject yourself to the degrading treatment you might experience should you again enter our house. We are, Sir, yours etc. John Broadwood and Son.

The result of that meeting in Sam and Emily Chappell's rooms above the shop in New Bond Street was the foundation of the Philharmonic Society.[1] Originally it was intended that there should be thirty members; this was expanded to forty. There were to be seven Directors to manage the concerts (all professional musicians, probably because the Antient Concerts had been at times 'directed' by royalty, and by an Archbishop of York). An unlimited number of Associate Members might attend. Members paid a subscription of three guineas a year, Associate Members two guineas.

The season began with eight Monday concerts at the Argyll Rooms in Regent Street. The Philharmonic Society's orchestra was led by John Peter Salomon, and directed from the pianoforte by Muzio Clementi. Subsequent concerts were directed alternately by Clementi and Cramer (presumably from a Clementi piano, if not a Chappell). George Smart became conductor in 1816. But it was not until seven years later that Louis Spohr, the violinist, invited to conduct a Philharmonic Society, did so with a baton and without a piano.

Until 1820 the convention was that the director would work from the piano, following the custom of eighteenth-century chamber concerts where the director sat at the harpsichord. But by then the concert grand piano with its iron supports and greater power was coming into existence, and the new breed of virtuoso piano soloist was on the horizon.

The spread of orchestral concerts in this decade produced a further problem for the piano makers.

Throughout the nineteenth century orchestral pitch rose. The early eighteenth-century pianos were tuned to an A between 415 and 430 vibrations per second (this is confirmed by Handel's tuning-fork, which survives, and gives an A of 422 vibrations per second).

It was Sir George Smart, as conductor of the Philharmonic Society, who set a 'Philharmonic pitch' with A at 452·5 vibrations

1. The Royal Philharmonic Society from 1912, its centenary year.

per second.[1] A Victorian writer of reminiscences (Dr J. E. Cox) says that it happened at the Italian Opera at the King's Theatre, where

the principal oboe was Griesenbach who, with Mrs Billington and Sir George Smart, settled what is called the Philharmonic orchestral pitch – a medium tone between that of Handel's tuning-fork and the recognised Paris Conservatoire diapason.

Some attribute the rise to a set of sharp wind instruments presented to an Austrian regiment by the Emperor of Russia at the Congress of Vienna. Regimental bands supplied many opera orchestras, and so the higher pitch became standard.

Piano makers had to devise ways of tuning pianos sharper, with additional stress on the strings and thus a more imperative need for strengthening, particularly as once peace had been concluded after Waterloo there was a constant movement of music and musicians between London, Paris and Vienna. Beethoven, in Vienna, was now the lion of modern music and the Philharmonic Society – regardless of 'public indifference' – often included his works in their concerts. He was a musician's composer in those years.

Beethoven was beginning to suffer from the deafness that was to darken his last years. The light tone of the German pianos dissatisfied him. He was pleased with his Streicher piano (Nanette Streicher, daughter of the great Andreas Stein, had successfully continued his piano-making business); Beethoven asked Frau Streicher to make him a piano with a stronger tone.

Broadwood pianos were already familiar in Vienna and Beethoven must have admired them for their six-octave range and their sonorous bass notes. But no doubt he preferred a German piano because he believed that the instrument had been a German invention. Cristofori was forgotten, and it annoyed Beethoven that the instrument should be known by an Italian name, whether 'Pianoforte' or 'Fortepiano'. He gave it a German name, the Hammerclavier, and labelled his Sonata in A major, Op. 101 'for the Pianoforte or Hammerclavier'. His next Sonata, Op. 106, was specifically designated for the 'Hammerclavier' –

1. This was later lowered, at the end of the nineteenth century, to the 'New Philharmonic Pitch' of A = 439.

by which title it is still known. But evidently his publishers refused
to go on humouring this whim and Beethoven's later piano works
are titled 'for the Pianoforte'.

Somehow Broadwoods heard of Beethoven's admiration –
perhaps from his pupil and family friend Ferdinand Ries who
was by this time living and playing in London, perhaps from one
of the number of English musicians who visited him in Vienna to
pay their respects. Thomas Broadwood wrote to Beethoven
offering him the gift of a piano. Beethoven wrote back in February 1818, enthusiastically accepting the present. 'I shall regard
it as an altar upon which I will place the choicest offerings of my
mind to the divine Apollo', he wrote.

The Broadwood grand was dispatched that spring, by sea to
Trieste and then overland to Vienna where it arrived in less than
perfect condition. Fortunately the English pianist Cipriani
Potter was in Vienna at the time, and was able to put the instrument into working order. Sadly, Beethoven's deafness was now
increasing and though he was inordinately proud of his Broadwood, seldom allowing anyone else to touch it, he could not fully
appreciate its tone. But his subsequent piano works exploit the
piano's full six octaves.

That the links between composers, performers and music
publishers were still close and important is demonstrated by a
letter written by Beethoven in 1819 to his friend and ex-pupil
Ferdinand Ries in London, enclosing two new works.

Taken to a publisher in London, they would sell easily for, perhaps,
fifty ducats in gold . . . Potter (Cipriani) says that Chappell in Bond
Street is now one of the best publishers . . .

Clementi was now getting on in years; and perhaps his relations
with Beethoven, at least in business, never fully recovered from
that unhappy wartime period in the 1800s when the composer
had to wait more than two years to be paid for his MS. Clementi
was moving into retirement, though his partner Collard was still
an important piano maker. The Cramer–Chappell business had
indeed now moved into the forefront of London music publishing,
though Cramer dissolved his partnership at the end of his seven-
year agreement (1818). Cramer was to start his own publishing
firm, J. B. Cramer and Company, ten years later.

Chappells prospered. Old Sam Chappell took his eldest son William into the business, and then his second son Thomas – who left school at fifteen when his father was afflicted by blindness. But when Sam Chappell died in 1834 it was his formidable widow, Emily, who became the matriarch-manager. By 1840 the 'E. Chappell' who was music seller to Queen Victoria was Mrs Emily Chappell, who proved to be a woman of business every whit as sharp as her husband.

Perhaps that was not considered surprising or 'unsuitable' because by that time music, and especially competence at the piano, was regarded as a necessary accomplishment for a well-brought-up young lady.

Since there were too few virtuosi available to teach, music schools had to be started. This pressure for lessons for amateurs coincided with the impulse to provide a school for musical education in London. The Paris Conservatoire had already earned a high reputation throughout Europe in the forty years of its existence; the Vienna Conservatoire had been started in 1817. A committee chaired by a notable amateur musician, Lord Burghersh, opened the Royal Academy of Music in 1822. At first it was a school for children, with a Headmaster as well as a musical Principal (Dr William Crotch). The children lived in cramped quarters in Tenterden Street, giving concerts at the Hanover Square Rooms. William Gardiner gives an account of the congestion at Tenterden Street:

I was requested to call upon a lad in the Royal Academy of Music. Having rapped at the door, for the life of me I could not recollect the name of the boy. 'Did he sing or play?' I was asked. I could not tell. I might take a peep into the different rooms, and see if I could find him.

In a large apartment were near twenty pupils, strumming upon as many piano-fortes, producing an instant jingle. In the singing-room they were sol-fa-ing in every kind of voice. Such a Babel I never wish to hear again. We then visited the violin department, the horrid scraping of which I could not endure. The horns were in a double closet, the oboes and flutes in the garret, and the trumpets in a cockloft under the skylight. In a small out-office in the yard the drummer was at work, and near him the trombone was darting his instrument down a long entry. In returning I was mightily struck by a loud voice practising a shake shut up in a shower-bath. My youth I could not find, but, just as I was departing, the porter bethought himself of the fagotto, when lo! on opening a door, I beheld the object of my search on the cellar steps, pumping on his bassoon with all his might in the dark.

Schools such as the Royal Academy of Music were at least an improvement upon such academies as that introduced by an Alsace-born wind player, John Baptist Logier, who observed the popularity of the piano and hit upon the scheme of teaching a number of pupils simultaneously. Today it sounds rather like the modern Japanese system of music teaching, but it was novel in 1814.

Gardiner also visited one of Logier's academies.

I was present at one of those exhibitions that so much occupied the public mind. At not less than twenty piano-fortes were seated nearly thirty young ladies, some not more than five years of age. The lessons, in which they all joined, were so composed that the difficult and showy passages were given to the best players, and those of lesser talent had parts of easier execution. When the whole was put in motion, the sounds, rising from so many instruments of different make and shape, produced an effect rich and curious.

Professional musicians were less impressed by the method. Moscheles came across it in Dublin:

Mr Allan, son-in-law of Logier, gave a public performance, where his pupils played. Pieces of my own were made to suffer. I repeat the word *suffer*. I feel more and more that this Logier system may produce good timeists, but what becomes of the right understanding and grasp of the composition? What of its poetry, when eight pianos are drilled into playing together with unerring precision?

Logier also devised and marketed a strange instrument which he called the Chiroplast, which supposedly when placed over the keyboard kept the pupil's hands and wrists in the correct playing position. Logier even managed to persuade Clementi to issue a statement approving this device (even though it obstructed the thumb and so made the playing of scales impossible); but that may not have been unconnected with the fact that in London the Chiroplast was being sold by Clementi and Company.

Nor may that obstructed thumb have been as odd in the early nineteenth century as it seems to us. Gardiner, writing in the

1830s, felt it necessary to explain the careful touch needed to play the piano:

No two authors agree upon the mode of fingering. In the time of Bach, the thumb, now become so important, was seldom used. That lightness of touch, which is the first qualification of a good performer, is soonest obtained by putting the hand into the same easy curved position as when we collect and pick up crumbs off a tablecloth – the tips of the fingers just touching the keys.

It was by teaching, and especially by teaching young ladies, that the most notable pianists of the day earned an appreciable proportion of their income. Several followed Clementi into piano-making or music publishing, or both. All played piano concertos at the concerts of the Philharmonic Society, and gave private performances (not yet 'recitals') in the houses of the rich, at which they were expected to show off the quality of the host's piano by extemporizing dramatically upon folksongs or popular tunes of the day.

The foremost among them in London between 1810 and 1830 was certainly John Baptist Cramer: 'glorious John', they called him.

I was not prepared for such effects as he produced [writes Dr Cox], the charm of which was not so much derived from his brilliant manipu- lation as from the feeling his exquisitely pure *cantabile* produced. In point of taste, expression and sensibility, I believe John Baptist Cramer to have been unrivalled; for he possessed the power of making the pianoforte 'sing' as if it were a human voice perfectly under control.

Cramer managed to preserve his musical integrity while sailing with the tide of popular acclaim. So did Ferdinand Ries, Beethoven's pupil, who was making a successful career in London as pianist and composer. There were others who seem to have capitalized on the flashier effects of which the piano was now becoming capable.

One was Friedrich Kalkbrenner, a prize pupil of the Paris Conservatoire at twelve. His ambition was to be an army officer, but he settled for fighting the keyboard instead. He began in Bath during the season, and soon became the popular delight. He attracted huge crowds to his concerts, but the purist musicians were less adulatory.

He was much feted and followed, but he never by any chance touched the feelings, or gave an indication of being anything else than a mere brilliant mechanist [writes Dr Cox]. His execution was indeed prodigious; but he could play scarcely any other compositions than his own with anything like taste or proficiency, and the almost total absence of genuine method or phrasing therein caused a repetition to be both tedious and wearisome. Most of Kalkbrenner's compositions were little else than frivolous *fantasias*, consisting of five or six variations upon some popular Italian (operatic) air, an English ballad, or a vulgar Scotch song, which, being anything but agreeable when even performed by himself, were absolutely intolerable whenever they were attempted either by inferior performers or mere commonplace amateurs.

Dr Cox, who heard them, placed second in quality (after Cramer) Cipriani Potter – the one English-born pianist who reached first rank in his own country in those years, and now remembered only by the title of the exhibition founded in his memory at the Royal Academy of Music where he once taught.

Cox calls him

a really sound musician and a genuine artiste, who must always be remembered with gratitude for having at a very early period of his career manifested a decided preference for Beethoven's works, as he in later years manfully stood up against unmitigated opposition to those of Schumann.

Philip Cipriani Hambly Potter was born in London in 1792. His godmother was a sister of the painter G. B. Cipriani, from whom he took his Christian name (probably no disadvantage in a London that expected its pianists to be foreign). His father was a piano teacher, and young Cipriani Potter was admitted early to the ranks of London professional musicians. He was an Associate Member of the Philharmonic Society from its foundation, and elected a full Member on his twenty-first birthday. The following year the Society commissioned and played an overture by their young member. He then went to Vienna to study and, an admirer of Beethoven at a time when the great composer was considered dangerously *avant-garde*, went to see him.

Beethoven did not take kindly to visitors but he liked young Potter. 'Potter has visited me several times', he wrote to Ries in London. 'He seems to be a good man, and has talent for composition.' Fortunately he also had talent for repairing and putting together Beethoven's Broadwood piano when it arrived in Vienna in 1818.

Potter returned to London in 1821. The next year he became first Professor of the Pianoforte at the Royal Academy of Music on its foundation. He also gave the first performances in England, with the Philharmonic Society's orchestra, of Beethoven's piano concertos in C major, C minor and G major. In 1832 he followed Crotch as Principal of the Royal Academy of Music, and died in 1871. Never showy, never 'fashionable', his name has been forgotten but his musical judgement has been amply justified by the years.

Ignaz Moscheles certainly was fashionable. He had written a brilliant show-piece, Variations on the Alexander March, that he played often. He was, and acknowledged that he was, a *bravura* pianist: he loved showing off the piano, and he loved showing off. Born in Vienna, he came to London and soon was playing at all the best soirées. His wife was related to the Rothschilds.

Moscheles' playing was dramatic. A contemporary wrote:

There was a spring and an elasticity in his fingers when applied to quick arpeggio passages, that brought out the most brilliant tones, whilst in those touching movements that constitute generally what is termed expression, his manner was no less effective. But the most extraordinary part of Moscheles' playing was perhaps the velocity and certainty with which he passed from one distant interval to another. His thumbs – they were very large and thick – seemed to act as intermediate points, from which his fingers were directed to almost the remote parts of the instrument, over which they flew with a rapidity wholly inconceivable; yet the uniformity of his touch and tone were so strictly preserved, that an imperfect note was never, and an unfinished note seldom, heard.

He had a passion for ornament and octaves. He (like Liszt after him) would decorate a composer's score at will if he felt that it would add sparkle to the piano and to his performance.

Yet he had great personal charm. Clementi and Cramer liked him; he was encouraging to the young, and was among the first to recognize and help the young Felix Mendelssohn.

Cramer welcomed Moscheles to London in 1822 and invited him to share a concert, and to contribute the last movement of a

Sonata they might play together: 'only I was not to put any of my octave passages into his part, which he pretended he could not play'.

Moscheles kept a diary throughout his concert career, and his widow later expanded it into a biography that illustrates vividly the pleasures and problems of a pianist's life in the 1820s. It also indicates the relationship between the pianist and the piano maker, and the methods used by piano makers to draw their improved instruments to the public attention under the fingers of a popular public figure.

The distinguished pianist on tour would give a few 'concerts' with a local orchestra. Few towns could raise more musicians, professional and amateur, to make up more than one small chamber orchestra, and so the local soldiery might be called in. At Liverpool in 1825 Moscheles found himself accompanied by 'a band consisting of a double quartet and four halting wind-instruments'. The occasion was slightly redeemed: 'I was enchanted with my Clementi piano.' In Edinburgh, three years later, he discovered that he had arrived a day or two after the Italian opera had gone there for a season – and recruited all the competent local players. So he was 'obliged to put up with a third-rate orchestra, got together anyhow from regimental bandsmen; the Highlanders, with their bare legs and kilts, being the poor substitutes for a well-trained orchestra'. Later that same year he was in Brighton, accompanied by 'a wretched orchestra'.

Moscheles was fortunate to find that good Clementi in Liverpool. In other cities he would try to borrow a good piano from a friend, or be faced with the local offering.

Just how profoundly pianos differed in character, and how devoted pianists were to their favourite make, is shown by Moscheles' comment when Cramer persuaded him to play a Broadwood at a double concert they gave together in London in 1822.

The strong metal plates used by Broadwood in building his instruments [wrote Moscheles] gives a heaviness to the touch, but a fulness and vocal resonance to the tone, which are well adapted to Cramer's legato, and those fingers softly gliding from key to key; I, however, use Clementi's more supple mechanism for my repeating notes, skips and full chords.

His reputation as a bravura player had gone before him into Europe. When he played at Spa the next year he tried to borrow Lady Portland's piano but she refused to lend it, 'declaring that I should damage her instrument: I, who am so averse to all thumping. She actually told a friend of hers present at the ball that I played with my feet!'

Apparently Moscheles, as a joke, used to pretend to play with his fists, playing in thirds so that he could strike the lower note with his closed thumb. Lady Portland could not be convinced that he would not ruin her piano for ever, and he had to make do with a Broadwood 'which, although it had seen its best days, did not prejudice his success'.

Beethoven, for once, was not so possessive and when Moscheles gave a recital in Vienna in 1823 he borrowed Beethoven's Broadwood. He had on arrival in the city toured the piano makers, 'whose progress he always diligently watched'. He chose a Graf to use at the concert, so as 'to bring out the good qualities of both'. Unfortunately by this time Beethoven was so deaf that he had completely ruined his Broadwood. Graf, the Viennese piano maker, probably realized that he could not come badly out of the comparison and so agreed to put the Broadwood into working order.

I tried in my Fantasia to show the value of the broad, full, although somewhat muffled tone of the Broadwood piano [said Moscheles] but in vain. My Vienna public remained loyal to their countryman – the clear, ringing tones of the Graf were more pleasing to their ears.

When he was being lionized, it was difficult to refuse to play whatever instrument he found himself facing. In Dublin, he was invited to the Anacreontic Society, 'consisting of amateurs who perform admirably the best orchestral works'.

After supper, Moscheles was shown a piano and invited to play. He did not trust the 'old worn-out instrument', and only gave them the Overture to *Figaro*. It was worse in Rotterdam, where he was so distressed by the piano that he 'extemporized on Mozart's air "I can do nought but pity you", and applied the words to myself'. He refused to play an encore because 'I would not a second time face a struggle with the refractory keys of the pianoforte'.

When fulfilling Royal Command performances, he could hardly argue about the quality of the piano. In 1827 he was asked to play at the Duchess of Kent's home in Kensington Palace – mother of the future Queen Victoria.

The little Princess Victoria was present, and the Duchess begged me to play at once, so that the Princess, who was obliged to go to bed early, might hear me. She left the room after my second piece. I had to play a great deal (on a Broadwood), and accompanied the Duchess in a song of Beethoven's.

In 1832 Moscheles was commanded down to Brighton to play before the court in the Royal Pavilion. It was December, and cold, and the great pianist was kept waiting.

Sir Andrew Barnard apologized for having kept me, and after a few polite phrases, asked me if I would try the Erard in the Pavilion. I found the instrument stiff and unmanageable from having stood so long in a cold room, but I was obliged to get my hand in somehow, and had not a single moment to spare for rehearsal with the King's Band. We met in the evening in the fantastically decorated and beautifully lighted music-room attached to the Pavilion. The scene was a brilliant one, King William IV, Queen Adelaide and their suite sat at the farthest corner of the room. The guests were a long way from the piano, and I was not presented . . .

During my performance the King approached me, and seemed to be listening; he bowed condescendingly when I rose, but did not say a syllable; the company talked loudly . . .

This was, no doubt, the obverse of being a fashionable pianist; one had to put up with this sort of treatment. But he had gone through the same experience in London on the night after the great Reform Bill was passed, that same spring.

Yesterday the Reform Bill was passed, and today, at a dinner party, we heard interesting discussions on this subject; but alas! a great musical soirée followed, attended by the whole Tory party, the Duke of Wellington at the head. One cannot play one's best in the presence of these great men, who concentrate all their attention upon an Italian prima donna; it doesn't matter whether I or any other artist plays the piano, they don't care about it; their applause on these occasions I regard as an expression of delight that they have got rid of me.

Moscheles lamented that at evening parties he often had to endure
so much amateur music, that he sometimes agreed to play out of
a desire for self-protection.

Nor was he always safe on the concert platform. Classical
music was still the possession of a limited circle, as in the Philharmonic Society with its forty 'Members' and its few hundred
'Associates' who might be confidently expected to give a polite
hearing to any work (though they found Beethoven hard going).
But the fashionable pianist who was caught in a 'popular' concert-
hall was there at his peril. The London public had its favourites,
mainly among the opera singers, and the audience assertively
knew what they liked.

In May 1826, Braham, a popular opera singer, organized his
'annual benefit' at Covent Garden and Moscheles agreed to take
part in the second half, which was to be an anthology of serious
music under the title of 'Apollo's Festival'. It turned into a
disaster.

Braham, the most popular of English singers, used always on this
occasion to please the 'gods' by singing sailors' songs, so we had to
endure a similar state of things tonight. Madame Vestris, the popular
singer, found willing listeners who were delighted with such nursery
ditties as 'Goosie, Goosie Gander', etc.

So far so well, but Braham had calculated without his host in
setting before such an audience as this, good music. Could no one see
that Weber himself was conducting? I'm sure I don't know, but the
screams and hubbub in the gallery while the overture was played,
without a note being heard from beginning to end, made my blood
boil; and in a state of high indignation, I sat down to my piano on the
stage, and gave a sign to the band beneath me to begin my 'Recollections
of Ireland'. At the opening bar of the introduction, the roughs in the
gallery made themselves heard by whistling, hissing, shouting, and
calling out 'Are you comfortable, Jack?' accompanying the question
with volleys of orange peel . . .

I stooped down to the leading violinist and said, 'I shall continue to
move my hands on the keyboard, as though really playing. Make your
band pretend to be playing also; after a short time I will give you a
signal and we will leave off together.' No sooner said than done. On
making my bow as I retired, I was overwhelmed with a hurricane of
applause.

No doubt Moscheles was glad to escape to the world of sympathetic musicians, such as Clementi. Moscheles and his wife often spent their Sundays at the Clementis' house at Elstree, where they sometimes met the Collards, Clementi's partner in the piano-making business. Moscheles particularly admired the younger Collard, William, whom he said was the most intelligent man he ever met. He also liked the Clementi pianos because of their touch, which he considered lighter than the Broadwood. He thought their tone was clearer, although the heavier Broadwood action produced a fuller sound.

Moscheles remained loyal to the Clementi piano for many years; and when he and his wife settled down in London in 1825, at 77 Norton Street, Clementi gave them 'the most valuable addition to their household goods', a splendid piano, inscribed above the keyboard with the words: '*Muzio Clementi e Socj. all' ingegnosissimo J. Moscheles, ed alla sua amabilissima consorte*'.

However, this was the 1820s, and in London and Paris the Erard Brothers were improving their pianos and anxious to have them played by so eminent and popular a man as Moscheles. Their agent in London was Sebastian Erard's nephew Pierre, who was in charge of the showroom in Great Marlborough Street. The Erards had been acute enough to build rehearsal rooms in association with the showrooms, and such men as Cramer and Moscheles frequently met at Erards to practise.

So in June 1825 Pierre Erard took the opportunity of telling Moscheles of a new development in piano action invented by his uncle Sebastian.

Pierre Erard showed and explained to me on a dumb keyboard his uncle Sebastian's now completed invention, for which the firm has just taken out a patent. I saw the earliest experiment of this invention in Paris. It consists in the key, when only sunk half way, again rising and repeating the note.

I was the first to play upon one of the newly completed instruments, and found it of priceless value for the repetition of notes. In the matter of fulness and softness of tone, there is something yet to be desired, and I had a long conversation on the subject with Erard.

Six months later, after a provincial tour, Moscheles was again back in London and Pierre Erard brought up the subject again – this time, evidently, with a discreet financial inducement.

I was at Erard's today, and saw his excellent pianos, which are built upon the new principle; but I decidedly refused his proposal to bind myself down to play solely on them, in spite of the profitable conditions he offered me. I intend for the future to be as perfectly free in this respect as heretofore.

Erards went on pushing; Moscheles could not escape the sales pitch even when he went to Berlin a year later.

Practised a great deal on an instrument which Madame Spontini (Erard's sister) sent me, with an urgent request that I would play on it at my concert.

Back in Britain, Moscheles went to give a concert at Bath, and found that Erards had sent a piano there for him. He spoke of it in 'the highest terms'. In 1828, Erards went as far as they could go, and still could not buy the great Moscheles.

Erard presented me today with a grand concert piano, of the value of 160 guineas. I certainly owe him my best thanks for such a present. Externally the instrument is all that can be wished for; but the tone of the higher notes is somewhat dry, and I find the touch still too heavy. My Clementi, therefore, still remains my favourite, although Erard's instruments have begun steadily to make their way. Madame de Rothschild, now that she has heard my Erard, wants to invest in one.

Two years later, Moscheles was virtually convinced. 'The touch in particular is vastly improved: I begin to revel in these instruments.' That was the year that Moscheles moved to 3 Chester Place, Regent's Park, where he was to live for sixteen years before retiring from London to Leipzig. His wife seems to have liked the Erard sound, for she felt that his playing improved in those years.

Moscheles, starting as a bravura player, gradually took a broader view of his art both as a composer and player. His powers steadily matured . . . It should, however, be stated here that this progress, though mainly originating with Moscheles himself, was greatly favoured by the improvements made in Erard's pianos; their organ-like tone and full resonant sounds gave Moscheles such pleasure that no doubt he had every incentive to bring into relief those great excellences, and display them in his adagios. 'A very violoncello,' he used to say, praising the tone, which he could prolong without using the pedals; to the excessive use of these he had a rooted aversion. 'A good player,' he used to say, 'must only rarely use the assistance of either pedal, otherwise he misuses it.' Frequently he would listen to an excellent pianoforte player, praise him in many respects, adding: 'I wish he had not his feet so perpetually upon the pedals. All effects now it seems must be produced by the feet – what is the good of people having hands? It is just as if a good rider wanted for ever to use spurs.'

Nevertheless, despite his conversion to Erards, Moscheles remained on good terms with Clementi and his piano makers, the Collard brothers. It was in that year that Collard introduced to him a boy of ten, Henry Litolff, 'a poor, clever but rather neglected child'. Litolff's father was from Alsace, and played dance-music, but was too poor to provide his son with a piano. So Collards allowed young Litolff to play the pianos in their workshop. Moscheles took him on as a pupil.

The Erard 'repetition action', which Sebastian had perfected over a period of some twenty years, proved to be one of the great advances in the construction of the concert grand. Later it was simplified by the pianist-piano-maker Henri Hertz, and as the Herz–Erard action was adopted by most piano makers for their grands.

Simultaneously several makers were experimenting in the strengthening of the case with metal, to hold the tensions that would be required by the seven-octave keyboard that was clearly on the way. Broadwoods have a piano made by the firm in 1823 with steel tension bars above the strings, and believe that the use of such bars had been usual for some years then. Erards took out a patent in England in 1825 for fixing iron bars to the piano's wooden braces, and using sheet iron to unite the 'wrest-pin block with the key-bottom so as to form almost an entire block'.

In 1820 Thom and Allen, two workmen employed by William Stodart (who joined them in its exploitation), invented a compensation frame to prevent the piano going out of tune in extremes of atmospheric temperature. This included tubes of brass and steel fixed above the strings. Pierre Erard, in Paris, took out a similar patent in France two years later.

Erards had obviously noted the marketing success of Broadwood in the early years of the century, and the commercial advantage of giving away pianos to great composers and executants. The pursuit of Moscheles indicates how hard Erards were working at the sales and publicity side of the business, as well as the technical development. In 1824–5 they had their greatest stroke of good fortune from the publicity viewpoint. A young Hungarian piano-prodigy arrived in Paris and created a furore. Erards put him under contract. So when the boy set out to tour England he was at the keyboard of 'Erard's New Patent Grand Piano Forte'. His name was Franz Liszt.

Franz (or Ferencz) Liszt was the son of a land steward on the great Esterhazy estates. The boy was born in 1811, 'the year of the comet', when all Europe was under the shadow of war. His childhood was divided between 'the great house' and the country-side; from the first he picked up sophistication, from the second a love of gipsy music and the timeless rituals of rural life. Young Franz displayed brilliance early, and gave his first concert at the age of nine. A group of Hungarian nobles paid for him to be taken the thirty miles to Vienna, where the boy became the pupil of Salieri and Czerny, Beethoven's pupil, who had already gained the reputation of being the best teacher and composer of piano studies.

Beethoven himself, it is said, heard the boy Liszt play and was so impressed that he marched on to the platform and kissed the child. In Vienna, Liszt also met Schubert. In 1822 he was taken by his parents to Paris, and two years later (at the age of thirteen) launched as a prodigy of the pianoforte. The Erards discerned his quality, and sponsored him in a tour of England.

The *Morning Post* contained this advertisement:

NEW ARGYLL ROOMS

Master Liszt, aged twelve years, a native of Hungary, respectfully informs the Nobility, the Gentry and the Public in general, that his benefit concert will take place this evening, June 21, 1824, to commence at half-past eight precisely, when he will perform on Sebastian Erard's new patent Grand Pianoforte a Concerto by Hummel, New Variations by Winkhler, and play extempore on a written Thema, which Master Liszt will request any person of the company to give him.

It must have been a notable début in London. In the audience were Clementi, Cramer, Ries, Kalkbrenner, Cipriani Potter, and virtually every leading musician in London. The theme given for his improvisation was selected by Sir George Smart, then conductor at Covent Garden and organist of the Chapel Royal.

He chose a theme from *The Barber of Seville* (Rossini was then the popular success of the Italian opera),

whereupon the boy began to 'work' without a moment's hesitation, winding up with a tremendous fugue, or what the audience accepted as such.

Liszt's success was total: it was agreed that his technique would have been remarkable in an adult, and that it was phenomenal in a boy.

The following year Liszt returned, and after playing in London toured the country. For his Manchester concert (for which he was announced as 'still only twelve years old', which would indeed have been remarkable had it been true – he was now nearly fourteen) he was part of a concert programme typical of the style of the period. It was a series of 'acts', none very long, employing singers and soloists in pieces that seem to owe more to the music-hall than what would be familiar on the modern concert platform.

This, despite the fact that the orchestra was considerably augmented for the occasion to the following 'Grand Scale': '12 violins, 4 tenors, 6 basses, 2 flutes, 2 oboes, 2 clarionets, 4 horns, 2 trumpets, 2 bassoons, 3 trombones, and drums.' The evening began with the 'highly celebrated Overture to *Der Freischutz*, composed by C. M. von Weber, which received the most decided marks of approbation at Mr Hughes's concert on Monday evening last'. Then came three vocal gems: Mr Roylance singing 'The Eagle o'er the Victor's Head', by Rook; Messrs Broadhurst and Isherwood in the duet 'Gay Being Born', by Dale; and Miss Symonds fluting Rossini's 'Una Voce poco fa'.

Then came Master Liszt, playing Czerny's 'Reichstardt' Variations, with orchestra, 'on Erard's New Patent Grand Piano Forte of Seven Octaves'. Following this, Mr Broadhurst returned to sing the ballad 'My ain kind dearie, O!', and then the other singers performed Bishop's round 'Yes, 'tis the Indian Drum'.

The first half concluded with Liszt and the orchestra playing Hummel's Concerto in A minor (yet again on 'Erard's New Patent Grand Piano Forte'). The second half opened with a local prodigy, Master Banks ('only 9 years old') leading the orchestra in Kreutzer's Overture to 'Lodoiska'. Then came a song from Mr Isherwood, Shield's 'The Spring with Smiling Face', and a duet 'When Thy Bosom' by the popular operatic star Braham sung by Miss Symonds and Mr Broadhurst.

Then there was the *pièce de résistance*: 'An Extempore Fantasia on the Grand Piano Forte by Master Liszt, who will respectfully request a written Thema from any Person present'. The concert was brought to an end with three songs, one of them the Scottish ballad 'John Anderson, my Jo'.

Improvisations were greatly favoured by the public. The pianist was expected to demonstrate his extraordinary virtuosity, and the capabilities of the 'New Patent Grand Piano Forte of Seven Octaves' as a barely secondary necessity. The flashier the performance, the wilder the applause; and musical standards were wholly sacrificed to ingenuity and athleticism. The Philharmonic Society, with its professional membership and rigorous musicality, was in part a defence against this sort of thing. However, it sold pianos.

A Victorian music critic looked back on those 'good old days' with acerbity.

The change which has come over the spirit of modern music can scarcely be more strongly emphasised than by comparing one of these old-world programmes with what would now be done at a high-class concert. For this was evidently a high-class concert, at which a gigantic orchestra of forty players cooperated, not a mere ballad affair . . . The worship of clever infants marked, in the opinion of all sensible persons, the lowest depths of musical cretinism. Sixty years ago [Francis Hueffer was writing in 1889] this was different, and, as we have already seen, the first virtuosi of the age countenanced the marvellous doings of the little wonder who, for a wonder, grew up to be a great man.

The popular pianists were admired for their digital athleticism. Moscheles was rather proud of the octave passages he inserted into many works, and what he proudly called his 'little skips' up and down the keyboard. No doubt Cramer, being a better musician and a purist, was trying delicately to discourage such tricks when he asked Moscheles not to write octaves into the sonata they performed together. Liszt, too, was not above 'decor-

20.   Upright piano by Lambert of London, made for the Great Exhibition of 1851.
The case is lavishly gilded, and the keys are inlaid with tortoiseshell

The two cuts, figure C and figure D, show the first United States patent and original construction of STEINWAY AND SONS' overstrung Grand piano, and also their first Upright overstrung scale, which is the main basis of construction up to the present time for all makers following the Steinway system.

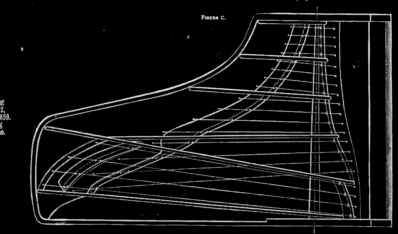

FIGURE C.

U.S. Patent
No. 26,532,
Dec. 20th, 1859.
Overstrung
Grand Piano.

Figure C represents the original drawing in STEINWAY AND SONS' patent for the overstrung scale, and the disposition of the strings in the form of a *fan*.

21. *Opposite, top*, plan of
the original Steinway
overstrung grand, from
the United States patent
of 1859 illustrating the
disposition of the strings
in the form of a fan

22. *Bottom*, the down-
striking Robert Wornum
grand designed in 1868/9
by James Gamble for Sir
Henry Cole, first director
of the Victoria and Albert
Museum. The decoration
is achieved by a wood-
staining process

23. *Right*, the Priestly
three-foot-high upright in
unpolished American
walnut given to Edward
Burne-Jones on his
marriage in 1860, and
decorated by him

24. An inlaid upright of
the 1860s by Collard and
Collard

25.   One of the most ornate pianos ever manufactured. This piano was made by Bösendorfer of Vienna to the order of the Emperor Louis Philippe, Napoleon III, as a birthday gift for his wife the Empress Eugénie. She brought the instrument to Britain on her exile in 1871 and it was for many years in her house in Torquay. On her death it was bequeathed to friends in the town. Many years later it was purchased by Harrods, from whom it passed to the present owner, a film producer. The wood is principally mahogany, inlaid with kingwood in a Greek key design. The legs and the angels at each end of the keyboard are af hollow-cast brass, crafted in remarkable detail, with an ormolu finish

26.   *Opposite,* a detail of the brasswork of the 'Empress Eugénie' piano

27. *Opposite, top,* the Byzantine Broadwood grand designed in 1878, with its accompanying bench, by G. E. Fox for Sir Lawrence Alma Tadema. Sheets of parchment were fixed inside the lid, on which visitors could sign their names. It was autographed by, among others, Tschaikowsky, Clara Schumann, Paderewski, Saint-Saëns, Joachim and Melba. Designed for Alma Tadema's Regent's Park home, with a room to house it, the piano was destroyed during an air raid in the 1939–45 war

28. *Opposite,* giraffe piano by Van der Hoef, Amsterdam, about 1810

29. *Top left, right, and bottom left,* three types of case for the upright piano of the early twentieth century

30. *Bottom right,* Broadwood grand designed by Edwin Lutyens, 1901

31. Jacob Blüthner (centre), with his British agents W. J. Whelpdale (left) and
W. M. Y. Maxwell, about 1890

32. Arthur M. Whelpdale, head of Whelpdale and Maxwell

33. Ignacy Jan Paderewski (1860–1941), as seen at the height of his popularity by a
contemporary caricaturist

ating' a composer's work with octaves, trills and cascading arpeggios; and indeed the public demanded it.

At a concert at the Paris Conservatoire some years later, when Liszt's great party-piece of virtuosity was a transcription of music from Meyerbeer's opera *Robert le Diable*, he was playing Beethoven's Kreutzer Sonata with the violinist Massart. By the end of the first movement the audience was bored with Beethoven and shouted for Liszt to play 'Robert le Diable'. They would not be denied; and the unfortunate violinist had to retire to the back of the platform while Liszt went through the gyrations of Meyerbeer before being allowed to complete the Beethoven sonata.

That was in 1841, by which time Liszt had become renowned throughout Europe as the 'Paganini of the keyboard'. Paganini first played in Paris in 1831, where Liszt heard him. He noted, too, the emotional public response to that master of the violin who had by unremitting practice turned himself into a magician on that instrument, who could conjure unprecedented and dramatic effects from any number of strings from four to one. The technical development of the piano, now extended to seven octaves, enabled Liszt to be the first to achieve the same effect on the new instrument.

Even so, it was not until the strengthening of the soundboard within a metal-supported frame (when Liszt forsook Erards for Bosendorfers, in the 1830s) that a piano could be guaranteed to stand up to the immense demands Liszt made on it. Sometimes proud owners of the lighter pianos of earlier days would lend them for the maestro to play at concerts in provincial towns; often the strings snapped or the soundboards cracked under the pressure of those terrible fingers, and it is said that his progress through England left a litter of broken woodwork and twisted wire.

Professional musicians and critics tended to sneer at such bravura playing, while they admired the technical skill of it. When John Nepomuk Hummel came back to London in 1830 after an absence of forty years he gave two concerts with the Philharmonic Society. A leading critic said that

as a performer he is master of all styles, but excels rather more in the brilliant than in the pathetic, though he never carries the former to excess. His touch is the true one, and more resembles Cramer's than any we have heard. The strength, and still more the equality, of his fingers are among the distinguishing features of his playing: and the pendulum-like accuracy of his time is too remarkable not to be noticed by all who hear him, though he occasionally makes this yield to expression; not, however, quite so often or in so great a degree as those who have a strong predilection for that manner, which denotes much sensibility, would wish. His execution is perfect, but we believe he does not consider great rapidity as an essential quality. We observed, and with infinite satisfaction, that his allegro movements were considerably slower than most of the pianists of the present day would have taken them. His good sense teaches him that great velocity renders it next to impossible to discern the delicacy of an air or the beauty of a modulation; that racing and leaping on the piano are generally resorted to by those who are conscious of possessing none of the higher powers, and feel obliged to supply the want of pure taste and deep feeling by mechanical dexterity.

However, Hummel did not draw in the crowds; Liszt most certainly did.

There were probably about fifty piano makers in London in 1830, and intense competition was arising between them. Erards were at this time the most successful piano makers in Europe, and their policy of providing pianos for the leading pianists (a policy copied from Broadwoods) had paid dividends in that Erards were usually to be found on the concert platform. They were normally used at Philharmonic Society concerts in London. Some sort of lobby seems to have been organized against them, for in 1835 Pierre Erard petitioned the Privy Council claiming that in this country 'certain unfounded notions were circulated to their disadvantage'. During the court of inquiry that followed, the leader of the Opera averred that Erard's pianos had 'a great deal more strength and power than any other instrument and greater effect in accompanying the voice'. The battle for supremacy in the piano trade had begun. If Broadwoods had won the first skirmish, Erards had won the second. But now there were more combatants in the field.

4
The Domestic Instrument

In the twenty years between 1830 and 1850 the piano finally assumed the form and character that it was to retain with very little change for almost a century afterwards. This happened at a time when Britain was undergoing a social and political transformation. If this country did not suffer the major political conflicts that disturbed much of Europe in 1830 and again in 1848, 'the year of revolution', it was partly because political power had been more peaceably rearranged by the effects of the Great Reform Bill, which was passed in 1832. This enfranchised the middle classes and gave them power, and a greater share in the wealth produced by the Industrial Revolution.

With wealth came leisure, and with leisure came a wider appreciation of the arts. In the next half-century it became the fashion for any 'respectable' home to be furnished with a piano, and for daughters of the household to learn to play it with often a high degree of competence. Nor was it uncommon for them to achieve the concert platform: Mrs Anderson and Madame Dulcken were as distinguished in their day as Liszt or Chopin.

Halévy wrote:

The piano lends itself to the most frivolous pastimes as well as the most serious studies. But it conceals within its bosom all the treasures of harmony, it is of all instruments the one which has contributed most towards popularising a taste for music and facilitating its study. Adopted by the greatest artists, it is at the same time to be found in the most humble dwellings.

Thalberg, himself a noted pianist of the time, pointed out the social influence of the piano in early Victorian England:

One of the most marked changes in the habits of society, as civilisation advances, is with respect to the character of its amusements. Formerly, nearly all such amusements were away from home and in public; now, with the more educated portion of society, the greater part is at home and within the family circle, music on the piano contributing the principal portion of it. In the more fashionable circles of society, private concerts increase year by year, and in them the piano is the principal feature. Many a man engaged in commercial and other active pursuits finds the chief charm of his drawing-room in the intellectual enjoyment offered by the piano.

Even steam and sailing vessels for passengers on long voyages are now obliged, by the fixed habits of society, to be furnished with pianofortes; thus transferring to the ocean itself something of the character of home enjoyments. By the use of the piano, many who never visit the opera or concerts become thoroughly acquainted with the choicest dramatic and orchestral compositions.

So vast libraries of piano music were published, including transcriptions for two hands or four of many popular operas and symphonies. Composers and teachers found a great demand for pieces that were 'brilliant but not difficult', that could be played by the daughters of the house in the drawing-room to admiring relatives and potential suitors. The piano came into its own as an accompaniment; many young men of fashion found it an asset to be able to sing the popular ballads of the day. This presented problems when the capability of a young woman did not extend to transposing at sight, to the most comfortable key for the voice.

So there was a ready sale for the 'transposing piano', which did all the work. There were several types. On one, the keyboard could be moved up or down, by a system of slots. On others, the whole action moved; in one transposing piano, the strings and frame were on rollers. The first patent for a transposing piano was taken out by Edward Ryley in 1801; John Broadwood made one in 1808.[1]

1. Transposing pianos were still in use in the twentieth century, notably by the popular songwriter Irving Berlin.
'He has never learnt how to play a conventional piano properly. He has created something like 3000 songs and influenced practically every song-writer for three generations by pounding the black notes in the key of F sharp and by using that little lever [of the transposing piano] make them come out sounding different.
'He could play – all ten fingers moving hesitantly over the black keys. What he could not do, was make the white keys sound half as effective. So whatever he touched, out it would come in the key of F sharp. This was 1909 . . .
'A century earlier the firm of Norris and Hyde in London had produced a

Music at home was given an additional stimulus in the 1840s by the music-making at Buckingham Palace by the young Queen Victoria and her husband: London was still the showplace for the leading European soloists, and most of them were invited to the Palace. After the extravagances and excesses of the Regency, Victoria's morality, propriety, and devotion to family life set a pattern that was copied throughout the country.

To many girls the piano came to represent a powerful weapon in courtship. Mary Gladstone, daughter of William Ewart Gladstone, regarded herself as poorly educated (though she could speak French and Italian and knew some German); but she learnt to play the piano well, no doubt because she was acute enough to recognize its advantages.

As a girl staying at Wilton she listened to Hubert Parry playing a Schubert Reverie and a Chopin Prelude, and wrote later:

Never in this life can I forget the effect on me of his rendering of those two pieces. Shall I not remember them in another? . . . Anything that is appealing in my pianoforte playing, anything that is tender or wistful or passionate is entirely owing to Hubert; it was he who first revealed to me how to express in music the emotion of a human heart.

Mary Gladstone was not the first Victorian girl to lose her heart to her piano teacher and thrill to the romance of the keyboard with all its potential. As Walter Savage Landor wrote:

> Many love music but for music's sake,
> Many because her touches can awake
> Thoughts that repose within the breast half-dead,
> And rise to follow where she loves to lead.
> What various feelings come from days gone by!
> What tears from far-off sources dim the eye!
> Few, when light fingers with sweet voices play
> And melodies swell, pause, and melt away,
> Mind how at every touch, at every tone,
> A spark of life hath glisten'd and hath gone.

---

piano that could change key for the pianist. He made inquiries and found tha the Weser Company in the United States could make a similar one for him . .. It cost him 100 dollars.' [Michael Freedland: *Irving Berlin*]

The poem is a celebration of the Victorian drawing-room, and could not have been written before the piano was developed to the point where it could express emotion.

The mood was encouraged by the popular pianists of the day. When 'Russian Field' came back to London in 1832 – and attended the funeral of his sometime master Clementi – he played his Piano Concerto in E Flat at a Philharmonic Concert; the slow movement, a *Pastorale*, was spontaneously encored. That May, Mendelssohn gave the first London performance of his Piano Concerto No. 1 (with Cipriani Potter conducting) at a Philharmonic Society concert: it was so popular that it was repeated at a concert in June, this time with Cramer conducting. A contemporary wrote:

The exquisite precision of the first *motivo*, lighted up with impulsive bursts of passion, bringing out a meaning which no one has since seemed capable of realising, together with the delicacy of the manner in which the instrument was, in the andante, made to sing, as if it gave out a combination of exquisitely attuned voices – it is not within the compass of words to describe.

In 1835 the star virtuoso in London was Henri Herz, the Viennese composer renowned for his keyboard agility but less for his interpretation: he later turned to piano making, in Paris. Herz was notorious for playing almost nothing but his own compositions. Sigismond Thalberg did the same thing, exploiting to the full the character of the piano at the expense of musicianship. Dr Cox despised his showmanship:

The fact was that Thalberg astonished the ears of the million rather than gratified the taste of the refined. Like Herz, he adhered wholly to his own compositions, not a bar of which was above mediocrity, his sole object having been to show off his wonderful powers of mechanism. For this end and purpose he covered sheet after sheet of music-paper with such an overwhelmingly increasing multitude of notes as could only be rightly expressed by the saying 'Rubbish shot here!' The torment he was to learners, both professional and amateur, no tongue can tell.

When Liszt returned to London in 1840 he was not immune from the same sort of criticism. In those years (though not when he was older) he allowed the genius of the great improviser to abandon respect for the intentions of other composers Mendelssohn wrote:

Liszt has forfeited a good part of my esteem thanks to the idiotic pranks he played, not only with the public – which matters little – but with the music itself. He performed works by Beethoven, Bach, Handel, Mozart and Weber in such a lamentably imperfect style . . . Here six bars were added, there seven left out: now he plays wrong harmonies which were subsequently cancelled out by others equally false. Then we had a horrible fortissimo employed in passages marked pianissimo – and so on, all kinds of deplorable misdeeds.

In fairness to Liszt, it could be said that this was what the public wanted; and more pertinently, that it was the debased style that Herz and Moscheles had made popular. If the music as written did not demonstrate the power of the piano and the skill of the executant, then he must 'improvise'. Emotion must be given full rein, however inappropriate to the composer's wishes. But together with the bravura compositions that attracted the crowds, Liszt was capable of very sensitive chamber playing. The Philharmonic Society long remembered a performance of the Kreutzer Sonata by Liszt with Ole Bull, the Norwegian violinist.

A single piano was soon no novelty in public, and the vogue for multi-piano concerts began. At one in London during Liszt's visit in 1840 he played with Herz, Thalberg and Moscheles. Liszt had arrived late. The four of them sat down to play, and discovered that each had the wrong part. They carried on regardless, which suggests a cavalier approach by each of them to the niceties of rehearsal. Four pianos were comparatively modest: Chopin's first appearance in Paris in 1831 had been in a concert given by Kalkbrenner with six pianos.

Erards now had a rival as the leading piano maker in Paris: Ignaz Pleyel, Clementi's music publishing agent, had begun to manufacture pianos, and to make them well. In 1825 he had produced a 'Unicord' piano with an iron frame – an early adoption of the full metal frame. But he is thought to have been anticipated by a piano maker in Boston, USA, Alpheus Babcock, who early the same year produced a square piano with an iron frame complete with hitch-pin block.

The fact that by 1830 Pleyel's pianos were rivalling Erard's was partly due to the technical innovations that he incorporated.

Many of them were the invention of a German-born employee, born Johann Heinrich Pape but by then calling himself Jean Henri Pape. Pape eventually started his own business as a supplier of piano parts in both Paris and London. He was responsible for a remarkable number of changes that eventually became accepted as standard. In particular, he devised the felt covering for the hammer, in place of traditional leather; and he was among the first to use tempered steel wire for the strings (Pleyel took out a patent for it in 1810; Broadwood was using English and German steel wire in 1815). Some of Pape's inventions were more abstruse. Recognizing that the piano must be level on the floor, he devised a system of spring castors. He also made a piano with eight and a half octaves.

By the 1840s Birmingham manufacturers had the reputation of producing the best brass strings; and by this time it had become fairly common for the bass strings to be wound with copper. It was in 1827 that James Stewart discovered that a single string could be hitched and wound back to form the second string of a bichord piano: he had been a partner of Jonas Chickering in Boston, and was said to have brought the idea to London from America. Perhaps the greatest breakthrough in this period was the invention by Antoine Bord in 1843 of the Capo Tasto bar, in effect an improvement of Erard's agraffe – a blunt metal bar, pressing across the strings like a wrest-plank bridge and defining the length of vibration. There were also refinements of the soundboard, and in 1845 Henri Pape glued metal rods to the soundboard, recognizing that this did not hinder the vibration as earlier manufacturers had believed it would, but in fact improved the tone.

Pleyel copied Clementi, Broadwood and Erard in promoting his pianos with every device that the social world and fashion might make available. As Erards had taken the young Liszt under their wing, Pleyel adopted a young Polish pianist – Fryderyk Chopin. Chopin had arrived in Paris from Warsaw, and had presented himself as a pupil before the most distinguished pianist then in the French capital. That was Kalkbrenner, who shortly before had gone into partnership with Pleyel. Partly to exploit this association, and no doubt noting that Erards attracted pianists to their showrooms in Paris and London by providing rehearsal rooms as well as their sales facilities, the Pleyels – Ignaz and Camille, father and son – opened their first Salle Pleyel. This small concert hall, mainly intended for piano concerts, was added to the showrooms at 9 Rue Cadet.

When Chopin played for the first time in Paris in public, it was in the Pleyel hall, on a Pleyel piano. It was at that famous six-piano concert, and Kalkbrenner nearly achieved a remarkable double since he advertised another young pianist to be part of the sextet – Felix Mendelssohn-Bartholdy, then aged twenty-three. In fact Mendelssohn did not join in, though he was in the audience.

Chopin paid his first visit to London six years later, in the Coronation Year of 1837. He was supposedly incognito, and travelled about the south of England seeing the sights, visiting Chichester, Arundel and Hampton Court. But he did play privately at one soirée, at 46 Bryanston Square, the home of James Shudi Broadwood. By this time Broadwood was a figure of considerable importance in the musical world of London, though nominally on the point of retirement. The business was in the hands of his son Henry Fowler Broadwood.

On a later visit in 1848 Chopin took lodgings at 48 Dover Street, and in a letter to a friend in Paris showed that he was being courted earnestly by the three leading piano makers of the day:

I have at last managed to get a foothold in this abyss called London. I have only just begun to breathe more freely these last few days, now that the sun has begun to shine.

Erard hastened to offer his services and he has placed one of his pianos at my disposal. I have a Broadwood and a Pleyel – three pianos in all, but what's the use of them, since I have no time to play.

Broadwood became a reliable personal friend, organizing the travel arrangements (by the newly completed railway) for his tour of the North of England and Scotland, sending Broadwood pianos ahead of him, and generally providing competent administration. Henry Fowler Broadwood might perhaps not have welcomed the analogy that Chopin chose to use of him in another letter, however flatteringly it was intended:

Broadwood, who is a real London Pleyel, has been my best and truest friend. He is, as you know, a very rich and well-educated man whose father transferred to him his property and factory and then retired to the country. He has splendid connections.

Despite the financial success of his tour – young ladies of the best families clamoured to be given even one piano lesson by him – Chopin felt himself under the shadow of another visitor to London: 'You have to play Mendelssohn if you wish to have a great success.'

Britain had by this time earned the reputation abroad of being a profoundly unmusical country, but one in which foreign musicians could make a fortune. It is ironical that during the half-century from 1770 when British piano makers led the world and their instruments were regarded throughout Europe and North America as incontestably the best, virtually no British-born pianist emerged to challenge Clementi, Cramer, Hummel, Moscheles and the rest. Few appeared during the years of Liszt, Chopin, Herz, Thalberg and Mendelssohn.

Clementi was born in Rome, Cramer in Mannheim, Hummel in what is now Bratislava, and Moscheles in Prague. Liszt was born in Raiding, Hungary, Chopin near Warsaw, Herz in Vienna, Thalberg in Geneva and Mendelssohn in Hamburg.

Was it no more than the British tradition that great musicians must have foreign names? Was it a result of the British educational system, so early teaching that proficiency in the arts was unmasculine and appearances in public (other than as a singer) unfeminine?

It would be tempting to blame Britain's dilatoriness in founding a school of music – the Royal Academy of Music was not founded until 1822 though Charles Burney and others had been pressing for a national music school half a century earlier. It would be tempting, if the Royal Academy of Music had produced more than one or two pianists of remembered genius during its early years. But it did not.

A nation of shopkeepers, said Napoleon scornfully. He might have been nearer the mark had he called the British a nation of manufacturers, explorers and inventors.

Perhaps there seemed to be something un-English in the bravura performances for which the piano was principally famed in the early nineteenth century. The one English pianist of international reputation who could certainly play technically as well as, say, Moscheles chose deliberately not to do it. The London-born Cipriani Potter went to Vienna, and became a friend of Beethoven (whose Broadwood piano he repaired after its journey from London); then he came back home, and settled into the comparatively introspective world of the highly professional Philharmonic Society where he gave a series of first performances in London of the Beethoven piano concertos. Then he became professor of piano at the Royal Academy of Music on its foundation, and its second Principal. It is a quiet, rather academic career (and a long one: Cipriani Potter died in 1871, aged nearly seventy-nine).

But no one clamoured to hear him play 'Robert le Diable', and no crowds cheered him in the streets as they cheered the venerable Liszt. There is no doubt that the continental virtuosi of the piano had a charisma, a personal attraction that was almost sexual. Liszt's attraction for (and attraction to) women is well documented. Chopin also had more than technical accomplishment. As Liszt wrote of him:

He had so distinguished an air and his manners displayed such perfect breeding that instinctively one treated him as an aristocrat. His whole appearance in fact made one think of the convolvulus that swings its exquisitely coloured cups, of a texture so delicate that the least touch will tear them, on stalks of an incredible fineness.

In mimicry he displayed a spirited drollery which seemed to be inexhaustible. He enjoyed making comic improvisations in which he reproduced the musical formulas and particular mannerisms of certain virtuosos, aping their gestures and movements, and the expression of their faces with a dexterity that provided in a flash a comment on their whole personalities.

That is very Latin, very un-English: and it does not seem that Cipriani Potter was ever tempted to emulate it. Not for him the exotic drama of the incredible octave-work or the 'little skips' of Moscheles and his kind. He preferred straightforward, faithful and (if his contemporaries are to be believed) beautiful performances of Beethoven with his colleagues of the Philharmonic Society.

There is a hint of promise cut short in the career of George Aspull, who was born in Nottingham in 1813. He toured the country as a prodigy, and won a number of gold medals, mainly for his improvisations. He died in his nineteenth year, and having written down very little music he left no memorial other than the affectionate reminiscences of his friends.

It could be that the emptiness of the ranks of British pianists of the period is due to a political and social phenomenon – the ending of the era of patronage. The social reformation epitomized by the 1832 Reform Act handed over much political and financial power to the middle classes; but it was many years before they began to come to terms with the felicities of the arts. It was said of 'one of the most pushing and rich of our enterprising merchants' that he was 'marvellously at home in arithmetic, compound addition, the rule of three, multiplication and so forth', but he had 'not much studied history, poetics, and the other graces and, as by many they were then thought, exotics of education'. That merchant was not untypical. No more did the Peter Beckfords do the grand tour and discovering small boys such as Clementi, spend minor fortunes to train and promote them.

The career of the first pianist of international note to be produced by the Royal Academy of Music – and indeed almost the only one for many years – illustrates this. William Sterndale Bennett was born in Sheffield in 1816, the son of the organist of the parish church. Both his parents dying while he was still an infant he was adopted by his grandfather John Bennett, who was a vicar choral or lay clerk at King's College, Cambridge. At the age of eight young William became a chorister of King's, but as he showed unusual musical promise he was sent at the age of ten (the earliest permitted age in those days) to the Royal Academy of Music, his fees being paid by a friendly member of Peterhouse.

At the Royal Academy he became a pupil of Cipriani Potter; and before Sterndale Bennett was twenty he had written five piano concertos (two of which he played at Philharmonic Society concerts) and a number of other works. Mendelssohn heard him play, and invited him to Leipzig. The boy was still poor: 'his published compositions were much too classical to command a rapid sale', says a contemporary.

So the Broadwood firm stepped in as sponsor, enabling Sterndale Bennett to study in Leipzig for two years. During that time he played his piano concertos at a number of concerts, with Mendelssohn conducting; he had invited Bennett, he said, 'not as my pupil, but as my friend'.

Schumann was greatly impressed by him.

From the cocoon of the schools so brilliant a butterfly has taken wing [he wrote] that we would fain follow its flight with outstretched arms as it bathes in the ether and gives to or takes from the flowers.

But when this 'thorough Englishman, glorious artist, and beautiful and poetic soul' (Schumann again) returned to London and married, he was drawn into the mesh of the musical establishment.

He was at one time Principal of the Royal Academy of Music, Professor of Music at Cambridge, and conductor of the Philharmonic Society. Not surprisingly, the duties of these offices virtually ended his career as a concert pianist, and severely curtailed his output as a composer. He was knighted: he turned into a much-respected administrator. He exemplified the Victorian virtues of moderation, of essentially English restraint, of submission to convention.

In the distant light of that Leipzig promise it is difficult not to see in him the butterfly broken on the wheel of routine. One wonders whether, as Sir William Sterndale Bennett, he ever attended a recital by his slightly younger contemporary Anton Rubinstein and remembered those days when he bathed in the ether of Mendelssohn's friendship and encouragement as he poured out his 'beautiful and poetic soul' on the piano keyboard.

When in 1842 the twelve-year-old Artur Rubinstein played in London for the first time he impressed his audience profoundly because of the breadth of his repertoire and the seriousness with which he approached it, even at that young age. Not only did he play Bach fugues accurately and from memory (and Bach was in those days a somewhat unfashionable composer), but he included some delicate romantic studies played with grace and expression, and also tackled successfully some of the more dramatic and difficult of Liszt's works. From this point, the age of the piano athlete, determined to match his courage against the Everest of technique, was drawing to a close.

A new seriousness had begun to affect the concert platform. The old idea of the Antient Concerts, where a ballad was followed by a piano fantasia, that by a glee, and that by a piano improvisation on a given theme handed up from the audience, was going out of fashion. One result of the greater availability of the piano was that it encouraged the practice of singing at home; and that, by a natural progression, led to the expansion of choral singing.

The Sacred Harmonic Society was founded in 1832; and though it preceded Queen Victoria's accession by five years, nothing could have been more thoroughly Victorian than this society of amateurs, pledged to meet together to perform 'the sublime compositions of Handel, Haydn and other eminent sacred composers, with that degree of precision and effect which their worth entitles them to, and which the development of their inherent beauties requires'.

In one year, 1836, the Society sang St Paul, the Creation, Israel in Egypt, the Dettingen Te Deum, Mozart's 'Mass No. 12' and, at Christmas, Messiah. Mendelssohn attended one performance of St Paul.

With this flowering of sacred music, Mendelssohn became more familiar to the majority of English audiences, particularly at provincial musical festivals, as a composer and conductor of oratarios, and as an organist, than as a pianist and composer for the piano. He twice conducted St Paul for the Sacred Harmonic Society in 1844, and wrote Elijah for the Birmingham Festival of 1846. Mendelssohn conducted it in London the following year, shortly before his death at the age of thirty-eight; Queen Victoria and Prince Albert were in the audience.

This seriousness also affected the use of the piano in public performance. Until the 1830s the piano was not regarded as an instrument that could hold the attention of an audience for a full concert. It was played as part of the orchestra, as the harpsichord had been; and the development of the piano concerto from Mozart to Beethoven mirrors precisely the technical development of the piano in those years. Increasingly the pianist would be given a solo 'spot', but almost invariably he would also play in partnership with the orchestra at some other stage in the evening.

The pianist might also be invited to play at a soirée at a great house; but then, as Moscheles found, even the most distinguished virtuoso would have to contend with conversation and the serving of refreshments; his delicate pianissimo might be drowned by the popping of champagne corks or the trumpeting of political debate.

From the 1830s Paganini, the 'devil's violinist', could attract an audience that would fill a large concert-hall; but a violinist needs an accompanist, and so he was not strictly a solo performer. Moscheles claimed to have been the first to dare to appear on the concert platform alone with his piano. That was in 1837. Two years later in Paris (and not, apparently, aware that Moscheles had preceded him) Liszt did the same thing. It was then called a solo performance.

The term 'recital' was first used in 1840, when an English musician, Frederick Beale, referred to Liszt's 'recitals on the pianoforte'. Some thought the term 'recitals' pretentious, but it caught on, and was first used to advertise a programme by Liszt at the Hanover Square Rooms in that year. His programme, however, was in the traditional showy form. First, a piano transcription of the Overture to William Tell; then a fantasia 'on reminiscences of I Puritani'; then some of his studies and, as he called them, 'fragments'; and finally, the customary bravura improvisation on a theme handed up from the audience.

There were fifty piano makers in London in 1830. But the next twenty years saw the most extraordinary expansion of piano manufacture to satisfy the apparently insatiable public demand. Many of these piano makers were former apprentices of the great houses of Broadwood, Erard and Stodart who had dared to branch out on their own. Some thrived; others, no doubt, built a piano laboriously in a one-man business, selling it to buy more materials until such time as the business built up.

But the one-man business was by no means to be despised. A similar expansion in piano manufacture was taking place in Germany. It was in 1836 that Heinrich Engelhard Steinweg built a piano in the kitchen of his little house in Seesen in the Harz mountains; the family emigrated to the United States in 1850 and anglicized its name to Steinway.

As the piano became a feature of many homes, practising was almost fashionable – though not popular with the neighbours, then as now. It is easy to feel some sympathy for that Frenchman who one day in the 1830s, maddened by the sound of pianos in the rooms above, below and on either side of his, rushed out of his house and set fire to a neighbouring piano factory, burning it to the ground.

5
The Exhibited Definition

During the second half of the nineteenth century the art of piano-making was largely concerned with refinement – especially refinement in two areas. These were the strengthening of the frame by the general adoption of cast-iron, and the improvement of the tone of all pianos by overstringing (setting the longer strings at an angle across the shorter).

As the tension upon the strings had massively increased – by the use of stronger frames, thicker strings, larger hammers – metal supports had become necessary. Broadwoods had introduced an iron-braced frame in 1847; the piano they made for Chopin in the following year had five such iron bars. There was a danger that such bars could produce unfortunate harmonics and a 'tinny' sound in the notes adjacent to them. Broadwoods therefore added a diagonal bar to take the heaviest stress.

Collard and Collard introduced a 'reverberation bridge'; and there was still argument over whether a better tone was produced in grand pianos by 'up-striking' or 'down-striking' actions (the hammers coming up from below the strings, or down from above them). Down-striking grands fought a rearguard action for some years: one Daniel Hewitt lost £12 000 in an attempt to popularize the 'camel-back' piano – a grand with the action in a peculiar 'hump' on the top. It was Hewitt also who took out a patent to do away with the piano case altogether, by fixing the frame and strings to the living-room wall. This attempt to introduce a 'built-in' piano failed. Possibly the inventor overlooked the effect on the neighbours of having their living-rooms used as a perpetual soundbox.

Early in the century John Hawkins of Philadelphia and London had made his bid to introduce a full iron frame. But the first patent for a system of cast-iron framing 'with wrest-plank secured in a metal frame by bolts, and covered with a plate of soft metal' was taken out by John Dewrance in 1855.

By that date, however, the members of one vigorous family who divided themselves between the old world and the new were moving ahead rapidly in the development of both the iron frame and the principle of overstringing. It was the revolution of 1848 that drove Heinrich Steinweg to emigrate from Germany to America, taking with him four of his sons and his three daughters. He left his eldest son, C. F. Theodore Steinway, in Germany to run his own piano factory.

On their arrival in New York, the sons took jobs as workmen with other piano makers until they could get their own firm going. But they did this so effectively that only a year later, the overstrung square pianos by Steinway and Sons of New York were commended at the Great Exhibition in London. The Steinways were a close-knit family and long letters were exchanged between New York and Seesen, where Theodore Steinway (a qualified engineer) was recruiting expert technical advice from Hermann von Helmholtz, the Berlin physicist who developed the theory of overtones.

During the first twenty years of the American company Steinways took out eighteen patents, several derived from Theodore's experiments in Germany. But it was Henry Jr who in 1859 produced the overstrung grand piano that – allied to brilliant modern marketing techniques – was to conquer the world. The Steinways bought land on Long Island, New York (then undeveloped) and set a timber wharf, a foundry, and the piano factory there, giving their name to the district.

They made plans for a concert-hall to be built next to the New York showrooms, but this was not opened until 1866 having been delayed by the Civil War. The opening was overshadowed by the tragedies that had overtaken the family during the previous year: Henry Steinway Jr had died from tuberculosis, and while visiting his brother Theodore in Germany Charles Steinway died of typhoid. The firm was thus left in the hands of the elderly Henry Engelhard Steinway and his two youngest sons Albert and William. Theodore gave up the German factory and joined them in New York.

It was Theodore who pursued the technical excellence of the grand piano. He made a detailed study of the steel industry both in the United States and Europe, and by 1880 designed and manufactured a cast frame that enabled string tension to be nearly doubled. Allied with Theodore's research into acoustics this enabled the firm to produce a concert grand that was outstanding in both power and tone. It was Theodore, also, who designed a smaller grand only six feet long, and proved that it could be made with similar characteristics.

If Theodore was the engineer, his younger brother William was the salesman and contact man. He interested himself in local politics and charities, went into property, started a tramline and a ferry, was a co-founder of the district gas company and on the board of two banks. He was also an active Democrat and a friend of Grover Cleveland, to whom William Steinway gave a piano when the President was married in the White House.

But the Steinways maintained their links with the musical world of Europe. This enabled them to persuade the leading European pianists to make American tours, though some initially were nervous: when Artur Rubinstein was negotiating his contract for an American tour in 1872 he specified that he must not be required to play in beer-gardens. Instead, he played at the Steinway Hall on a Steinway grand.

Already Steinway pianos were earning a high reputation in Europe; and in 1877 the company opened a European sales office and service unit in London.

The Steinway square piano had been noticed with approval at the Great Exhibition in 1851. That exhibition was to be the precursor of a number of international exhibitions in the next half-century. These aimed at attracting the public, but were a means whereby manufacturers of many nations could see their rivals' products, identify new trends and techniques, and battle for the gold medals and commendations that the judging panels handed out.

The exhibition had been the idea of Prince Albert, to demonstrate the skill and standard of British manufacture (though the assembled results proved less advanced than had been hoped, and led to active lobbying for the setting up of schools of art and design where higher standards could be taught). The exhibition, organized by Henry Cole, was housed in Joseph Paxton's 'great glass hive' specially erected in Hyde Park approximately where the Albert Memorial now stands. There were more than 13 000 exhibitors, more than half of them British, and the event was immensely popular, attracting over six million visitors.

The Great Exhibition was an occasion for the various piano manufacturers to display the originality and distinction of their products. The catalogue gives an interesting cross-section of the trade at that point, and is significant both for the emphasis placed on technical advance (the main philosophy of the Exhibition in general) and also decoration. It is relevant, for instance, that Broadwoods considered cabinet-making and inlay of particular importance; and that other manufacturers were now concentrating on the 'cottage' piano at the expense of the square.

Joseph Kirkman and Son, of Soho Square and Dean Street (inheritors of that greatest of eighteenth-century harpsichord makers), showed 'a miniature model of a grand piano, $6\frac{3}{4}$ octaves, with metal braces and drilled bridges; a 7 octave full grand piano with repetition action, in rosewood case; a semi-grand piano in walnut case; and an oblique piccolo piano'. Thus Kirkmans were using metal braces, rather than the full iron frame; and they still felt it necessary to mention that the full grand had Erard's 'repetition action'. They too had by this time adopted oblique or cross-stringing for the small upright piano.

George Frederick Greiner of 51 Upper Marylebone Street was more inventive. His 'semi-grand piano' was constructed 'on the principle of the speaking trumpet, with unison tuning-screws, and repeat tongue action'. Greiner had used 'a newly-invented material' in place of ivory for the keys.

William Southall and William Stodart and Son were more conventional and showed, respectively, 'a grand piano', and 'a patent rosewood horizontal grand' and 'a compact rosewood square piano'.

C. Cadby of the Grays Inn Pianoforte Manufactory was still experimenting with suspended soundboards. His 'grand in rosewood' was 'on the exhibitor's new patent suspension principle: the sounding board, instead of being glued or permanently attached to the wooden frame is suspended from it by metallic attachments which, being adjustable, admit of its being tightly

strained to increase the tone'. Cadby also showed a grand in
zebra wood on the same principle, and an upright cottage piano
showing the same principle applied to 'the cheaper kind of
pianos'.

William Rolfe of Cheapside eschewed novelty in favour of a
'two-unison common cottage piano confirming the advantages of
the ordinary repetition and check or double actions; a piano in
which stability, economy and excellence are the objects aimed at'.

John Brinsmead put in a piano in which 'the long brass joint
generally seen upon the fall of pianos, is obviated when opening
by a simple contrivance. The case permits the instrument to be
placed in any part of a room.'

George Metzler's was a 'small size cottage piano, made of
pollard oak, "O.G." or arched fall with ornamental shell front'.
John and Henry Moore showed a 'grand cottage piano' – the best
of both worlds – 'of new design'.

George Luft and Son of Great Russell Street put in an 'Albert
cottage piano of new construction', a delicate tribute to the
Prince Consort whose design for the 'Albert cottage', a simple
home for the poorer classes, was being shown at the Exhibition.
They also showed a harmonium.

Richard Hunt of Blake Street went in for an extravaganza. His
'tavola piano' was 'a dining or drawing room table, standing upon
a centre block or pedestal, and containing a piano (opening with
spring bolts) on the grand principle, with a closet containing
music composed by the inventor. This piano has the ordinary
power of tone although occupying half the usual space, and can
be made the piccolo or grand size.' Clementi would have been
delighted by this device to sell the inventor's music with his
piano.

Enever and Steedman of George Street emphasized the case and
the exotic keys. 'An elegant walnut marqueterie semi-cottage
piano of new design, with double action. The pearl and tortoiseshell keys are made by T. & H. Brooks of Cumberland Market.
Also a plain walnut square-fall piccolo or microchordian piano
with single action.'

Robert Allison of Regent Street were concerned to make the
identification of piano keys simpler. Their 'walnut wood cottage
piano' was distinguished by 'the keys of the finger-board being

alternated in colour to show all the scales major and minor, according to a single rule for each mood, founded on the plan of the semi-tonic interval, which renders the seven notes to be touched for an octave of each of the other eleven scales, as evident as the scale of C'. Simplicity itself.

John Champion Jones of Soho Square was championing togetherness. His 'double or twin semi cottage piano' had 'two fronts and sets of keys, one on either side, suitable for any numbers of performers from one to six; case of walnut-tree'.

Charles Holderness of New Oxford Street and Ralph Allison of Wardour Street and Brook Street also showed walnut pianos; the former's was a 'cottage grand of $6\frac{7}{8}$ octaves', the latter's 'with carved figures and inlaid with flowers in woods of natural colours'.

William Jenkins and Son, of London Street, Fitzroy Square, were aiming at a more specific market with their 'expanding and collapsing piano for gentlemen's yachts, the saloons of steam-vessels, ladies' cabins etc., only $13\frac{1}{2}$ ins. from front to back when collapsed'. Jenkins also showed a 'cabinet pianoforte in figured walnut-tree, carved and ornamented in the Elizabethan style'.

Frederick Hund and Son of Ebury Street had devised 'a new kind of cottage piano' called the Lyra, which stood 'on a peculiar constructed platform or sound conductor, into which the bass strings extend; and although the instrument is only 3 feet 5 inches high, it produces a tone equal to a semi grand: the instrument has a grand check action with levers of great power and elasticity'.

Robert Addison of Regent Street produced a transposing piano. These had been in existence for some years, but most had hitherto required the player to lift the keyboard and transport it bodily up or down. In this Addison piano 'its novelty consists in the keyboard, hammers and strings being immovable'; instead, the whole action moved, thus allowing the player to transpose into three higher and three lower keys.

George H. Aggio of Colchester (an appropriate home for it) showed a 'piano fitted up in a plate glass case, and gold carvings with an embroidered curtain front'.

Abraham Dimoline of Bristol claimed for his seven-octave

compensation piano that 'the mechanism by its lightness etc. produces an agreeable touch'. There was an 'improved plan for uncovering the keys', and the panels were 'paintings of mother-of-pearl on glass'. His semi-cottage piano, also of seven octaves, was in a papier-mâché case with inlaid mother-of-pearl 'in the Italian style'.

William H. H. Akerman of Bridgwater, Somerset, was one of the few manufacturers to tackle the action rather than the case, with his 'piano with a new movement: a bevel action for the dampers, applicable to all kinds, intended to give precision of touch by the certain rising of the key; it preserves also the dampers by gentle instead of jerking movement'. Akerman also offered a form of octave coupler, intended no doubt to simplify the playing of the bravura octave work so common in mid-Victorian piano music.

Smyth and Roberts of Birmingham were interested in the problem of stress on the soundboard. Their seven-octave cottage piano, with its conventional grand action and repeat, had a sounding board and back 'on the principle of a violincello', which was achieved by mounting an iron frame between the sounding board and strings but allowing the sounding board to expand and contract: 'they are suitable for hot climates'.

T. Woolley of Nottingham was also concerned with this problem; his 'equilibrium' piano was also advertised as 'suitable for all climates'.

Joseph Harmar of Bloomsbury Street and Towns and Packer of Oxford Street were also showing transposing pianos with mobile action.

Pierre Orpheus Erard of Great Marlborough Street demonstrated their 'new patent metal frames for pianos, intended to carry the principal part of the weight or pull of the wires, independent of the wood frame, with a new screw apparatus for tuning attached to the same; particularly adapted to extreme climates'. Thus did the iron frame come into general commercial use. Erards were showing their full range of pianos: 'Ornamented extra-grand, extra grand with pedal keys; small grand, improved new scale; grand oblique, ornamented in the Elizabethan style, adapted to extreme climates; grand cottage; reduced cottage; extra grand, and grand oblique.'

Isaac Henry Robert Mott of the Strand showed a still more astonishing development: horizontal grand pianos 'with metallic frames above and beneath the strings capable of resisting change of climate, or great tension, without interfering with the freedom or vibration of the sounding board'. That was not uncommon; but the Mott pianos were of 'nearly 8 octaves, also an additional keyboard of five more octaves' – a range surely far beyond the human ear.

Robert Wornum of Store Street, that pioneering firm, still favoured the down-striking action for their semi-bichord grand piano.

J. and J. Hopkinson of Soho Square added a novelty to their 'horizontal grand piano with patent action on an entirely new principle giving increased power and certainty to the touch'; they added an invention by Mara, 'a tremolo similar in effect to that produced by the human voice'. Hopkinsons may also have been among the first to advertise a 'Boudoir' piano, in rosewood.

G. Peachey of Bishopsgate Street Within showed a pair of piccolo pianos, loyally named the Victoria (in improved pollard oak) and the Albert (in improved rosewood).

W. Matthews of Nottingham produced a model showing the strung frame of an upright piano 'with lever tuning apparatus, the object being to sustain the pressure of the strings and prevent the instrument getting out of tune'. They had also invented 'an upright piano in which an apparatus is introduced to keep the instrument in its upright position'. The first uprights, the great giraffes, did have a disconcerting habit of falling over.

Finally, among the British manufacturers at the Great Exhibition John Broadwood and Sons showed four grand pianos, remarkable for the elegance of their cases. Their four grands were: first, in ebony, seven octaves, designed by E. M. Barry (the twenty-one-year-old son of Sir Charles Barry, architect of the Houses of Parliament), inlaid, carved and gilt, with straight bracing. Second, in an amboyna case, seven octaves, carved and gilt, with diagonal bracing. Third, in an amboyna case, seven octaves, with diagonal bracing; and fourth, in an inlaid walnut case, seven octaves, with straight bracing.

These pianos were among the successes of the Great Exhibition, which was intended to demonstrate the advanced nature of

British craftsmanship and design; piano manufacture was one of the few areas in which it could truly be claimed that the British products were the best, in design and manufacture. The Gold Medal went to Erard of London.

Prince Albert persuaded his adopted countrymen to repeat the exhibition a decade later, at South Kensington in 1862. But the Prince's death at the end of 1861 clouded the occasion. Nevertheless international exhibitions became the fashion, and special mentions were given to several British piano makers – John Broadwood and Sons, Collard and Collard, Hopkinson, Kirkman, and John Brinsmead and Sons, each of which firms could claim to have patented improvements in grands or uprights. Overstrung square pianos by Steinway of New York and Chickering of Boston were also praised in the early sixties.

The French became especially persistent as exhibition organizers. For their 'Great Universal Exposition' of 1867 an immense iron building was erected on the Champs Elysées and became known as 'the cathedral of commerce'. That exhibition was most significant for the piano manufacturers; for Steinways triumphed there, technically and socially. Berlioz admired their pianos, as did the illustrator (and amateur musician) Gustav Doré.

Steinways became fashionable; and from 1867 their pianos were in demand in Europe in increasing numbers. That exhibition was also something of a triumph for the pianist-turned-pianomaker Henri Herz; the judges noted that he personally supervised the manufacture of the pianos sold under his name. Broadwoods also won a Supreme Gold Medal.

The makers vied with each other for gold medals. In 1878 the French marked their recovery from the Franco-Prussian War with the greatest international fair held up to that date. It was on a 66-acre site in the centre of Paris, held over 50 000 exhibits and attracted sixteen million visitors. The head of the firm of John Brinsmead and Sons was awarded the Cross of the Legion of Honour. Gold medals went to Erard, Pleyel Wolff and Company, Herz, Schroeder, and Hopkinson.

Europe was still the hub of the world, and English manufacturers may have overlooked the first major world's fair in North America held two years earlier in 1876 – the Philadelphia Centennial, marking a hundred years since the Declaration of

Independence. Steinways were there, winning (as their historian records with justifiable terseness) 'the usual medal for excellence'. So also were symbols of the new technology that was to revolutionize the craft-based industries: Alexander Graham Bell's telephone, Thomas Edison's duplex telegraph, the typewriter, and the sewing machine. But it was in Paris in 1889 that the public were able to see demonstrated for the first time (beneath the shadow of the newly erected Eiffel Tower) the one modern application that was to have a devastating effect on the piano trade – electricity, used to produce light and power. But it was some years before it was linked with the acoustic gramophone which had begun to emerge in 1877, when Thomas Edison first recorded the human voice on cylinders, in New York.

Meanwhile piano makers were proliferating in London. Increasingly successful was Chappell and Company, the inheritor of the business founded by Samuel Chappell early in the century. Sam's widow Emily had kept the business going, principally as music sellers but also from 1840 as piano manufacturers, first in Phoenix Street, Soho, and later at Chalk Farm. Emily Chappell was aided by her sons Thomas and Arthur. But she was a strong-willed and autocratic lady, and did not admit Thomas into partnership until 1856, when he was in his forties.

Thomas Patey Chappell was soon an outstanding leader of London musical life. In 1858 he initiated and financed the building of the St James's Hall in Regent Street. The hall had excellent acoustics, and soon became famous for the series of Popular Concerts each Monday and Saturday. These were sponsored by Tom Chappell and directed by his younger brother Arthur. Admission was one shilling, and the 'Pops' brought the works of great composers, performed by famous executants, within the reach of a wide public (and were thus the antecedents of the subsequent Proms).

The St James's Hall also housed piano recitals that enabled larger audiences to come to appreciate works that had once been thought obscure. The young Charles Hallé played the complete piano sonatas of Beethoven there in a series of recitals in 1861, and they proved so popular that the series was repeated in 1862 and again in 1863. (The St James's Hall was demolished in 1893 to make room for the Piccadilly Hotel.)

To mark the Thousandth Popular Concert on 4 April 1887 Robert Browning wrote a sonnet with the lines:

> Thanks, then, to Arthur Chappell, thanks to him
> Whose every guest henceforth not idly vaunts
> 'Sense has received the utmost Nature grants,
> My cup is filled with rapture to the brim,
> When, night by night – ah, memory, how it haunts!
> Music was poured by perfect ministrants,
> By Hallé, Schumann, Piatti, Joachim.'

The importance of the 'Pops' was that they widened the idea of concert-going and did so while maintaining the highest musical standards. But the Chappells were by no means pompous in their tastes: Tom Chappell had published most of the dance music of the early Victorian age, and in the 1840s was said to have himself demonstrated the then daring polka. But Gounod called him 'that prince of music publishers', and he was in the forefront of most London musical activities. He was one of the original governors of the Royal Albert Hall when it was built in 1871, and one of the sponsors two years later of the National Training School of Music, which subsequently became the Royal College of Music (Trinity College of Music was founded in 1872, and the Guildhall School of Music in 1880, two years before the 'National Training School' received the royal charter).

Tom Chappell's enterprises were diverse. It was he who engaged Charles Dickens to give his famous and successful readings from his works. Dickens said that he had been well treated by the Chappells, and averred that 'such people as the Chappells are very rarely to be found in human affairs'. Tom Chappell had a streak of boldness. At the age of twenty-three he bought the publishing rights of a musical show when his elder brother William was abroad. The show was *The Bohemian Girl*, and became a long-running success. It was Tom Chappell, too, who had faith in Gounod's *Faust* when it had failed in Paris: it proved to be a notable success in London.

He too recognized the potential of a lyricist and a church music composer who uneasily formed a partnership to write operettas: and it was an office boy from Chappells called Goodman who acted as the go-between in the troubled association of Gilbert and Sullivan. But Tom Chappell launched them with *Trial by Jury* in 1875, and was one of the financial sponsors of the Comedy Opera Company, which later became the D'Oyly Carte Opera Company.

Tom Chappell's life spanned a transformation in musical taste. When shortly before his father's death he was taken away from school at the age of fifteen to join the family firm, 'to study it from the stock room upwards' at £26 per year, the piano was still in process of development and the musical world was a small and élite confraternity (exemplified by the very private and professional foundation of the Philharmonic Society in his parents' home). When his life ended at the age of eighty-three, in 1902, the modern piano had been defined, and the London concert world was open to a much wider and equally receptive audience. He could also claim that Chappells had earned the reputation of being fine piano makers. As Broadwood and Clementi had done in the earlier years, Tom Chappell did in the second half of the nineteenth century, mingling craftsmanship with salesmanship in the right proportions.

Dickens, clear-sighted as ever, said of the family: 'The Chappells are speculators, though of the worthiest and most honourable kind.' Tom Chappell's successor as managing director, William Boosey, wrote of him after his death:

In all the many departments of business which he controlled, to clearness of judgement and broadness of views he added a splendid liberality . . . Added to which he possessed that rarest of qualities, the gift of being successful without making enemies . . . He was the personification of that old school of English gentleman that it is so often asserted has died out . . . As a young man, old people leaned on him; and as an old man, young people leaned on him.

There was one other poignant bridge between the early century and the late. Franz Liszt, now the venerable 'Abbé Liszt', returned to England in 1886. It was sixty years since he had toured Britain as a boy prodigy, forty-five years since his last appearance (not wholly successfully) as a soloist. He was persuaded back to attend a performance of his oratorio 'St Elizabeth' at the St James's Hall, by the Novello Oratorio Choir, conducted by Alexander Mackenzie (later Sir Alexander). He was treated with reverential awe; the Dover train was stopped at Penge so that Liszt could alight near the home of Henry Littleton, the head of the Novello publishing firm, with whom Liszt was staying. He was seventy-five, and far from well (he died the following July).

But he was cheered in the streets, which was more than had happened to him on earlier visits. He was tired, and fell asleep during the performance of 'St Elizabeth' at the St James's Hall. Queen Victoria summoned him to Windsor, where (a touching relic of a former age) he played an improvisation, before a Hungarian Rhapsody and a Chopin Nocturne. 'The Queen was delighted, and expressed her delight in her own gracious manner', wrote a contemporary.

At an evening party in the same week Liszt was persuaded to play 'what appeared to be an improvisation, taking for his theme the March from Schubert's "Divertissement a l'Hongroise" '. At the invitation of the Prince of Wales he went to a smoking-concert at the Prince's Hall, where he particularly commended the playing of the young Pachmann. Asleep or no, Liszt must have approved the ambience of London, for he stayed, unexpectedly, for a second week. In that week he specifically chose to attend two piano recitals, one by Frederick Lamond ('the young Scottish pianist'), and the other by his own pupil, Stavenhagen.

From the contemporary accounts it is clear that Liszt's 'improvisations' were received respectfully, but were regarded as a rather outdated device. Music had become much more formal.

The rivalry between the piano makers was becoming acute. They were suppliants for the public favours of the great composers and pianists: the new techniques of advertising were coming into use and the public approval of a great name was valuable.

During his London visit Liszt was persuaded to write to Broadwoods commending the tone of a piano he had heard at the Grosvenor Gallery. 'No pianofortes last so well as those of Broadwoods', he wrote. Tennyson took up his pen: 'The pianoforte is an excellent one and has kept in marvellously good tune', he wrote. 'It was used as an accompaniment to Herr Joachim [the violinist] on this last day (after six weeks' use without being tuned) and approved by him.'

Sir Charles Hallé – who founded the famous Manchester orchestra in 1857 and became first Principal of the Royal Manchester College of Music in 1893 – wrote: 'I can highly recommend the Broadwood Pianoforte, as I have used them in public and private for the last forty two years and prefer them to any other.' Sir William Sterndale Bennett said that 'after seeing the instruments in Pulteney Street [the Broadwood factory], my only fear was that they were too perfect . . . I have never heard any finer pianos than those you sent over, and shall remember them for years to come, if I live.'

Richard Wagner – Liszt's son-in-law – wrote that 'the tone of the Broadwood pianofortes reminds me of the character of the old Cremona violins . . .'

That last testimonial, in an age of testimonials, must have been particularly frustrating to the Brinsmead family. For they had just launched the 'Cremona' piano. Like other piano makers, they had studied the violins of the Cremona school – the Amatis, Stradivarius, Guarnerius and Bergonzi.

The insignificant little instrument seemed to offer no mystery of construction, no secret of material, and yet it was endued with a power of producing sounds so magnetically harmonising, so delicate, that baffled enquirers came to regard it as something mysterious, if not actually uncanny! No attempts have succeeded up to the present to reproduce the Cremona, even this boastful age of science has made not one step towards the solution of the mystery. Like a faithful and intelligent copy of an old master, the spirit is wanting – that intangible something which in all things is felt, not seen.

Brinsmeads analysed the Cremona violins with scrupulous care, even making technical tests on the pores of the wood and the characteristics of the varnish. They then produced a Cremona piano, and despite the Wagner testimonial used the name for many years.

But the value of these Victorian testimonials is in some doubt. The generous hearts and artistic appreciation of musical virtuosi enabled them to warm to any piano maker who would give them a good piano. Perhaps the saddest marketing story is that of Frank Chickering, son of the Boston piano manufactory, who hauled a Chickering grand across the Alps and set it up in Liszt's apartment in Rome.

Liszt played it. 'I never thought a piano could have such qualities . . . I congratulate you', wrote the maestro. But even in his old age, with a lifetime of broken pianos behind him, Liszt was eager to keep up with the latest developments in piano manufacture. 'When Mr Steinway gets here', he wrote from Weimar in 1884, 'I shall have a piano shop talk with him, about the new construction of his grands.' He approved the Steinway grand too. The Chickerings, then fighting a losing battle against the Steinway inroads, cannot have been pleased.

Similarly Richard Wagner may have approved the tone of the Broadwood; but when Steinways gave him a grand piano to mark the opening of Bayreuth in 1876, having loaned him another for a concert tour the previous year, he wrote:

Sincere thanks for the incomparably beautiful Steinway Grand, which certainly is worthy of a better piano player than, yours gratefully, Richard Wagner.

Lord Tennyson's testimonial in his letter to Broadwoods that his piano had kept in tune 'after six weeks' use' indicates the weakness of the mid-Victorian pianos in this respect, a characteristic they had inherited from the harpsichord. As long as wood remained the customary material for the piano frame, the wrest-pins (tuning-pins) had to be embedded in wood, and were thus liable to move and put the strings out of tune.

The piano tuner was therefore a familiar figure in musical households, and the principal piano makers kept a small army of them whose duty was to visit the great houses at regular intervals. The Morley family preserves a sheaf of the 'duty-sheets' carried by one such tuner on his rounds, from which it is clear that ladies of fashion would invariably call round the piano tuner on the morning before a musical soirée.

The need for this service declined with the introduction of the iron frame and the setting of the wrest-pins in metal. Brinsmead patented such a system in 1884, incorporating a metal flange on the cast frame perforated to take octagonal nuts around a screw-threaded bolt to which the strings were attached. Tuning then became a matter of adjusting these nuts, a far simpler matter than the tedious and delicate business of adjusting the wrest-pins themselves. This system also kept the piano more securely in tune for much longer periods.

In 1893 London gained a new concert-hall – the Queen's Hall in Langham Place. The lease of the hall was taken by Chappells, and William Boosey transferred his Ballad Concerts there. Boosey was the adopted son of John Boosey and worked for that company from the age of sixteen: but Tom Chappell recruited him to organize Ballad Concerts at which songs such as 'Because', the 'Floral Dance', and 'Little Grey Home in the West' (all, of course, published by Chappells) were interspersed with piano solos by such established artists as Pachmann and young hopefuls such as Moiseiwitsch and Solomon.

Boosey succeeded Tom Chappell as managing director of that company in 1902, and remained a leading London music publisher and concert impresario until 1929, presenting at the Queen's Hall such pianists as Paderewski, Schnabel, and Cortot.

With its excellent acoustic properties, the Queen's Hall became the centre of orchestral music in London, and largely due to the enthusiasm of its first lessee and manager Robert Newman, the home of the Proms from 1895 until the hall's destruction by bombing in 1941. The Queen's Hall piano was a newly patented instrument – the Broadwood barless-steel concert grand, a formidable instrument employing rolled boiler steel of graduated thickness in place of cast iron. It was patented by the head of the firm, Henry John Tschudi Broadwood.

By 1894 Broadwoods had made 195 420 instruments. The list of standard models available from stock illustrates the scope of piano manufacture in that decade, the apogee of the British Empire, the years of the Diamond Jubilee of the Queen-Empress, the high-water mark of British confidence and expansion.

The 8 ft 6 in. Concert Grand was the showpiece. There were four other grands in the standard list: the Drawing-Room Concert Grand (7 ft 9 in.), the Semi Grand (7 ft 3 in.), the Boudoir Grand (7 ft 1 in.) and the Short Grand (6 ft 3 in.). All were available ebonized, or in rosewood or burr walnut. The *Timber Trades Journal* described Broadwoods' timber yard in lyrical terms:

This Thames wharf offers therefore an unique object-lesson in dendrology. Inside, we were brought face to face with fallen giants from the tropical jungle, from the silent Australian bush, from the dense backwoods of the Wild West, and from the stately and historic wealds of England . . .

The list contained several varieties of 'Upright Grand' distinguished by their casework; and the already changing social customs of the time were demonstrated by a Bijou Pianoforte only 3 ft 8 in. high and 4 ft 5 in. wide. People were beginning to live in flats in the cities.

Customers who live in residential flats with artistically furnished rooms of a small size have often-times raised an objection that pianofortes of good tone occupy too much space. The extreme portability of this class of piano has rendered it in request, not only by purchasers living in residential flats many storeys above ground – where a lift is seldom provided of sufficient strength to bear the weight of so heavy an instrument as a full-sized piano – but by military officers on foreign service constantly moving from one station to another, to whom every extra inch in height or extra pound in weight is of consideration.

This was the sales pitch of the Empire on which the sun never set, within which the Army even took along its pianos. So did the Royal Navy, for a Morning-room Piano is advertised 'as supplied to HRH the Duke of York on board HMS *Melampus*'. The Duke of York (afterwards King George V) was frequently seasick on board *Melampus*, so it seems improbable, to say the least, that he ever played it.

The advantages of the smallest piano, the Pianette, made by Broadwoods in common with other manufacturers at this time, give further illumination of the lives of the late Victorians.

For Chambers, Schools, Barrack-rooms, Houseboats, Shooting Lodges and Yachts. It has been transported on camel-back across sandy deserts or on the heads of coolies through rugged wilds in other tropical parts, on the other hand it has well withstood the rigours of an Arctic winter, as when an instrument was taken to the far North in the British Polar expedition of 1875 by Captain Nares for the entertainment of the crew of HMS *Discovery*

There was also provision for the modern style of illumination.

For rooms lighted by electricity, John Broadwood and Sons provide their Upright instruments with almost invisible electric connections

34. *Top*, the Broadwood solid-tyre delivery lorry

35. *Above*, preparing aircraft fuselages for despatch from the Broadwood piano factory during the 1914–18 war

36–42. **A selection of photographs from the Broadwood album, showing the Broadwood factory, 1903**

36. *Opposite*, fixing steel barless frames. The frames are dropped in and lifted out by the overhead runways

37. *Above*, French polishing grand tops. These would be subjected to six different processes to obtain the high finished gloss

38. *Opposite*, key making. The keys are fitted to the key frame

39. *Above*, finishing grand pianos – the fitting and adjustment of the action is one of the final processes in the completion of a grand piano

40.   *Opposite, top*, regulating the upright mechanism. In upright pianos the action mechanism is set in a vertical position

41.   *Opposite*, regulating the grand mechanism. This action is horizontally set

42.   *Above*, the final touches and tuning. This process is performed on the piano before leaving the factory. Each piano will have been tuned several times during the course of manufacture

43-45. Apprentices at the London County Council piano course at Bethnal Street, about 1910

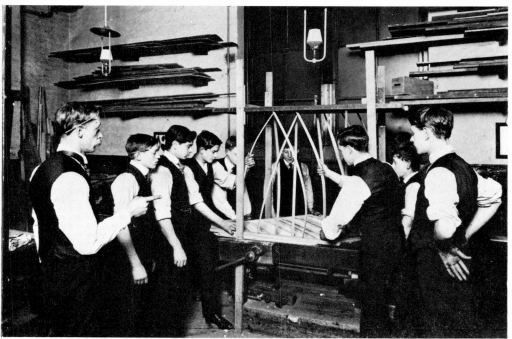

46. *Opposite, top left*, preparing to cast the iron frame of a grand piano at the Booth and Brookes foundry, Burnham

47. *Opposite, top right*, the finished cast frame of a grand piano

48–55. **Eight stages in the manufacture of a modern piano**

48. *Opposite*, laying the soundboard, known as the 'heart of the piano'. Soundboards must be made of special woods, usually spruce or Romanian pine

49. *Above*, the modern process of barring the soundboard. Some factories still use the original process of 'go bars' using yew or lance wood bent under pressure to secure and mould the soundboard

50. Carving the bridge, a highly skilled operation. This bridge must carry the strings at exact distances apart

51. Checking the bridge levels

52. *Opposite*, fitting the bass strings. The strings and frame of a grand piano must withstand about 20 tons of pressure

53.   *Opposite, top*, fitting dampers. Dampers rest on the strings. When the sustaining (loud) pedal is pressed, the damper is lifted away from the string

54.   *Opposite*, regulating the keys. These must be carefully spaced and balanced. To achieve perfect level, thin paper washers are placed under the felt washers on the middle rail

55.   *Above*, bodying up the parts. After the first staining, filling and the first application of polish, 'bodying up' completes the final polishing process

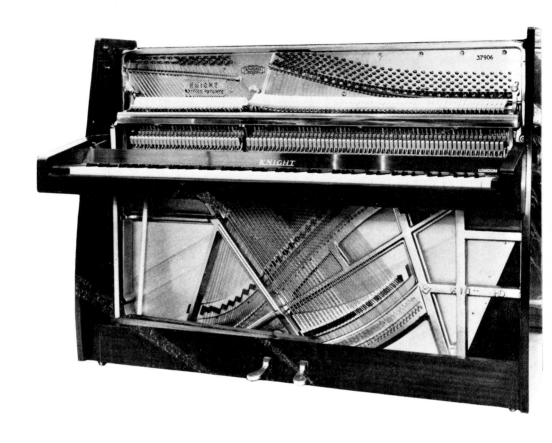

56. The Knight piano, a high quality upright showing the overstrung construction

fitted to the existing candle brackets at a slight extra cost. Such fittings not only obviate the guttering of wax and the constant attention necessary when candles are used, but a couple of prettily shaded incandescent lights, whilst being of great convenience to the player, set off the appearance of the ornaments and the good figure of the wood in a manner which is absolutely brilliant.

As the technology of the piano was established, and only comparatively minor improvements remained to be made to the standard instrument, the case once more became the focus of attention. The late Victorian age was fascinated by ornament and decoration; and Englishmen travelling all over the world for trade or conquest came home with novelties and design ideas from all over the world. As the eighteenth century discovered China and furniture design responded to Chinoiserie, and subsequently the bamboo craze, so at the end of the nineteenth century the fashion was for Japanese crafts. Broadwoods produced a Japanese Upright:

The external appearance of this piano is quaint to a degree. Japanese fashions and industrial artwork have become endued with absorbing interest. The casing is of Andaman Redwood or Padouk. The surface is here stained a subdued violet-black, or brown-black, according to the tint of the panels, being finished off dull, with the grain or pores of the wood left open. The panels are embellished with skilfully manipulated reliefs of coloured ivory, mother-of-pearl, and metal, executed by an accomplished native artist in Osaka, Japan.

Japan had the attraction of novelty. It was only in 1854 that the American Commander Perry managed to break through the reserve of the hitherto closed and medieval Japanese society, and lay the foundations for trade with the West. The Japanese proved to be as interested in the rest of the world as others were in oriental traditions. For there was a square piano made in Japan at the Paris Exposition of 1878, and two years later Torakasu Yamaha set up his musical instrument factory (he was making 600 pianos a year by 1910). Europe's fascination with Japan has two enduring memorials in music: Gilbert and Sullivan's *The Mikado* (1885) and Puccini's *Madam Butterfly* (1904).

The Japanese style was only one of a remarkable number of styles of piano-case then available. Broadwoods, who had employed Sheraton to design early pianos, still offered a Sheraton style – as well as Jacobean, François I, Tudor Gothic, Elizabethan, Louis XIII, XIV, XV and XVI, Flemish Renaissance, Cinquecento, Queen Anne, Adam, Chippendale, Alma-Tadema (Byzantine), Classic Greek, First Empire, Burne-Jones, and Moorish.

Decorating the cases of musical instruments was not, of course, new. The great harpsichord makers had employed artists to paint often ornate pictures, usually inside the lid of their instruments. The Victorian age was enthusiastic about decoration and ornament. The philosophical theory that moved John Ruskin and William Morris was a desire to escape from the proliferation of machine-made ornamentation back to the old English tradition of craftsmanship, the self-expression of the worker in wood, metal and colours. The Great Exhibition of 1851 set in train many debates about design and decoration in furniture and interior decoration: the piano, being a bulky and expensive item of furniture, was not left out of these arguments.

The design and application of ornament thus became a critical issue (but when the Victorians put frills on their piano legs they did so to protect them from dust and damage, not out of reasons of prudery). Some 'specials' were so overloaded with ornament that the function of the piano seems almost to have been subordinated to the extravagance of the case. The Alma Tadema 'Byzantine' piano was one such. This extraordinary instrument – a Broadwood – was made for the Royal Academician Sir Lawrence Alma Tadema, and sat (there is no other word for it) in a 'Byzantine' room at Townsend House near Regent's Park illuminated by windows glazed with Mexican onyx – no doubt a 'dim religious light'. The piano case and the room were designed and in part executed by G. E. Fox. The case was on columnar legs of rosewood and ivory, and itself was oak inlaid with ebony, tortoiseshell, mother-of-pearl, mahogany, ebony, gilding, brass and ivory. The frieze round the edge of the case was inspired by decoration in the church of St Sophia in Constantinople. The inside lid was left comparatively plain, so that Alma Tadema could pin sheets of parchment to it upon which distinguished visitors were invited to sign their names.[1]

1. The Alma Tadema 'Byzantine' piano was destroyed in an air raid during the 1939–45 war. See Michael I. Wilson: 'The Case of the Victorian Piano' (*Victoria and Albert Museum Year Book*, 1972).

The Broadwood grand designed by E. M. Barry and shown at the Great Exhibition has already been mentioned (see page 103). The argument over decoration tended to divide into two schools: those who believed that ornament should emerge from the character of the wood used for the case, and those who used the piano-case as a canvas upon which to paint pictures (as the harpsichord makers had often done).

Wood-carving lent itself to the expression of the Victorian passion for Gothic styles, and many Gothic and 'Ecclesiastical' pianos were produced, complete with perpendicular and ogee arches. Pugin, high priest of Victorian Gothic, produced several designs.

Edward Burne-Jones, as a young man a member of the Pre-Raphaelite Brotherhood, spanned the late Victorian period. As a young man he decorated his own piano in the Pre-Raphaelite style; later in life, as Sir Edward Burne-Jones the knighted Academician, he turned to the school of applied ornament.

His own piano was given to him by his aunt as a wedding present in 1860. It was a 'pianino' by Priestly of Berners Street, and only three feet high. Its case of unpolished American walnut was left plain so that he could paint it, which he did with delicacy and restraint. He put a pair of angelic figures at one end of the inside of the keyboard lid, and a frieze of Pre-Raphaelite women awaiting Death, crowned and carrying a scythe, on the front panel beneath the keyboard.[1] Burne-Jones painted another pianino in a similar style for the artist George Pryce Boyce.

At some point Henry Broadwood commissioned Burne-Jones to design a piano. His reaction is interesting, for he chose to re-design the case, returning it nearer to the traditional harpsichord shape. He chose a softer curve for the side, taking it to an acute angle at the tapering end; and he placed the case upon a simple trestle, of the type common in the eighteenth century.

In 1878–80 he designed the 'Orpheus' piano for William Graham, M.P., again following the harpsichord tradition by painting inside the lid a vigorous picture of Mother Earth surrounded by her children.

This was very different from the more symbolic Wornum piano designed by James Gamble for Sir Henry Cole, first director of the Victoria and Albert Museum. This piano – with a down-striking

1. Now in the Victoria and Albert Museum, London.

action – uses a technique of wood-staining to give the effect of inlay.

Probably it was Burne-Jones's friendship with William Morris that led Broadwoods to produce a number of grands designed by Burne-Jones and executed by Kate Faulkner in gesso-work, a technique using plaster decorations subsequently painted and gilt or silvered. The background of these extravagant floral designs was customarily stained wood, often in a deep rich green (unfortunately the dye has proved to be fugitive and the surviving pianos have lost their depth of contrast).

The first of these Burne-Jones/Faulkner Broadwoods was probably produced in 1881 (and is now in the Birmingham City Museum). Another of them, two years later, was produced for Alexander Ionides: 'Groups of spring flowers in raised and silvered gesso adorn the top and sides of this case . . . Varying tints of coloured silver upon a groundwork of celadon green produce a very fine effect.' Yet another, for the Emir of Kabul, also had raised silver gesso: 'Upon a groundwork of granulated Rose du Barry is a pattern of various spring flowers, and these are wrought in flowering lines and curves, coloured by various shades of silver.'

Alfred Waterhouse, architect of Keble College, Oxford, also designed a Broadwood, but not ornately, putting modest floral patterns in boxwood and mother-of-pearl around the edge of the lid and on the side but otherwise leaving the case plain.

The same could not be said of the piano designed by T. G. Jackson, R.A., for Athelstan Riley. A contemporary account describes it thus:

The outside of the case is veneered with purple wood stained dark green, and the effect of the natural dye in the wood, combined with the chemical used, produces the appearance of very fine old ebony. Elaborate intarsiatura, representing a profusion of lily stems, leaves and blossoms, in satinwood and pear-tree, dissipate the sombreness of the dark green in a striking manner. To heighten the effect, the blooms are made to scintillate with the iridiscent tints of mother-of-pearl, each lily centre being overlaid with transparent and variegated tortoiseshell, through which a rich red enamel effectively gleams. On raising the top of the piano, a dazzling effect is produced, the inside of the top and case being enamelled vermillion and Japanese lacquered. Upon this surface, golden laurel boughs, laden with gold berries, sway in graceful curves.

After that, the Broadwoods produced for the Duke of West-minster (in parquetry rosewood with ormolu mouldings) and Henry Irving (Adam style, in satinwood with inlays) seem positively modest; so does the Czar of Russia's grand (white enamel, gilt).

These pianos were 'specials', produced for customers whose pockets were deep enough to sustain their taste. Increasingly there were attempts to redesign the case of the cheaper upright. The *Building News* organized a competition for the design of a cottage piano in 1877, as did *The Studio* in 1894. The Arts and Crafts movement was having an impact on interior design, and its emphasis on materials rather than ornament was gaining support. At the Arts and Crafts Exhibition of 1893 Walter Cave produced an upright in a plain oak case, the front legs carried upwards to form candle-holders. This was produced commercially (by Bechstein) as the 'Medieval English Upright Grand'.

Stimulated perhaps by this competition, Broadwood went to the leading young domestic architects of the day – Baillie Scott, C. R. Ashbee, and Edwin Lutyens. In 1896 Baillie Scott produced a highly successful design that was nevertheless one of the most radical re-thinkings of piano-case organization. This was the 'Manxman' (Baillie Scott came from the Isle of Man). It was in the form of a plain closed cupboard on a pedestal; when the doors with their 'wrought-iron' medieval hinges were folded sideways and back, the keyboard, music-stand and candle-holders were revealed.

C. R. Ashbee (now best remembered for his group of houses on Cheyne Walk, London) designed an upright for Peter Jones which was based on the Manxman but made more use of decora-tive beaten metal for the hinges, turning them into bands of ornament. Ashbee also designed a remarkable grand, made by Broadwood, which he gave to his wife as a wedding present in 1898. It is virtually square, and the top is hinged centrally across the case.

Several pianos were designed for Broadwood by Edwin Lutyens, then a promising young architect making a reputation with his country houses, many of them in the Surrey hills. At least one of these pianos was designed to be placed in a particular Lutyens house (Marshcourt, Hampshire): this was in character with the philosophy of Voysey, Ashbee and their school, who decreed that a house and its furniture were a whole and should be designed with a unity of expression.

Lutyens himself was not uninterested in the painted piano. In 1897 he wrote to his wife:

What about a piano? This I shall design when the time comes – small, square and refined, and the colour inside gorgeous. I shall try to get Guthrie of the Glasgow School to paint whispers – I almost prefer his painting in this sort of decoration to E. Burne-Jones.[1]

Yet Lutyens' own piano designs were architectural rather than ornamental, drawing their distinction from structure rather than applied decoration.

His first Broadwood grand was in light oak, panelled round the sides. The decoration was in the under-frame – a complex arrangement of irregular scroll-like curves connected near the floor by an irregularly curved stretcher – and in the pedal-lyre and music stand of beaten ironwork. This case, built round a steel barless frame, was shown in the Royal Pavilion at the Paris Universal Exhibition of 1900 and won the Grand Prix, the highest possible award.

Lutyens designed two more Broadwoods, in 1901. In both he kept the case simple. In the first, for Marshcourt, he put the case on a seven-legged trestle. In the second, he devised an extraordinary and somewhat incongruous underframe in the shape of a drum-like cylinder of columns, adding decoration to the case with large metal candle-holders.

These 'special' grands were to be among the last flowerings of the world of artistic patronage, when rich men paid large sums for the construction of beautiful objects. The standardization of the twentieth century ended such extravagance. Henry Broadwood (who died in 1911) was among the last craftsmen to benefit from it. To his credit he was in the forefront of piano-case design, always ready to welcome change. But with the new century came a new world: and with it new methods of entertainment. In 1895 Marconi had demonstrated his system of wireless communication. To many it seemed no more than a technical toy.

1. Michael I. Wilson, op. cit.

6
A Foreign Threat

The era of Free Trade meant that Britain was an open market for foreign manufacturers. Steinways received their first Royal Warrant in 1890, and in an advertisement in the *Musical Courier*[1] in the following year they were able to list as patrons, besides Queen Victoria, the Prince and Princess of Wales, five dukes and duchesses, twenty-seven earls and countesses, and an army of lesser nobility.

You too can be a duke [ran the advertisement]. Well, not quite, really. But you can acquire a tinge of the celestial dukishness by buying the same brand of piano as did His Grace. Then you can use its keyboard to play 'Nearer, My Lord, to Thee'.

By the reign of King Edward VII Steinways could stencil on their pianos the titles of HM the King of England, HM the Emperor of Russia, HM the King of Sweden and Norway, HM the King of Saxony, HM the German Emperor, HM the Emperor of Austria and King of Hungary, HM the Queen of Spain and HM the King of Italy.

But it was not from America that the main challenge to the British piano industry was coming. It was from Germany. In the years following the end of the Franco-Prussian War in 1870 and the unification of Germany, the German industrial machine began to roll into full production.

Increasingly and in all aspects of commercial life, manufacturers began to fear the encroachment of German precision and German trading upon the British Empire. The British might have been great soldiers, sailors and explorers, and their traders in the late eighteenth and early nineteenth centuries went into the world to find markets and exploit them. But now the rest of

1. Quoted by Arthur Loesser, op. cit.

Europe, comparatively pacific after the internal revolutions and wars of 1830, 1848 and 1870, turned to making things to sell.

The Germans not only made pianos: they made them well, and in considerable quantity. By 1886 the annual production of pianos in America was said to be about 25000, in France 20000, in England 35000, and in Germany – 73000. That was what the Germans claimed. The British refused to believe it.

When Chappells supplied Richard Strauss with one of their pianos for the studio he used for composition, he wrote:

Dear Sirs: I consider the tone of a remarkably sweet and sympathetic quality, and of unusual sustaining power, the touch very responsive and light. Having always been used to pianos of German make, it was a great and agreeable surprise to me to find such a perfect instrument of English manufacture.

Yours faithfully, Richard Strauss.

In their enthusiasm for this testimonial, Chappells seem to have overlooked its implicit reflection on the standards of British piano manufacture in general.

The most distinguished German house was that of Bechstein. Carl Bechstein had begun making pianos in Berlin in 1853. He set up a London showroom in Wigmore Street in 1879 within a few years of the resumption of trade between Britain and Germany. In the 1890s he followed the pattern set by Pleyel in Paris and Steinway in New York, and opened the Bechstein Hall in Berlin.

In 1901 he built and opened the Bechstein Hall next door to his Wigmore Street showrooms. The hall cost nearly £100000. The architect was T. E. Colcutt, designer of the Imperial Institute in South Kensington; the symbolic paintings were by Moira. At the first invitation recital on 31 May 1901, the artists included Busoni (playing a Bechstein grand, naturally), and the violinist Ysaÿe.[1]

At about the same time as Bechstein was starting piano manufacture in Berlin, Julius Ferdinand Blüthner began to make

1. On the outbreak of war in 1914 Bechstein's business in Britain, including the hall, was sequestrated. The name was changed, and the property bought at auction by Debenhams. Part of the premises, including the hall, was then leased to the Wigmore Hall and Piano Galleries Limited: the Wigmore Hall was reopened under its new name on 17 January 1917. After the Second World War it was leased to the Arts Council.

pianos in Leipzig. He, too, prospered; and Blüthners opened a London showroom in 1896.

Ignaz Bosendorfer was a Viennese, and of a slightly older generation. A pupil of Joseph Brodmann, instrument maker, by 1828 he was granted the right to trade as a piano maker in his native city. A few years later Liszt expressed his approval of a Bosendorfer grand; and in 1839 the Emperor of Austria appointed Bosendorfer 'Piano-Maker to the Royal and Imperial Court'. Ignaz's son Ludwig succeeded him as head of the firm in 1859 and built the Bosendorfer Hall, the best concert-hall in the city. The firm expanded with the prosperity of Vienna as one of the musical centres of Europe.

The firm of Grotrian–Steinweg was created by Friedrich Grotrian and Heinrich Steinweg of Seesen (the founder of the American Steinways). Together in 1835 they built a square piano to Grotrian's design.

Grotrian then went to Moscow where he worked for some years as a piano maker. But he kept in touch with Heinrich Steinweg and, after Heinrich emigrated to New York in 1850, with his son Theodore. The Grotrian–Steinweg factory was transferred to Brunswick; and gradually, as the Steinways were more and more concerned with their New York business, the Grotrians took sole control of the German company.

Johannes Adolf Ibach built pianos in Germany from 1794, through wars and rumours of wars. Two of his sons expanded the firm in the 1830s, with a factory in Cologne. In 1880 they opened a London showroom for their own and other Westphalian pianos (the author has a piano built by Gerhard Adam of Wesel which bears the agency stencil of 'Ibach Ltd, London W1' above the keyboard).

Finally there was the firm of Schiedmayer of Stuttgart, at one time the leader of the German piano industry.

The expansion of the German piano trade in the years before 1914 is illustrated by the lists published by Alfred Dolge in his book on *Pianos and Their Makers* (1911). The lists are clearly not exhaustive; not every manufacturer gives the date of his company's foundation.

But the pattern that emerges is of a rapidly expanding industry, both in Germany and in Austro-Hungary where the inheritors of the early 'German' piano makers continued their tradition. The records show that rather more than 200 piano factories were started in Germany between 1850 and 1890.

Many of these companies, both British and German, were one-man factories making one piano each week or fortnight, buying in the keys, actions and strings, and carpentering a simple case. Already the major piano-making countries had substantial companies making components for many big manufacturers in common.

Cut-price competition was threatening the survival of many companies. Too much employment was on a 'jobbing' basis – there was no security in the trade and thus the standard of work declined. The tradition of craft apprenticeship had withered under the pressures of industrial mechanization, and by 1912 the trade was discussing ways of initiating an apprenticeship scheme to bring more skilled men into piano-making.

At least one firm, Hopkinson, instituted such a scheme, and arrangements were being sought to include a piano-making course in the curriculum of a London technical college.

The Pianomaker, the vociferous journal of the piano trade under the brilliantly idiosyncratic editorship of Herbert Sinclair for many years, was staunch in the defence of British industry against German encroachment.

'All the great inventions in connection with the industry have come from the brains of Englishmen', he wrote, with pardonable if excessive zeal, listing these:

Overstrung – Tompkinson
Tape action – Wornum
Repeating action – Brinsmead
Regulating screw to grand action – A. Squire
Barless iron frame – Broadwood
Piano player – Mr White (who went to US)
Tapered Hammer felt – Jones, sold to Whitehead
Planing Flange of Iron Frame & drilling with holes on the rake –
  Smith & Wellstood.

It was not, unfortunately, quite as simple as that. Many developments were made in Britain, but (for example) the repeating action owed far more to Erard than Brinsmead (who did deserve credit, however, for work on the iron frame).

Comparative export figures for pianos and piano parts (excluding keys and actions) for 1912 told a sadder tale. German piano exports totalled £2 136 700. British piano exports totalled £325 280. The only two countries where British pianos were outselling German, and then only narrowly, were France and New Zealand. Australia was buying German pianos, despite preferential import duty on British pianos (30 per cent against 35 per cent).

But freight rates were such that it was cheaper to ship a German piano from Hamburg to Wellington, Adelaide or Brisbane *via London* than to ship a British piano direct from London to New Zealand or Australia. The result was to be seen in comparative exports to Australia in 1912: German pianos, £371 900; British pianos, £75 200.

No doubt the most depressing statistic for the British piano manufacturers was the figure of German piano exports to Britain – well over £500 000 in 1912. The situation is demonstrated in the pages of the Army and Navy Stores catalogue for 1907, which lists 'Pianos Manufactured for the Society in London' at prices from £28.10s to £42, and 'Good German Pianos, Sold at Moderate Prices, and imported direct from the Factory by the Society' at prices from £33 to £42.

The largest and most expensive piano available from the general list was the Bechstein concert grand at 300 guineas; eight other Bechsteins were listed at prices from 58 guineas. Another German manufacturer represented was Ibach.

The two British manufacturers represented in the catalogue were Broadwood, from a boudoir upright at 42 guineas to semi-grand in a rosewood case at 160 guineas, and Collard and Collard, from a 'Cottage Overstrung' at 50 guineas and the 'Shortest Horizontal Grand Overstrung' in rosewood at 100 guineas.

Of the seventy-three pianos listed as standard in the Army and Navy Stores general catalogue, fifty-five were of German manufacture.

The Pianomaker battled valiantly, writing in March 1913:

We must fight the impression that a good piano must bear a German name. British instruments are a credit to the country. 'However did you allow the Germans to creep into your markets? You must have been asleep.' This was felt to be true – English manufacturers rested on their world wide reputation. However the Germans set out to improve on all the well-known features of the British piano and started to 'dump' their goods on the English market. To secure a foothold they sacrificed profit and were prepared to give long-term credit. Once in then the prices rose above the UK manufactured ones. For a long time the UK manufacturers were unable to fight – they didn't know what had hit them. But not surrendering, they fought for the British name. 'We know that there are English pianos that are a credit to the best traditions of English brains and craftsmanship.' In outward details some of the foreign houses may be given a point, yet as musical instruments there is nothing to surpass the products of the prominent London manufacturers.

In the summer of 1913 *The Pianomaker* tackled the retailers on the subject.

Some dealers can't afford to allow patriotism to interfere with business. They *may* be able to make more profit on a German piano, but this is not always so.

The answer might lie in a truce to the cut-throat competition that was bedevilling the British piano trade.

What we want is a united retail trade giving the productions of our own houses a fair chance with those of their foreign competitors.

But even the passionately British-minded *The Pianomaker* had to admit that hard-headed marketing was the basis of the German success.

We must admit a praiseworthy characteristic of the German nation is perseverance. The greatest reason they monopolise so many of the world's piano markets is that they have pushed their goods to the front with a commercial militancy. The British manufacturers were unable to tackle foreign markets in the same way as the Germans because they were so busy defending foreign competition in the UK: But this has resulted in the UK instrument becoming even better – 'British pianos are the world's best'. How can British pianos be introduced into continental markets? By linguist commercial reps. German travellers are to be found everywhere.

Sadly for the British piano makers, most musicians now considered that the best pianos in Europe were Bechstein and

Blüthner, both German makes. This would hardly have been questioned in the British musical world of the time, outside the piano industry.

Nevertheless there was a storm when Landon Ronald,[1] who had been appointed Principal of the Guildhall School of Music two years earlier, accepted an offer from Bechstein to equip the school with their pianos at a nominal charge of £6 per piano per year. Previously Brinsmead had the contract, at £4 per piano.

The Pianomaker called this arrangement 'inexplicable'. The ultimate authority over the Guildhall School is the Court of Common Council of the City of London, and that tuneful nest of singing birds resolved by 112 votes to 26 that 'the art of pianoforte playing will in no degree be impaired by the instruction of British students on pianos of the best standard British makers'.

Approving this, *The Pianomaker* commented that

the Principal of the Guildhall School may be an excellent musician. But whatever his position may be in the musical world we have never heard it stated that he is an expert in the selection of pianos. Very often it is the case that even the most distinguished musicians are very poor judges of the inherent qualities of a piano.

Evidently Landon Ronald refused to give way: there remained twenty-seven Bechsteins at the Guildhall School (described as 'Foreign: all supplied by one firm') against forty-four British pianos.

The Pianomaker descended to a wholly unworthy smear campaign.

It seems to us there is something of a mutual admiration society about the affair for we believe that the erstwhile manager of the firm in question gave a complimentary dinner to the Principal on the occasion of the latter's appointment.

Once more *The Pianomaker* appealed to the City Corporation to change the contracts for the supply of pianos when these came up for renewal.

In honest justice to our manufacturers these foreign pianos should be unceremoniously bundled out of the Guildhall School of Music.

1. Afterwards Sir Landon Ronald (1873–1938), orchestral conductor, Principal of the Guildhall School of Music 1910–37.

In the years before the 1914–18 war a further challenge faced the British piano industry – the development, mainly in the United States, of the player-piano. If the girls of 1840 had wanted music that was 'brilliant but not difficult', the girls of 1900 wanted music that sounded brilliant without the need for boring practice. With the suffragette movement came the first stirrings of female emancipation, and the daughters of the household were no longer prepared to sit quietly at home learning the accompaniments to drawing-room ballads.

Acute as ever, Herbert Sinclair analysed the social change in *The Pianomaker* in July 1913:

In the days of our great grandmothers when an indoor life and an acquaintance with the finer arts were more in accord with the up-bringing of a young lady than the participation in outdoor exercises, more time and care were devoted to the piano. Social conditions have altered very much, and what with motoring, golf, hockey, and the great travelling facilities the rising generation, more particularly that part which is not possessed of latent musical taste, will not take the time to be properly taught piano playing, and it is often the case that a hostess has to fall back upon the player piano when in the natural course of things she should call upon one of her daughters to entertain her guests.

The player-piano concept was developed originally from the reed organ or harmonium. That worked on a system of air pressure, the player pumping at the pedals. Throughout the nineteenth century inventors were working at the idea of making a keyboard instrument sound on a pre-programmed system: it is, after all, the barrel-organ principle by which a cylinder studded with spikes activates the notes or (in the case of the hurdy-gurdy and similar instruments) the strings.

By the 1880s an American company had marketed an instrument named the Mechanical Orguinette. This was a reed organ, pedalled as usual but containing a paper roll, appropriately punched to sound the correct notes. The result tended to be noisy and loud, since the air-pressure required was considerable. But the device was successful enough for the company to try and apply it to the piano. In 1897 an American inventor, E. S. Votey, patented a mechanical piano which he called the 'Pianola'. The invention and the name were taken up by the Aeolian Company of New York.

A claimant to the title of inventor of the piano-roll was a Scot, John McTammany, who died at the age of seventy in 1915. Taken to America when a child, he is said to have conceived the idea of the piano-roll while in hospital with war wounds (presumably the American Civil War). He gave a public showing of his invention in 1876 but could not raise the money to develop it, and a number of manufacturers then took it up.

The Aeolian Company was the most successful, in Europe as well as the United States. A London showroom was opened in Regent Street, London, in 1899, and the Pianola sold well under the slogan 'So simple a child can play it'. The Aeolian Company had a head start in Britain largely due to the conservatism of British piano retailers: they refused to believe that this new-fangled invention would catch on, until they saw the business results of the player-piano companies. Patents flooded in like confetti, for player-piano improvements and the innate reserve of the retail trade and the piano tuners wilted under the popular success of the new instrument.

The main improvements in the player-piano were of two kinds: devices to enable the player to add expression to the necessarily mechanical performance of the player-roll; and following on this, the emergence of piano-rolls made by distinguished pianists.

Many of the Aeolian improvements were introduced by the English-born American, William Braid White, who wrote a standard work on the subject. But the first expressive player action came not from America but from Germany, manufactured from 1904 by the Welte Company. A few years later the Aeolian company launched the Duo-Art system, which enabled the roll to reproduce a piece of music at two strengths simultaneously, for theme and accompaniment. The American Piano Company answered them with the Ampico system.

The next development was the reproducing roll, which enabled the player to reproduce exactly the performance of a piece by a great composer and executant. Once again the Welte Company led, with rolls by Grieg, Debussy and Ravel.

Stravinsky wrote an Étude for Pianola. Rachmaninov recorded a number of piano-rolls. The early masters of jazz piano improvised on piano-rolls; Scott Joplin recorded many of his Rags.[1]

The basic player-piano was a specially built instrument with the player system incorporated (though it could be cut out and the instrument used as a normal piano). The reproducing systems could be adapted to play existing pianos.

British retailers were slow to meet this challenge partly because the cost of a player-piano was approximately twice that of an ordinary instrument. When the British makers began to move into this field they went through an uneasy period in which good player actions were incorporated into poor pianos, and poor actions into good pianos, with no good result.

Broadwoods were among the few British manufacturers to make their own player actions, which they patented under the name Artistone, and incorporated into all their pianos from the large barless grand to the baby uprights. The advantages claimed were:

It is so compressed that the tone and touch of the Piano are not affected to the slightest degree. All instruments are fitted with the Melotone accenting device, which enables the performer to accentuate the melody above the accompaniment when required, and also to vary the latter.

The sustaining pedal can be used either by hand, or brought into play automatically by means of perforations in the music-roll, whilst the Silencer enables the performer to run any part of the music-roll over the tracker-bar in silence. The larger models also contain a Transposer, by means of which accompaniments can be transposed six semi-tones – an invaluable addition, since accompaniment rolls, as a rule, are only cut in one key.

The Artistone player-piano sold at £84, and other makes at up to £125, or the price of a full-scale grand. The Orchestrelle Company, selling in Germany and France as well as in Britain from a saleroom in Bond Street, pushed up its profits by £12 300 to £80 000 in a single year, Hopkinsons launched an electric player-piano, the Electrelle; Strohmenger produced an all-metal player 'for foreign climates', with the larger capacity roll (they were produced in 65-note capacities or 88 notes).

1. Some of these have been heard again in London at concerts organized by the Player Piano Group in the Purcell Room at the South Bank, using a variety of pianos maintained at the British Piano Museum in High Street Brentford.

The Americans produced the felicitously named Pistonola, with a vacuum engine with exhaust cylinders in place of the traditional bellows and pedals. The American companies, led by Aeolian, campaigned vigorously through the schools of Britain, sending teams of articulate and well-bred young ladies round to demonstrate the advantages of player-pianos for 'concert and gymnasium work and folk dancing'. The piano teachers were not amused; but the piano teachers were seldom influential, being 'visitors' out of school hours and not permanent members of the staff. So more than a few schools were equipped with player-pianos.

So were many homes, despite the very considerable cost. The advantage of having Backhaus, Godowsky, Dohnànyi or Busoni actually playing in your living-room was a status-symbol not to be denied to a society that outside the big cities only heard music professionally performed during the occasional concert by some touring celebrity. 'Artists' Rolls' could be bought at prices from 2s 6d to 10s 6d from music shops and piano dealers.

The manufacturers and retailers were thus faced with the problem of an eager buyer who desperately wanted to possess the product but could not immediately raise the money. So it was that the piano industry followed the example of the sewing-machine industry into the field of hire-purchase.

It was not new for makers to hire out instruments. It had been commonplace in the eighteenth century, when Shudi and Kirckman had hired out their harpsichords and spinets by the day, week or month. The system was particularly appropriate for harpsichords since they needed regular tuning and maintenance.

Now the piano trade instituted the 'Deferred Payments' system of purchase over periods of one, two or three years. But the system was so foreign to the Victorian philosophy of financial probity and thrift that companies had to spell out the particular safeguards of their Deferred Payments system. Thus Broadwoods:

A serious objection to purchasing costly articles by monthly payments is the danger of loss through some unforeseen circumstance which prevents the completion of purchase. The musician of the family may leave home, and the piano may not be required. Death, or severe reverses in worldly circumstances, may make the instalments a burden, and the purchase must be given up.

Broadwoods offered a 'Surrender Value Contract', specifying the surrender value of the piano at each stage of hire-purchase.

Many retailers took up the hire-purchase system, and began to sell pianos stencilled with their own name. The Barnes company, with its chain of shops throughout East London and later in Oxford Street, prospered in this way and many 'Barnes' pianos were sold though the company never manufactured its own instruments.

Other retailers were less scrupulous and as the 'own name' system did not encourage quality control, over the years up to 1914 many pianos of doubtful quality were produced and sold with a variety of keyboard labels.

In that classic of late Victorian life *The Diary of a Nobody* by George and Weedon Grossmith (which was published in 1892) Mr Charles Pooter of The Laurels, Brickfield Terrace, Holloway, was particularly proud that his wife Carrie might be heard 'practising the "Sylvia Gavotte" on our new cottage piano (on the three years' system), manufactured by W. Bilkson (in small letters), from Collard and Collard (in very large letters)'.

The distinguished accompanist Ivor Newton recalls that Collard and Collard were such a familiar name in Edwardian England that when as a boy he played the piano in the pit of the Queen's Palace of Varieties in Poplar one comedian used the name in a gag: 'The bailiffs are always taking my piano back – it's Collard and Collard.'

When in 1911 the American piano maker Alfred Dolge published his 'comprehensive history of the development of the piano' he listed the known manufacturers of pianos throughout the world. There were 136 piano makers listed in Britain, of whom all but three were manufacturing in London. The remaining three, curiously, were all in Halifax, Yorkshire; and among them was a Pohlmann, presumably a descendant of the craftsman from Saxony who with Zumpe popularized the square piano in the 1770s.

Of the 133 London piano makers, the great majority were all working in one comparatively small district – Islington. The directories of the time indicate that nearly a third of them were in that borough, together with many of the associated suppliers of keys and actions, hammers, felts and wire. Others spread into the adjoining boroughs of Camden Town and Chalk Farm to the west, and Hackney and Stoke Newington to the east. But the piano trade of the time was concentrated within a few square miles of North London.

Only nine piano makers were south of the river, but they included Henry Hicks and Son in the New Kent Road; Albert and Jones in Stockwell; and in Lewisham, Murdoch, Murdoch and Company, and Morley and Company.

The story of the Hicks company was itself remarkable, since the business was founded by a man from outside the piano trade. Henry Hicks was the son of a farming family in Calne, Wiltshire. In 1865, when the Great Western Railway was still a comparative novelty, he and a group of young friends determined to take a cheap weekend excursion to see the sights of London, as young men from the provinces will.

Henry Hicks fell in love with London. On their last night, as the group stood on Waterloo Bridge, he asked his companions: 'Are you going back?' 'Of course,' they said. 'I'm not,' said Henry. He found somewhere to sleep for the night, and the next morning, walking up Moorgate in the City, he saw a notice in the window of Cramers the music shop. They needed a porter. He was a strong-built country lad, and he took the job.

At Cramers he learnt how to tune a piano. He became a salesman, and did well at it. Five years after deciding to stay in London he opened his own retail store at the Elephant and Castle. He remained loyal to Cramers, selling their pianos as his first line. Soon he married and produced a son. William Henry Hicks was equally strong-willed. Inevitably the boy was sent to serve his apprenticeship at Cramers. But when he completed his indentures he refused to go straight into the family company.

Instead he went into partnership with a friend to make pianos, as White and Hicks. They were successful. Hicks bought out White, and went back to his father to say that now they were both doing well independently, they should go into partnership as Henry Hicks and Son, piano manufacturers and retailers. This they did, taking a factory near the showroom at the Elephant and opening twenty shops in South London.

The Murdoch company had similarly romantic beginnings. John Gloag Murdoch was born in 1830 in Huntingtower, Perthshire. He first completed an apprenticeship in hand-block printing on cloth; but then machine printing came in, and Murdoch took an apprenticeship in that, until the age of twenty-seven. After a few years John Murdoch noted that Messrs William Collins of Glasgow were expanding their publishing business by selling family Bibles; Murdoch joined their staff and became their agent in the north-west of England. In 1871 he began business on his own account, and soon was selling 30000 family Bibles a year.

His business prospered, and he began to print coloured oleograph pictures. These too were a great success. As photography became generally available it was the custom to make provision in the family bible for family portraits; and from this Murdoch went on to produce photograph albums. Most of these goods were sold by travellers who toured the country districts selling on 'time-payment', one of the earliest instances of hire-purchase.

A popular type of photograph album had a small musical-box movement built into the cover so that a tune played when the album was opened. From selling musical albums, Murdoch developed the business with his associates John and Alexander Dow so that they were soon importing musical boxes of all sorts from Germany, some of them complicated and expensive. Musical boxes led to the sale of pianos and reed organs.

Since these were less portable, the company opened a warehouse, and then a shop, and then more shops, until Murdoch, Murdoch and Company became one of the largest retailers of musical instruments, making their own pianos with two subsidiary piano-making companies, Spencer and Company and Malcolm and Company. Other members of the family founded businesses to supply other necessities of the Victorian home, such as mangles and perambulators.

Only Morleys of those three South London firms had a musical background: the Morleys had been makers of musical instruments for many years, one of them had worked for Erard during the Frenchman's time in London at the end of the eighteenth century, and inheriting Erard's patent harp action became the leading manufacturer and salesman of that other essential instrument in the fashionable drawing-room, the harp.

The Morley family had ramifications throughout London musical life, and is remarkable for the number of instrument makers and music publishers it produced over a period of 150 years. There was a Morley in the music business in Bishopsgate at the end of the eighteenth century. The youngest of his seven sons, Robert, went to live in Lewisham and was a member of the Crystal Palace Orchestra when it was first formed. His son, also Robert, became a tuner with Erards in 1871, then went to Broadwoods, and finally started his own business in Lewisham in 1881 (where he was succeded by his son Douglas Morley, the present head of Robert Morley and Company, of which *his* son John S. P. Morley is director).

A second son of the Bishopsgate Morley was James Morley, who in 1816 had a music shop in Clapham. The family was deeply religious and his son Joseph George Morley rebelled against this, crossed the Channel and worked for Erard making harps in Paris. Later he returned to London and set up on his own as a harp maker, first in Earls Court and then in Kensington. In that business he was succeeded by his son, John Sebastian Morley, who on retirement in 1969 combined his business (including piano restoration) with that of Robert Morley and Company.

A cousin of Robert Morley the elder was William Morley, a leading Victorian music publisher with premises in Regent Street. The piano maker in the family was Henry Morley of Apollo House, Royal Hill, Greenwich. The Morley company still has one of his early upright pianos (with pleated cloth front) dated about 1810. An associated company was the Morley Phillips music shop in Bromley, later merged with Robert Morley and Company.

The reason for the concentration of piano makers north of the river was twofold. First, the piano trade was established before London had adequate bridges across the Thames, and roads to the south – and long before the development of the residential suburbs south of the river. Secondly, the established firms such as Broadwood were north of the river, and new companies tended to be started by former apprentices and employees of such companies within easy access of associated suppliers.

But change was taking place. In 1904 Broadwoods left Great Pulteney Street, Soho, after 150 years: the central showrooms were fitted into a building in Conduit Street, off Bond Street, that had formerly been Limmer's Hotel. The factory had moved from Westminster to Stour Road, Old Ford in Hackney.

The principal manufacturers, other than those already named, were Arthur Allison and Co, founded in 1840, at the Apollo Works in Leighton Road, Kentish Town; and Ralph Allison and Sons, of Prebend Street, Islington. Henry Ambridge and Son (1890) was in Fontayne Road, South Tottenham. Bansall and Sons (1883) were at the Albert Works, in Clarence Road, Hackney.

Barratt and Robinson (1877) were in York Road, Kentish Town, Nathaniel Berry (1866) in the City Road, and the Brasted Brothers (H. F. and R. A.) in Prince George Road, Stoke Newington. John Brinsmead and Sons (1836) boasted a showroom in Wigmore Street, and the works in Grafton Road, Kentish Town. Bernard Brock (1890) was making pianos at three addresses in Hackney. Burling and Mansfield were among several manufacturers in the streets round the Metropolitan Cattle Market in Islington.

Challen and Son are said by Alfred Dolge to have been founded in 1894: but Charles H. Challen made his first piano in 1804. Collard and Collard, inheritors of the Clementi firm, had three shops in the West End (at 26 Cheapside, the old Longman and Broderip emporium, 19 Tottenham Court Road and 16 Grosvenor Street) and a factory at Oval Road, Regent's Park. J. B. Cramer and Co had shops in Oxford Street, Moorgate, Notting Hill Gate and Kensington High Street. William Danemann (1892) had warehouses and offices in Paul Street, Finsbury, and factories in Northampton Street, Islington.

Eavestaff and Sons, then managed by the ageing son of the business, W. E. Eavestaff, who was known to everyone in the trade as 'young Eavestaff' up to his seventy-fifth year, were at 38 Baker Street. F. B. Lambert (1881) was in Cressy Road, Haverstock Hill, on the borders of Hampstead and Islington.

Moore and Moore (1837) had a showroom at 59A Oxford Street, and John Rintoul and Sons (1858) were in Berkeley Road, Islington. John Spencer and Company's works were in George Road, Regent's Park, and William Squire Jr's factory since 1881 not far away round the corner in George Road, Regent's Park. John Strohmenger's works were in Goswell Road, at the southern end of Islington, with showrooms in Brompton Road and High

Holborn. Broadwood White and Company (1879) had a factory in Hackney; Witton, Witton and Company (1838) in King's Cross; and Henry Zender and Company in Stamford Hill, Stoke Newington (his younger brother Sydney Zender, who had broken away in 1892, was as yet less well known).

As early as 1911 two of the most respected smaller firms had begun to form a business association. They were the early Victorian George Rogers and Sons (1843), with a showroom in Berners Street and a factory in Archer Street, Camden Town, and J. and J. Hopkinson, whose business was in a similar pattern – a showroom at 52 Wigmore Street, and a factory in Fitzroy Road, Camden Town.

This is only a partial selection of the 133 manufacturers in Edwardian London, chosen by a piano maker who was young in those days and remembers these as companies that made good pianos. The list indicates the scale of the piano trade at that time; but it also implies that most companies were still craft-based, relying on the skills of a few craftsmen to make a limited number of products. Not for those Edwardians the routine of modern mass-production.

A piano maker recalls how new companies started.

Everyone at the big companies, Broadwoods for example, was a craftsman. So Bill might say to Tom: 'Let's have a go – there's a demand.' They would decide to risk going out on their own. They could hire a railway arch or a little factory in a back street for thirty bob a week – they would only need a hundred pounds to get started, and a good craftsman could save that on piecework. They would buy some parts, and employ a fitter-up and a finisher – a man to put in actions and keys. Some of their pals would come in part-time to help them with some stringing or tuning – and that was the start of it. In those days in North London there was a piano factory in every street.

And yet the business association between Rogers and Hopkinson pointed the way that many other firms would soon have to follow. For one or two of the most notable Victorian companies were already showing signs of commercial uneasiness in the new century.

Monington and Weston had been among the leading piano makers for more than a quarter of a century, founded in 1858 in Bayham Street, Camden Town, by two men who rapidly took it to the forefront of the industry. Their pianos won gold medals in the London international exhibition of 1872, and the great Paris exhibition six years later. At one time the company employed 100 highly skilled woodcarvers, and in the years when heavy mahogany carving was popular Monington and Weston pianos were in great demand.

But in the Edwardian era the style had less appeal, and the company found itself in financial difficulties. It was bought in 1911 by a young man, William Shepherd Watts, who proved that his faith in the basic strength of the company, and in his own managerial skill, was not at all misplaced.

Other young men showed similar boldness. In the same year, 1911, Michael Kemble began making pianos in Carysfort Road, Stoke Newington. Also that same year another young piano maker took another sort of gamble. Douglas W. Grover was the descendant of London instrument makers for over 100 years – the name of Grover can be traced in the trade back to the eighteenth century. He had started his own piano-making company in 1906. In 1910 his wife fell ill, and went to stay with friends in Gloucestershire to recover and recuperate. Douglas Grover would take the train down to Stroud each weekend. He came to appreciate the countryside more and more. By the time his wife was cured, he had decided that it would be possible to transfer his piano factory to Gloucestershire. He found an empty Cotswold mill in the village of Woodchester, outside Stroud; and disregarding all the pessimists who pointed out that the piano industry and all its suppliers were almost wholly London-based, he began manufacture as the Stroud Piano Company,[1] training local labour in the craft of piano making.

It was a risky decision, but in the long run (despite perils and vicissitudes) it paid off. As, later in the century, a number of other piano makers found the need to leave London, Grovers could properly claim to have led the way.

As so often, the feeling for the craftsmanship of pianos seemed to be in the blood. The year 1912 was also significant. A small, stocky South London boy left school. His great-great-grandfather had been at Broadwoods. From the age of eight he had spent his evenings in the Hicks piano factory in the New Kent Road.

1. Now, still in the Grover family, the Bentley Piano Company.

When he left West Square Central Boys' School, Southwark, young Alfred Knight had 'very good' grades in practical handicraft in wood and metal. He enthusiastically joined the Hicks company as a piano-making apprentice, one of the new generation.

Despite the presence of such hopefuls as Alfred Knight, the tradition of apprenticeship in the piano trade had weakened. Many were keen to revive it, as a means of raising the general standard of craftsmanship. One or two companies, Hopkinsons among them, reintroduced formal apprenticeships. And in 1913 arrangements were completed for a piano-making course to be included in the curriculum of the Furniture Department of one of the London County Council's technical colleges.

In August 1913 an all-British Music Exhibition was held in London. Thirty-five of the leading British piano makers took part. Only nine of them claimed to be making player-pianos (though some of the others certainly were, or were installing foreign player-actions in their instruments).

Despite foreign inroads, they could claim evidence of a reasonably prosperous industry. British piano exports, it was reported, had doubled in ten years. The import of mahogany into Britain (the principal wood then used in piano manufacture, mainly obtained from the forests of British Honduras) had increased by 47 per cent in 1913.

There was considerable anger in the trade about the price-cutting activities of some piano retailers and furniture stores, which it was felt were lowering the acceptable standards of manufacture. A proposal was put forward to publish a 'black list' of unfair practices. Some stores were selling 'new' pianos at below list price – it was claimed that these were in fact reconditioned pianos. The hire-purchase schemes were running into deep waters and the problem of reclaiming pianos on default of payment was causing trouble. There were bitter price-cutting wars among the London stores: Selfridges were giving 20 per cent discounts for cash, and Whiteleys 33⅓ per cent. John Barkers felt themselves obliged to raise their cash discount from 20 per cent to match Whiteleys: but Harrods stuck to 25 per cent and refused to change. The battles were fought with floods of 'bargain' advertisements in the newspapers, which the makers called 'decoy-ducks'. Steinways threw the trade into confusion by announcing that they were about to cut out the retailers and launch their own chain of retail outlets in the provinces. The British manufacturers faced with these common problems and challenges were driven to sink their differences and form a Music Trades Association in self-defence.

The situation was not wholly bad. E. Goodman (who as a boy had acted as go-between in the partnership of Gilbert and Sullivan) was now director of Chappell's piano factory and wrote an optimistic prognostication of the future of the British piano industry. Chappell had increased piano production by a third within a few years, and the production of grands had increased sixfold.

Challen were in an equally successful phase. Frank Challen had backed the 'short grand', only 4 ft 9 in. long, and this piano, with its good performance and looks, proved popular: Challen marketed it as a distinguished piece of furniture.

Indeed the Challen short grand proved so successful that the company turned over almost all production to it, and for a period of years made very few uprights. Even so, the company was doing research into reducing the mechanical noise of the player-piano action, in view of the inroads made into the British market by the American player-piano.

Britain declared war on Germany in August 1914, and conflict was joined on grounds more desperate than those of piano making. A certain vindictiveness began to agitate the British public – a vindictiveness that was most bitterly and unreasonably exercised when the First Sea Lord, who had devotedly prepared the Royal Navy for war, was hounded from the Admiralty because he happened to have been born German.[1] German nationals living in Britain were interned, and their companies in Britain closed down. This was particularly unfair on those companies with German origins and names that were wholly British-owned in the United Kingdom. Bechstein was still German-owned. But the Blüthner company in Britain was a concession owned since 1876 by two Englishmen – W. M. Y. Maxwell and W. J. Whelpdale. Whelpdale had died in 1913, and the company was being run by his son Arthur Whelpdale – successfully, for in the first nine

1. He was Prince Louis of Battenberg, father of Earl Mountbatten of Burma.

months of 1914 he imported 1400 Blüthner pianos for Britain and the British Empire (particularly Australia). But Blüthner, with Bechstein, suffered from the prevailing jingoism and war fervour; a brick was thrown through the window of their Wigmore Street showroom.

Early in 1915 the annual list of Royal Warrant-Holders was published. This is a list of manufacturers whose products have been found to be satisfactory in use by the Royal Households over a set period, and who may be entitled to display the Royal Arms. On the list for 1915 were the names of Bechstein and Blüthner.

'A Public Scandal!' roared *The Pianomaker.*

7
Survival of the Fittest

Too many skilled men died in the mud of Flanders between 1914 and 1918. The piano trade lost its share. The Great War and its aftermath spelled doom to many of the little manufacturers who had been making pianos in back-street factories. Some of the greatest names suffered with the smallest. The world-renowned Broadwood barless concert grand, probably one of the best pianos ever manufactured, was extinguished by the shortage of steel and because of its extreme size and weight. Supplies of copper were diverted wholly to war purposes, and that in itself was enough to threaten the piano trade with closure. One or two manufacturers made brave improvisations: Sydney Zender, who had moved his works to Hackney in 1916, used iron for strings as a final expedient to avoid going out of business altogether.

Others turned to wartime manufacture. The Brasted brothers put their skills with wire and wood to making parts for the primitive biplanes used by the Royal Flying Corps in its fledgling years.

The piano had played a part in the war: 'sing-songs round the piano' were a feature of the life in the army messes and recreation centres such as Toc H behind the lines (the film *Oh What a Lovely War* included an accurate depiction of one such centre). But a new instrument was coming into popularity – the wind-up gramophone, which was even taken into the trenches. With the coming of peace in 1918 the gramophone, at first hand-wound and then rapidly superseded in the twenties and thirties by the electric machine, began to oust the piano as a means of popular entertainment.

For the 'gay young things' it was the perfect instrument, providing entertainment without the drudgery of work. The piano industry countered with the player-piano. In January 1920 the American Aeolian Company enlarged its factory at Hayes,

Middlesex: the mill alone covered 39000 square feet. The refinement of the 'reproducing' piano-roll meant that the player could enjoy the playing of such masters as Busoni in his or her living-room; and since the quality of reproduction of the gramophone was still comparatively poor, the player-piano offered a more direct aesthetic experience.

Ferruccio Busoni, born in Tuscany, had been a child prodigy, appearing in Vienna at the age of nine. He was the inheritor of Liszt's bravura style, which he greatly admired, though he never met Liszt. During the First World War he retired to Switzerland, refusing to play in any of the warring countries. But he made a great number of piano-rolls, and returned to the concert platform before his death in Berlin in 1924.

A still more famous international figure was Ignace Jan Paderewski, who was highly popular in London from his début in 1890. If Busoni was the inheritor of the Liszt tradition, Paderewski followed the style of his fellow-Pole Chopin (and supervised a classic edition of Chopin's works). During the Great War he raised substantial sums for Polish exiles. In 1919 he was elected Prime Minister of Poland, and represented that country at the Versailles Peace Conference – a rare example of a great pianist becoming a leader in public life. In 1920 he retired from politics and returned to the concert platform. Sadly, war overtook him for a second time and he died in exile in New York in 1941.

Another vastly popular pianist of the day was Vladimir von Pachmann. Born in Odessa of Austrian descent, he made his London début in 1882 playing the Chopin F minor Concerto. Over the years his platform manner became more and more idiosyncratic and extravagant – he would chat to the audience between and even during works. He died in Rome in 1933.

Despite the emergence of new challenges to the piano, Britain produced two world-famous virtuosi at this time, and gave a home to a third. In 1921 Solomon began his adult career with a recital at the Wigmore Hall. But he had appeared in London much earlier, at the age of eight, in a concert at the Queen's Hall in June 1911. The *Daily Telegraph* reported:

At the instrument specially constructed for him, with small keys, little Solomon, bare-legged and clad in a cool-looking white suit, cut a very diminutive figure. His frank engaging countenance was frequently suffused with smiles as the notes responded to the touch of his agile fingers. He was on the best of terms with himself and his audience, not to mention the orchestra with whom he exchanged friendly glances as they nodded approval of his precocious efforts. He played the Mozart Concerto in B flat (K 450), the slow movement of the Tschaikowsky Concerto in B flat minor, and a Polacca for piano and orchestra by Alice Verne Bredt. He played the Polacca 'con amore' and in the course of it compassed a couple of glissandos with surprising dexterity. And now that Solomon has shown us what an uncommonly clever, bright, amiable little fellow he is, let us add a hope that he will be given plenty of toys to play with in the next year or so, and not allowed to wear out Nature's gifts before they come to full maturity.

He was given a tricycle at the end of that concert, and delighted the audience by leaping on to the saddle and riding off the Queen's Hall platform on it. At the age of nine he was summoned to play for King George V, Queen Mary and their family at Buckingham Palace; and after a half-hour classical programme, asked to play 'something for the children', he obliged with a vivid performance of the 'Teddy Bears' Picnic'.

Born Solomon Cutner, the son of a tailor in the East End of London, he was discovered hammering the piano at a school concert, was taken up, and put before the public. From the age of eight to fourteen he gave concerts almost weekly. At sixteen a fund was started to give him a formal musical education. This proved his salvation, since he was able to withdraw from the concert platform for three years to study with Cortot and Lazare-Levy. In later years he wrote that 'no one should appear in public before he or she is 20'; and Solomon was effectively the last of the infant piano prodigies. His reputation as a pianist of world distinction grew, particularly in Chopin and Beethoven. During the Second World War he played often at the National Gallery concerts organized by Myra Hess. He was the first classical pianist to travel for ENSA to play for British troops overseas, and in July 1944 followed hard on the invasion of Europe to give a concert tour in Normandy, playing pianos that varied from 'upright grands to downright shams'. In 1955 he was at the Edinburgh Festival as a participant in one of the chamber groups of virtuosi that distinguished the Festival in those years, playing with Zino Francescatti and Pierre Fournier. In the following year his concert career was tragically ended by a stroke.

His contemporary Clifford Curzon had a more conventional musical education, entering the Royal Academy of Music at the age of twelve and making his début at the Queen's Hall under Sir Henry Wood at the age of sixteen in 1924. From that date he has followed a career of distinction in the leading ranks of classical pianists.

It was the First World War that determined Benno Moiseiwitsch to make his home in London. Born (like Pachmann) in Odessa, he studied under Leschetizsky in Vienna and made his London début in 1908. Long accepted as a jovial and popular figure on the British musical scene, he became a British subject in 1937.

Mark Hambourg had settled in England earlier, and married an English girl. He too became a naturalized British citizen. So did Louis Kentner, who was born in Silesia and educated in Budapest but made London his home and musical base.

The recovery of the piano trade after the First World War was slow and difficult. For Brinsmeads in particular the years after 1918 were tragic. The company had grown in the last quarter of the nineteenth century, winning prize after prize at the international exhibitions. With a showroom in Wigmore Street and a factory in Grafton Road, Kentish Town, Brinsmeads were in the front rank. The war dissipated all the company's tradition and energy, and towards the end of 1919 there were rumours that the company was to be closed. The workers went on strike. By April the Brinsmead works had shut its doors, and the strike was spreading to other companies. By July there was a compromise, and the piano strike ended. But it had broken Brinsmeads, and six months later a receiver was appointed. In the following year the company was wound up, and the historic name bought by Cramers for £4000. Cramers decided that the name was still marketable and re-launched the company as John Brinsmead and Sons (1921) Limited.

The same pattern was to be sadly repeated throughout the twenties. In April 1923 Frank Squire died; in July B. Squire and Son was bought by Kembles. Kemble and Company had been strengthened when Michael Kemble was joined by his wife's cousin Victor Jacobs, an accountant newly returned from the war in 1918. Within a few years they had bought up Cramers, John Brinsmead, and Moore and Moore in addition to B. Squire and Son.

In November 1923 George Hermitage, managing director of J. & J. Hopkinson died: the Hopkinson name and business were bought by George Rogers and Company, who had enlarged their factory the previous year. Other elderly piano makers saw how things were going. Between June and August 1924 seven manufacturers went into liquidation.

The end of the war meant that the Blüthner agents Whelpdale and Maxwell (now A. W. Whelpdale, the younger Maxwell, and their company secretary J. 'Jimmy' Meadmore) had to begin importing German pianos once more. The Blüthner factory at Leipzig had been virtually untouched by the war and was in full production. But there was a difficulty. While the musical profession recognized the high quality of the Blüthner piano, there was still an understandable popular antipathy to all German products in Britain. The company therefore began to investigate the possibility of manufacturing in their own right. The name 'Welmar' was coined in 1919, and a contract was made with Squire and Longson to manufacture Welmar pianos at their works in Medlar Street, Camberwell.

Squire and Longson were run by C. E. 'Clarrie' Lyon and his brother-in-law H. V. 'Bert' Shepperd – an effectively contrasting team since Lyon was a man of ideas and intuition while his brother-in-law was shrewd, straightforward and a good salesman. Working for them was Alfred Knight, who had joined them from Hicks. Between them they were making fine pianos, not only under their own Cremona name, but under a variety of names for other makers and retailers. The retailers would supply their own transfers to be put on the inner keyboard-lid – Barnes of London, Rushworth and Dreaper of Liverpool, Cranes of Manchester, and many more. Welmar discovered a particularly good market in Scotland, dourly unaffected by the frivolous ready-made entertainments of the pleasure-loving South. The first order from the Allied Music Traders of Scotland was for 150 Welmar uprights bought at £29 each, and sold retail at 49 guineas.

However, though the trade had doubled the value of exports between 1921 and 1924, the value of pianos imported into

57. 'The piano thumpers' – a sing-song round the family piano, about 1908.

58. The Steinway Duo-Art reproducing piano of the 1920s, from a contemporary advertisement

59. *Opposite, top,* Mantovani playing
the Eavestaff Minipiano, 1935. This is
the De Luxe model, with electric
lights topping the keyboard columns

60. *Opposite,* the Eavestaff Minigrand,
1935

61. *Above,* the Kemble overstrung
'Minx', 1936, in the 'Louis XV' style
in antique walnut. This piano was 2 ft
$10\frac{1}{2}$ ins high, and 4 ft 4 ins wide

62. *Right,* the Kemble 'Olympia' 4 ft
miniature grand, about 1936

63. The Kemble modern
'Cubist' upright, 1936, with chromium
fittings and lights

Harrods

invite you to try the new all-British

CHALLEN
'MINOR' GRAND

The
Piano of the
B.B.C.

FAMOUS as the Piano selected by the B.B.C., the Challen comes to you from the world's largest producers of Grand Pianos. In this 'Minor' Grand, which may be seen and tried at Harrods, you have the superlative tone and quality of the Pianos that delight you 'on the air,' in a conveniently small size.

Length 4ft. 3in., full compass (7¼ octaves), Ivory keys ; magnificent case of modern design. Fully guaranteed for 10 years.

In polished Mahogany or Oak, Satin Walnut, or Ebonized finish.

PRICE 65 Gns

Or delivered Free on the first of thirty-six monthly payments of

41/9

Harrods will make a generous allowance for your present instrument in part payment.

On receipt of a postcard, a paper pattern showing the exact area occupied by the instrument will be sent Free.

HARRODS LTD *SLOane 1234* **KNIGHTSBRIDGE SW1**

64. A contemporary newspaper advertisement for the Challen 'minor grand' of the 1930s

65–71. **Fifteen representative pianos made by the principal British manufacturers**

65. *Opposite, top left*, Bentley (The Bentley Piano Company Limited)

66. *Top right*, Danemann (W. Danemann and Company Limited)

67. *Bottom*, Kemble (Kemble and Company Limited)

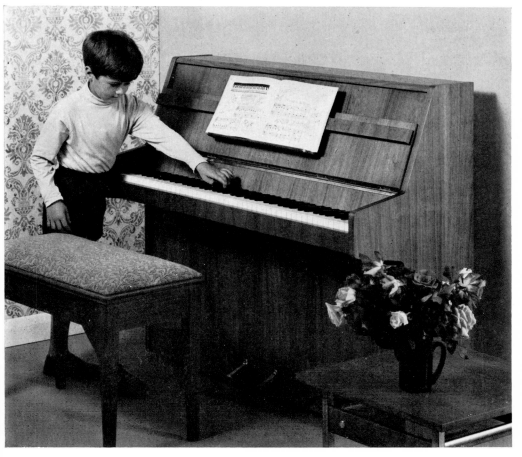

68. *Top left*, Barratt and Robinson (Barratt and Robinsom Limited)

Top right, Brinsmead

Bottom left, Broadwood (John Broadwood and Sons Limited)

Bottom right, Challen

Top left, Cramer

Top right, Eavestaff (Brasted Brothers Limited and W. G. Eavestaff and Sons Limited)

Bottom left, Knight (Alfred Knight Limited)

Bottom right, Zender (Sydney Zender Limited)

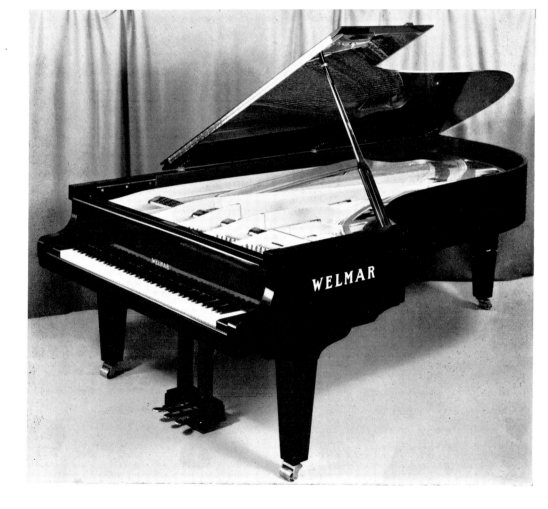

69. *Opposite, top left*, Monington and Weston (Monington and Weston)

70. *Opposite, top right*, Rogers (George Rogers and Sons)

71. *Opposite*, Welmar (Whelpdale, Maxwell and Codd Limited)

72. *Right*, Michael Kemble, co-founder of Kemble and Company

73. *Below, left*, Victor Jacobs, co-founder of Kemble and Company

74. *Below, right*, Denzil Jacobs, chairman of Kemble and Company

75. *Opposite, top left*, Robert Kemble, director of Kemble and Company

76. *Top right*, Jack Codd, of Whelpdale, Maxwell and Codd, makers of the Welmar piano

77. *Bottom left*, Captain Evelyn Broadwood M.C., chairman of John Broadwood and Sons

78. *Bottom right*, William Danemann, founder of W. Danemann and Company

79. *Above*, Edgar Danemann (left) and Tom Danemann (right), directors of W. Danemann and Company and sons of the founder, with the new generation in the company, Jacqui and Timothy Danemann

80. *Opposite, top*, William Shepherd Watts, former chairman of Monington and Weston

81. *Bottom left*, Bernard Watts, director of Monington and Weston

82. *Bottom right*, John Morley, director of Robert Morley and Company

83. *Above*, Alfred Knight, O.B.E., founder of the Knight Piano Company

84. *Left*, William Evans, C.B.E., creator of the successful Challen baby grand

85. *Below*, H. Tom Hicks, of Henry Hicks and Company

86. *Opposite, top left*, Frederick Saffell, chairman of Barratt and Robinson

87. *Top right*, Gerald Brasted, M.B.E., of Brasted Brothers and W. G. Eavestaff and Sons

88. *Opposite, left*, Douglas Brasted of Brasted Brothers and W. G. Eavestaff and Sons

89. *Opposite, right*, Stanley Murdoch, of Murdoch and Murdoch

90. *Left*, Richard Grover, M.B.E. (right), with his son David Grover and the portrait of his father Douglas Grover, founder of the Bentley Piano Company

91. *Below, left*, Herbert Lowry, director of George Rogers and Son

92. *Below*, Ivan Zender, director of Sydney Zender

Britain had also substantially increased. In 1921, 9079 pianos were imported to a value of £335000, while 1538 pianos were exported to a value of £150000. Three years later, 10797 pianos were imported to a value of £557000, while 6542 pianos were exported to a value of £315000. Evidently the trade was finding it difficult to hold even the traditional markets of the Empire, particularly Australia and New Zealand.

Within the piano-making trade there were different views of the future. Some made a success against all the odds. William Shepherd Watts had bought Monington and Weston in 1911. The company had been founded in Camden Town in 1858, and had won gold medals in both London and Paris at the international exhibitions. At one time the company employed a hundred wood-carvers, and was renowned for its ornate cases. Watts was undeterred by the prevailing economic conditions during and after the First World War, and opened a new factory at Kentish Town in 1921. Other makers were less sanguine of the future.

In 1926, no doubt as an encouragement to the trade, King George V and Queen Mary toured the factory of their oldest Royal Warrant-holder – the works at Bow of John Broadwood and Sons, who had made pianos for the Royal Family since the days of George I. In the following year King George bought a new Broadwood for Buckingham Palace, and Queen Mary a Broadwood-Ampico reproducing player-piano for Sandringham.

Industrial unrest, culminating in the General Strike of 1926, introduced a mood of pessimism that only the most determined could counter. When Arthur Whelpdale's nephew, Jack Codd, left school in 1924 he was taken into the business largely because of the want of other employment opportunities. After a period in Switzerland to learn German he was sent to the Blüthner factory in Leipzig to complete an apprenticeship there, as his uncle had done at the turn of the century. He worked at the bench, learning the Blüthner techniques for setting-up, the regulation of the touch, and toning. In contrast, and a year or two later, Douglas Grover in Gloucestershire felt that the trade faced a difficult and uncertain future. Feeling that his son should have an alternative skill, he sent him to learn estate agency (though some years later Richard Grover was to return to the business and become a leader in the piano trade).

Apart from the gramophone, there was another serious com-
petitor in the field of home entertainment. In November 1922 the
British Broadcasting Company began transmissions from radio
station 2LO at Savoy Hill, London. Its managing director John
Reith was not himself musical but strongly believed that it was
the duty of the BBC to offer the public the highest quality of
entertainment in all its forms. In 1924 he summoned Sir Henry
Walford Davies to attend an advisory committee on broadcast music.

Walford Davies was a great popularizer. A former organist of
the Temple Church, London, he had gone to be Professor of
Music at the University College of Wales at Aberystwyth where
he had established a reputation for being able to put good music
before ordinary people (largely through the Workers' Educational
Association) without 'talking down'. He had grasped the opportunity offered by the gramophone.

While most musicians were either treating the gramophone with con-
tempt or eyeing it greedily as a possible source of personal profit [writes
his biographer H. C. Colles], he had foreseen its immense potentiality
for bringing music to all and sundry.

While its music was still a travesty of the real thing, he could
imagine the symphonies of Beethoven so perfectly reproduced on it
that a man might sit with his feet on the fender and enjoy a concert
which would be virtually a replica of Queen's Hall.

Walford Davies recorded for His Master's Voice a set of lectures
about music, with illustrations played by himself on the piano.
These proved highly successful.

As he journeyed to and from Wales by train he observed the
poles and aerial wires sprouting in thousands of back gardens,
witness to the growing popularity of radio. When Reith asked
him to join the BBC's music advisory committee he accepted
eagerly, and at the first meeting spoke eloquently of the possibility
of summoning 'the great minds of all the ages to serve at the
microphone'. Walford Davies gave his first broadcast for schools,
talking at the piano, in April 1924. Two years later he began a
series of talks for adults under the title of 'Music and the Ordinary
Listener', which he kept up for four years. It was the beginning of
that pioneer work by the BBC to broaden the musical education
and awareness of the British people that has borne such remarkable fruit.

The coming of radio, allied to the change in social life inaugurated by the £100 motor car (the Ford, and then the Austin
Seven), was devastating for the piano trade. Then the player-
piano fashion was shattered virtually overnight. In America the
Aeolian Company's profits were eroded by the first thunder of
what was to be the 1929 Wall Street financial crash. A message
came from New York ordering the closure of the British branch.

Within little more than twenty-four hours the vast factory at
Hayes and the showroom and hall in Bond Street were shut down
(the Aeolian Hall was subsequently leased by the BBC).

The player-piano had never sold in such great quantity as the
conventional piano. At the height of its popularity about seventy
or eighty were manufactured in Britain a week, compared with
about 1500 ordinary pianos. But the two major companies in
Britain, the Aeolian Company in Bond Street and the Triumph
Auto Company in Regent Street, sold prestige player-pianos at
prices from 150 to 200 guineas. Triumph had a particularly
efficient sales and delivery organization, so that an enquiry
would produce a van outside the house the next day unloading a
piano complete with stool and a selection of rolls, which would be
left on a payment of £5 down and a signature on a hire-purchase
agreement.

The other piano manufacturers incorporated player-actions and
sold the result more cheaply, but the influence of the Aeolian (and
to a lesser extent Triumph) advertising was such that they, with
the American Ampico, virtually dominated the market. Then
came the crash. Triumph Auto could not hope to continue an
advertising campaign on the scale of the Aeolian operation, and
the company closed. It was a personal disaster for its energetic
managing director, Frederick Saffell.

As a youngster Fred Saffell had joined the Kastner Auto-piano
Company in 1907, and soon appreciated the potential of the player-
piano. In the anti-German fervour of 1915 the German-born head
of the firm, Maximilian Kastner, was interned. With a group of
associates Fred Saffell bought the company and kept it going. In
1917 he further diversified by acquiring the piano makers Barratt
and Robinson, which had been founded in 1877 in York Road,
Kentish Town, and had become among the foremost late Victorian piano makers.

With admirable resilience Fred Saffell emerged from the remains of Triumph Auto and the player-piano boom to build Barratt and Robinson once again into one of the leading British names, principally by selling through the furniture stores who supported him during this acutely difficult time.

Changes were also taking place within Chappell and Company. On Tom Chappell's death in 1902 William Boosey became managing director. He was the adopted son of John Boosey and had joined Chappells in 1894 to run a series of ballad concerts. His principal interests were music publishing and musical administration (the company owned the lease of the Queen's Hall). The company was reorganized in 1919 and the Chappell Piano Company incorporated as an autonomous subsidiary with Mr Healey as director. By 1922 the piano company had recovered remarkably from the war and was making 100 uprights and grands a week.

At the Queen's Hall, Chappells ran the Promenade Concerts until 1926, when the BBC took over their administration. At Queen's Hall concerts under the Chappell management many distinguished pianists appeared, including Paderewski, Schnabel, Cortot, Pachmann, Moisewitsch, Solomon and Curzon.

Chappells published most of the scores of the great musical shows of the period – *Merrie England*, *A Country Girl*, *The Arcadians*, and the *Merry Widow*. Then there were the lighter successes of the twenties – *Rose Marie*, the *Desert Song*, the *Student Prince*, and the success of 1929 – Noël Coward's *Bitter Sweet*.

It was in 1929 that the American music publisher Louis Dreyfus walked into 50 New Bond Street one day, and walked out having bought the business. His brother Max became chairman of the independent Chappell and Company Inc. of New York, and the partnership led to an internationalization of Chappell music publishing.

The piano company similarly set out on a programme of expansion, in 1929 buying the Allison company and also, most dramatically, Clementi's famous company Collard and Collard. (Chappells bought yet another distinguished piano firm, John Strohmenger and Sons, in 1938.)

In the early twenties a young man from Wales learnt the trade of piano making in the Chappell factory at Chalk Farm. He was William Evans. The son of a police inspector, he had trained as an engineer, but coming to London to seek his fortune he had found his way into the piano trade and proved to be one of its most notable businessmen and salesmen. In 1926 he left Chappells to join the then ailing family business of Challen.

Earlier in the century Frank Challen had produced a 5 ft small grand. It was a good piano, but produced in limited quantity. William Evans determined to bring the small grand back into popularity. By organizing larger-scale production and buying in actions, frames and pedals in greater quantity he was able to reduce the price from about £125 to £65, and put the small grand within the reach of the average home. The venture was a success. It was the salesmanship of William Evans, also, that put Challen pianos into many BBC studios. Evans became managing director of Challen in 1931. He had virtually revived the grand as a domestic, as distinct from a concert, instrument.

The idea of the piano as a mass-produced object was alien to many piano makers. The concept of the individually craftsman-built instrument remained. But it was in the twenties that the first elements of rationalization began to creep in. Some manu-facturers came to realize that the only solution to the economic challenges of the period was to adopt simpler and standardized procedures for those aspects of production to which such pro-cedures could be applied. There would always have to be elements of piano manufacture that would not be susceptible to such production methods, stringing and tuning among them. Though today computerized systems could no doubt be devised, the capital cost would not justify the outlay.

By the twenties, the first kilns were being introduced to mature wood and bring soundboards to the correct toughness by pro-viding artificial and speedy 'weathering' and humidity. The older makers stuck to their traditional method of storing timber out of doors for many months, refusing at first to recognize that a better result could be achieved in a kiln in a matter of hours.

The craft tradition was upheld by Strohmengers, with their ornate architect-designed cases for grands many of which went into ballrooms in the great ocean liners. In Lewisham, Douglas

Morley produced a number of original and unusual cases that attracted considerable interest, some of them reminiscent of the early nineteenth-century 'camel-back' pianos.

Tom Hicks, for many years Treasurer of the Pianoforte Manufacturers Association and first President of the Piano Publicity Association, recalls the production methods of a piano factory in the twenties:

Our workmen were craftsmen, and could hold their own against any modern workman. They had to be craftsmen to earn the money: they were on piecework. They had to be quick. The man who made the case was practically making it out of trees. Today a fitter-up takes all his parts, which are finished and milled, and glues them together. In those days a man had little more than a plank of wood. To put his ends on, he took another plank of wood, and had to plane it up and shape it and put on his cheeks (end-pieces). He had to bow-saw them into the right shape. The tops, the doors, the keyboard-cover all had to be moulded.

It was a seasonal trade. At Easter the average manufacturer sacked at least half his employees, keeping the others just making parts. This was because he could not store the pianos. Most factories were very small, and when a week's stock was made it had to be sold or the firm was finished.

During the summer the workmen went down to the seaside, and became waiters and did other jobs. Then after August Bank Holiday they all came back and worked flat out.

At Hicks we were among the few to manufacture all the year round, because of our retail establishments. In summer we took over a school in which we could store hundreds of pianos. The financing of the operation was so close that the bank manager used to come round to inspect the stock.

Another company that devised a way of improving conditions of work by ending the August-to-Easter pattern of employment was that of the Brasted Brothers. The company had been founded by Harry Brasted in 1870, in the heyday of piano production, and had built up a reputation for producing a sound commercial piano sold under retail dealers' 'Own name' labels. After the First World War the company was being run by Harry Brasted's three sons, Percy, Harry and Bert, respectively in charge of management, production and sales. When in 1925 the century-old Eavestaff company was on the market on the retirement of W. E.

Eavestaff, the Brasteds bought the name and began to manufacture a quality piano under it.

The original Brasted works had been in Clapton (the old tram terminus, with the disadvantage for a piano manufacturer of being on two floors). A new works was built in 1919 in Hermitage Road, Finsbury Park. There was plenty of room to incorporate the Eavestaff production, together with two other woodworking companies: H. & P. Ltd, mainly manufacturing bedroom furniture, and George Hammer & Co., the joinery business (later to earn distinction for its joinery in Coventry Cathedral: church and school furniture was its strong line).

In 1928 Brasteds merged with their Harringay neighbours Boyd Ltd and Barnett, Samuel to form the Associated Piano Company. Boyd Ltd was an old-established piano-making firm owned by the Samuel family, who were also owners of the Barnett, Samuel and Decca Company which made band instruments of all kinds and also gramophones at a factory in St Ann's Road, Harringay.

The merger, and the extra space available in the factory, enabled Percy Brasted to guarantee his employees year-round jobs. He reorganized production to allow for this, and during the summer the 27000 square feet of the Assembly Shop would gradually fill up with pianos, sometimes stacked three high.

These would melt away as the orders began to come in during the autumn. The system earned Brasteds a reputation as good and reliable employers.

Manufacturing methods were also being rationalized. The trade had for years bought in many of its components – wire, felts, and actions. Fletcher and Newman were leading suppliers. There were three leading manufacturers of actions – Herrburger Brooks, British Piano Actions, and John Malcolm and Son (the last a subsidiary of the manufacturing and retail company, Murdochs).

The majority of pianos being manufactured were straight-strung uprights, the action for which could be standardized. Herrburger Brooks were by this time producing a cheap and reliable action. The days had long gone when actions were produced individually for each piano. The Robert Wornum pianos of the late nineteenth century were probably the last with this characteristic, and they used to fascinate piano makers who opened them with curiosity to see what original type of action each might have (the Wornum grand produced for Sir Henry Cole at the Victoria and Albert Museum, for instance, has a downward-striking action).

Herrburger Brooks were on the way to achieving a world monopoly in the manufacture of piano actions. Louis Sterling (afterwards Sir Louis Sterling, and the creator of the Columbia Gramophone Company), having bought Herrburger Brooks decided to go for the monopoly situation. In 1928 he approached John Malcolm and Son with a takeover proposal. Initially James Murdoch, director of the parent company, was willing to sell. But William Evans, by this time a substantial customer on behalf of Challen, was disturbed at the prospect of two vital supplies – piano actions and keys – being in the hands of a monopoly.

He therefore appealed to Murdoch for time to form a consortium, and found that he could only be given a week. Within that period he assembled a group of piano makers, including Hicks, Kemble, King Brothers, Murdoch, Squire and Longson and Waddingtons. Between them they raised £32000 to buy the company – a remarkable achievement in a time of financial stringency. The members of the group could guarantee production.

About a year later Louis Sterling approached the company again; and this time it was incorporated into Herrburger Brooks, but under contracts that ensured supplies and a percentage of profit to the participants for some years afterwards.

There were still many characters in the trade. One was Arthur Hughes, who made strings for most of the piano firms. He would go round from company to company collecting his money, and exchanging hospitality on the way. He was a convivial man, and sometimes rashly generous. He once drove a contact up to the Spaniards on Hampstead Heath, by pony and trap. The landlord liked the pony, and bought it. Afterwards Hughes looked somewhat abashed and his friend asked why. 'Well, I believe I only hired it,' said Arthur.

8
Challenge of Electronics

At the end of the 1920s international piano production had reached around 500 000 a year. Within a matter of a year or two production had dropped to almost a half. The Great Depression hit hard at a trade already devastated by the gramophone, radio, and finally the cinema. In each High Street a new cinema opened; and with the coming of the 'talkies' the pianos that had given such eloquent accompaniment to the earlier silent films were replaced, if they were replaced at all, by the Mighty Wurlitzer arising from the depths bathed in a pink flood.

The fire that burnt down the Camberwell factory of Squire and Longson in 1929 seemed symptomatic of the blows that were raining down one after the other upon the piano makers. One of the principal manufacturers of pianos sold through the retail music-stores was virtually out of business. Again, it seemed not unexpected when in 1931 the doyen of British piano manufacturers, John Broadwood and Sons, proved to be in financial difficulties. William Evans, now managing director of Challen, agreed to make the Broadwood piano under licence. Broadwoods retained the factory at Bow. This was found to contain at least one relic of a more graceful age. In a part of the factory were found a row of Broadwood grands, apparently new, stacked on their sides. These were classified as 'used stock'. They represented the result of the company's honourable if quixotic practice of hiring out new pianos from the London showroom for elegant evening soirées in Mayfair drawing-rooms.

Once played, the pianos were returned to the factory and stored as 'used stock'. The practice probably dated from the eighteenth century when a stock of harpsichords was kept by Shudi and Broadwood for hiring purposes. In Edwardian England the custom was worthy; in the harsher economic

climate of the thirties it was extravagant. But at least the Broadwood piano was kept in existence and the tradition maintained,
as it has been since by Captain Evelyn Broadwood, MC.

It took great optimism and purposefulness to start a new
company at that unpromising time. Alfred Knight did it. He
found a factory at Carysfort Road, Stoke Newington, and with the
expertise inherited from his ancestors who had been Broadwood
workmen, and from his own experience at Hicks and at Squire and
Longson, he began business as Baker and Knight. In 1935 he
became sole proprietor of the Knight Piano Company, within a
few years was exporting all over the world, and by the end of the
decade was manufacturing 1000 pianos a year – a triumph of
determination over adversity. He was himself a pianist, had
studied music with Tracy Robson at Steinways, and had played
with bands and in cabaret: he delighted in demonstrating his
pianos wherever he went.

The Squire and Longson factory was rebuilt, but could not
recover from the decline in business and in 1933 the name was
bought by Kembles. The Welmar company (now Whelpdale,
Maxwell and Codd, for Jack Codd had completed his apprenticeship with Blüthners and returned to London to join the firm) had
also suffered from the loss of production when Squire and Longson
burnt down. In 1933 they decided to manufacture on their own
account, and began in a factory in Clapham, taking C. E. Lyon
and H. V. Shepperd of Squire and Longson into the business.
After a year they were producing about ten quality pianos a week:
Welmar determined to concentrate on the 'Blüthner' tone. From
the beginning they made a 4 ft 6 in. grand, and then began
manufacture of a 6 ft grand.

A pleasant association was maintained when the heir of the
Blüthner company in Leipzig, Ingbert Blüthner – the great-
grandson of the founder – came to serve his apprenticeship in the
Welmar factory in Clapham.

Meanwhile the trade was earnestly looking for some novelty to
revive public interest in the piano, and to stimulate the flagging
trade that was driving still more companies to the wall. There
had for many years been small pianos – indeed the original
Zumpe square pianos were only four and a half octaves, 'not
much bigger than two writing-desks put together'. In Victorian

England Broadwoods and many other manufacturers had produced 'yacht pianos' for shipboard use. In the twenties the Hicks company had found a small single-string piano of German design, strung from the back. They contracted to make them under licence and produced fifty or so: but they did not catch on, and the licence was allowed to lapse.

Then in 1934 Percy Brasted discovered a miniature piano made by Messrs Lundholm of Stockholm. It was comparatively expensive, because made in small quantity, but had three important advantages over the conventional upright. The player could look over the top at an audience, the instrument was so small that it made a small room look larger, and a case could be designed round it to fit appropriately into modern styles of interior decoration.

Brasteds bought the rights from Lundholm, which ceased manufacturing it and contracted to import the British-made version, receiving a royalty on sales. Percy Brasted thought 'miniature piano' too cumbersome a description and named the instrument the 'Minipiano'. It was the first registered use of the prefix 'Mini', and was registered world-wide.

The first Minipianos were six-octave bichords, and had a simple mechanism linking a rod directly to the action at the back of the instrument. The soundboard or 'belly' was therefore at the front – a reversal of the usual practice. This made it initially unpopular with piano tuners who did not like the fact that the tuning pins were beneath the keyboard. The tone was sweet and small, and that was another appealing feature for popular taste was just beginning to turn towards the baroque in organ music and interest in early keyboard instruments such as the spinet and harpsichord was growing.

One of the designers from Brasted's associated furniture company, Mr Gosling, was commissioned to design three cases. These were the Ritz, a simple and graceful version of the Scandinavian Lundholm; the Modern, a plain wood case with horizontal chrome bands (this was the period when the Bauhaus design school was propagating chrome as a furniture material); and the De Luxe, which was a version of the Modern with narrow pillars at each end of the keyboard, topped with electric lights. There was also a Period version with applied classical decoration.

The Minipianos were produced in a variety of finishes – birch ply, mahogany or walnut colour, stained black, or enamelled white, cream, black or green. The 'black' notes could also be coloured to tone. There was even a crackle finish, a satin finish, and a high gloss for the North of England (New Zealand also preferred high gloss). Many of these design ideas came from the furniture fashions of the day. They shocked the traditional piano makers.

They were even more shocked when, on the day the coloured Minipianos first appeared in the windows of the Barnes music shop in Oxford Street, London, and Wilson Peck in Sheffield, police had to be called to control the crowds.

The trade was agog when, by the end of the first year, Brasteds' sale of Minipianos topped 7000, at 28 to 38 guineas apiece. A second factory had to be rented in Stoke Newington to cope with the demand. The ghost of Johannes Zumpe must have smiled at the resurgence of his little piano.

The popularity of the Minipiano was gratifying, but Brasteds determined to produce a seven-octave trichord piano which, though not much bigger than the original Minipiano, would give a much rounder tone. Originally the frame and case had been fastened to a back-piece braced with wood. Now in the factory Jack Davis designed a flanged iron frame, to which the case could be bolted. This frame, subsequently copied by many European manufacturers of uprights, enabled higher string tensions to be employed, and reduced the width of the instrument from back to front by about eight inches.

With this construction the design of the action had to be reversed back to the more conventional style with tuning pins at the back (to the satisfaction of piano tuners). But to keep the width of the piano down, the keys had to be shortened which gave a curious touch. This was solved by introducing a lever action.

The Duke of York (afterwards King George VI) accepted a Minipiano for his daughters, and allowed the company to add to the key-slip the legend 'As used by Their Royal Highnesses the Princess Elizabeth and the Princess Margaret Rose'. The 1935 Radio Show opened with Paula Green singing 'Oh! Oh! You Radio!' from the top of a pyramid of (apparently) a hundred Minipianos (the effect was achieved with mirrors: there were only twenty-five). The distinguished concert pianist Solomon played it, the popular Charlie Kunz broadcast on it. Few dance bands and dance-halls were without one (and thousands went to the local dance-hall on a Saturday night).

Percy Brasted went to the United States and arranged for the Minipiano to be made under licence by the American Hardman Peck Company. The editor of the *Piano Trades Magazine of America* wrote that Percy Brasted had 'revolutionised and saved the piano trade'. By 1939 the Brasted firm, the Associated Piano Company, was producing 10000 of the 50000 pianos made in Britain.

Other manufacturers were thinking along similar lines and the success of the Minipiano redoubled their efforts. At Barratt and Robinson in 1935 Fred Saffell designed and manufactured a miniature piano, the Ministrelle, which improved on the previous pianos of this type by repositioning the action and making other modifications so that the Ministrelle would be more convenient to tune. The speed with which this small piano was designed and launched – and achieved commercial success – was entirely due to the fact that unlike most piano manufacturers Fred Saffell did not have to negotiate with other suppliers (by this time nearly all piano makers bought in a great number of parts): Barratt and Robinson were making their own actions, keys, hammers, wrestpins and soundboards, and thus were able to reorganize and rejig rapidly to meet the new requirements.

Kembles also joined the battle. In 1935, by which time Michael Kemble's son Robert had joined the company, they launched three new models to join their range of grands and conventional uprights. These were the Jubilee (named in honour of the Silver Jubilee of King George V in that year), the Cubist, and the Minx Miniature. When the new pianos were shown at the British Industries Fair in that year another piano manufacturer looked at the Jubilee and commented 'You'll never sell that thing!' Kembles themselves were not entirely sure of the public response, and the demand when it came stretched their production capacity to the limit. The Jubilee was to continue in the catalogue for thirty years, and the Minx Miniature is still in production.

Monington and Weston also contributed a development to the 'small piano' success story. William Shepherd Watts, with his sons Terry and Bernard, invented and developed the Tuplex Double Iron Frame, which reduced the thickness of the frame by about half and thus enabled them to make a 'slimline' miniature piano which was launched in 1936.

The general market for pianos had slumped completely in the first half of the thirties and it was the adaptation, improvement and promotion of the small piano that by capturing the public interest enabled a number of firms to keep going. The market for full-scale concert grands was increasingly dominated by Steinway, Bechstein and Blüthner. William Evans had taken most of the market for the smaller 'boudoir' grand, and his Challen pianos, grands and uprights, were in extensive use at the expanding British Broadcasting Corporation.

Despite the promotion of the Minipiano at the 1935 Radio Show, relations between the piano trade and the infant science of radio were far from good. Conscious that this new branch of entertainment had driven many of their contemporaries out of business, the piano makers were heartily suspicious of the BBC. Some regarded it as very clever of William Evans to have got the contract to supply the BBC with pianos. Others, envious of his success, regarded it as akin to supping with the devil.

With the refinement of electronic technology and the resultant improvement in quality achieved both by the BBC and the radio industry, more classical music was broadcast, and not only in adult programmes. To Walford Davies's popular talks was added the Foundations of Music series – a broadcast library of good music, a regular feature on one musical topic each week with a twenty-five-minute slot every day of the week.

This series was directed by the young Anthony Lewis,[1] newly down from Cambridge. Sir Anthony comments:

I always like in this context to pay a tribute to Lord Reith. He was not a great musician, nor even as far as I know a great music-lover. But he was quite determined that classical music should have its due place in the broadcasting service.

I think the musical profession should be very grateful to him for his stand on this point. He was under great pressure from all sides to reduce the emphasis on classical music on the grounds of economy. But the development of the Third Programme after the war, and all

1. Later Sir Anthony Lewis, Principal of the Royal Academy of Music.

that stems from this, is due to him. He was responsible for establishing the status of music in broadcasting.

Not all the administrators at Broadcasting House were sympathetic to the expense that would be incurred in taking music seriously. There is a legend that when one such functionary was asked for permission to hire a second oboe for the BBC Orchestra he queried: 'Can't you put the first oboe nearer the microphone?'

But music was aired, and not only in the adult programmes. Many listeners who were young in those days recall the talks on music given by Helen Henschel, with her familiar signature tune the theme from Brahms' First Symphony, played with sonorous affection on the piano.

Despite his company's own success with the BBC, William Evans had long argued within the piano trade and the BBC that that institution should seriously examine the various types of piano available for broadcasting, and lay down guidelines that would be acceptable not only in London but in the regional studios then being set up in lavish profusion.

In 1936 the BBC determined to choose the best pianos for broadcasting. A Great Piano Test (as it came to be known) was organized. For the best part of a week Studio One at the newly opened Maida Vale Studios was filled with pianos sent in by virtually every major piano maker from Britain and abroad. A series of BBC staff pianists was set to playing each of the pianos in turn, while a panel of judges listened in a closed-off control room.

Among the pianists, Cecil Dixon played Mendelssohn's Bees' Wedding, Ernest Lush the opening of the Tschaikowsky B♭ minor Concerto, and Irene Kohler the Ravel Toccata. The judges, chaired by Godfrey Brown (at that time musical director of the Northern Ireland Orchestra), included Victor Hely-Hutchinson (Professor of Music at Birmingham University), Frank Merrick, and Anthony Lewis.

After listening to the same pieces for a week, the judges were more than a little bemused. Broadcasting was still technically uncertain, and none of them could be sure whether the quality of piano tone might be significantly affected by the placing of the piano in relation to the microphone, or in relation to the acoustics of the hall. They were also aware, as were the pianists, that contracts of considerable value might hinge on their decision.

There were three categories: Concert Grand, Medium range pianos, and Small pianos. The judges placed a first, second and third in each category, and there was considerable relief when the names chosen turned out to be makes of universal repute, with a fair proportion of British pianos among them.

The piano trade was in an uncertain condition as the thirties progressed. Then another piano maker suffered a heavy blow. In 1938 the Woodchester Mill of the Bentley Piano Company near Stroud in Gloucestershire was almost totally destroyed by fire. It was an old Cotswold cloth mill, and in 1788 it had been visited by King George IV and bore a plaque to commemorate the fact. The greater part of the factory was completely destroyed together with most of the plant and machinery.

But on the day following the fire a local estate agent offered the company a single-storey factory on the opposite side of the main road; the Bentley directors had not known that the premises were even on the market.

Despite the severe competition within the piano trade, fellow piano makers and suppliers rallied to help – as, it may be remembered, Broadwoods' workmen rallied to help their Clementi colleagues after that factory had burnt down 130 years earlier. Within a week the Bentley company were occupying their new factory and the first new machines were running. Within nine months the output of pianos was back to the same level as before the fire. An outstanding example of the cooperation received was the gesture of Messrs Wadkin, the woodworking machinery manufacturers, who dispatched to Bentleys the first off the line of each machine required.

And then, in September 1939, Britain was once more at war with Germany.

For a time piano production went on much as before. Then the Government brought in a regulation that piano production must be concentrated. Whelpdale, Maxwell and Codd were approached by Sir Herbert Marshall and Sons (manufacturing the Marshall and Rose piano), George Rogers, and Broadwoods. These other names were then manufactured at Clapham together with Welmar.

Alfred Knight continued to manufacture pianos under Government contract, specifically NAAFI pianos (specially strengthened with metal trim and proofed to withstand the quantities of beer liable to be spilt on them). Alfred Knight also made pianos for ENSA (Entertainments National Service Association – the organization that provided entertainment on an extensive scale for troops in the field, often taking distinguished pianists with the 'concert parties' that sometimes performed within the sound of gunfire to large and appreciative audiences). Nine Knight pianos went ashore in Normandy immediately after the invasion of Europe in 1944.

Barratt and Robinson also produced some NAAFI pianos, but most of the factory was turned over to the production of parts for wooden-clad aircraft, such as the Mosquito. Other piano manufacturers made aircraft parts, among them Kembles and Danemann. Danemann also made army stretchers, and wheels for gun-carriages.

Pianists who travelled the world in considerable discomfort to give pleasure to the troops sometimes had curious encounters. The accompanist Ivor Newton recalls:

By the time we reached the island of Miserah at the extreme end of the Persian Gulf, where the pirate Captain Kidd reputedly buried his treasure, my unfortunate piano, suffering from too many ups and downs of altitude and too much rough handling, was badly out of tune.

There was little that I could do except lament its condition to a young American soldier who was standing near. 'Gee,' he said, 'you won't find a piano tuner here. These native people live on a diet of ship-wrecked sailors.' He paused and meditated. 'Gee,' he repeated at last, 'If I could only get a socket wrench from one of the Air Force guys, I'd have a go at it myself.'

I decided I could do nothing, so went away to rest before the evening's work. To my amazement when I arrived for the concert, the piano was in perfect condition. When I told the C.O. about this afterwards, he ordered the young soldier to be found for me.

'I don't know how to thank you,' I said. 'You've made a wonderful job of it. That can't be the first piano you've tuned.'

'Well,' he said, 'perhaps you know my family.'

'Why, what's your name?' I asked.

'Steinway,' he said as though it meant no more than Smith or Jones.

In 1974 John H. Steinway, Vice-President of the Steinway Company, remembered:

'We did have a wonderful time on the Masira Islands – perhaps the most god-forsaken air base that we operated jointly with the RAF during the Second World War.'

9
Post-war Rationalization

Many of the piano makers whose businesses were not destroyed by enemy action during the war found that the peace brought little improvement in conditions. Because the piano-making industry was concentrated almost entirely in London it had suffered grievously from bombing and rocket attacks. Henry Hicks and Company's factory at the Elephant and Castle had been flattened, as had many of their South London shops. Retaining the company's property interests, the directors decided not to rebuild or reopen the piano factory. Tom Hicks went to Challen.

John Broadwood and Company opened a new factory at Acton, and began to make pianos on their own account once more, under the leadership of John Broadwood's great-great-grandson Captain Evelyn Broadwood, M.C., who was himself to become doyen of the British piano trade.

Brasteds brought their pre-war success, the Minipiano, up to date by extending the overstringing from corner to corner of the frame, giving the bass strings the length and tone of a five-foot grand. The Eavestaff Miniroyal, as they named it, also became one of the first post-war pianos to be designed (by a Danish designer) in the 'Scandinavian' style, and to be offered in oiled teak.

But these were brave efforts to fight against the times. The piano makers who had been able to continue during the war, and those who had turned to aircraft manufacture, had the advantage of technical improvements that had been introduced under the stress of war, particularly in the field of heat-resistant glues which revolutionized and speeded up the assembly of the piano-case.

In the years of Government control immediately after the war, two factors pressed particularly heavily on the piano trade. The first was that all production had to be directed to export. The piano trade had always enjoyed a considerable export trade, but in the turbulent world recovering from almost universal war the export markets had to be fought over and recovered slowly and persistently. The second adverse factor was the branding of the piano as a 'luxury' item that could not be permitted in a home market where food, clothes and many other essentials were still rationed. In 1945 pianos were obliged to carry a purchase tax of 100 per cent – the price of a piano was effectively doubled.

The trade challenged this imposition on the grounds that the piano was a musician's tool in trade, that it was a vital instrument in education, and finally that because of the austere conditions being endured by the trade very few pianos were being made and sold, and the amount of purchase tax being obtained by the Exchequer was minimal. William Evans led a succession of delegates to the Treasury; in 1950 purchase tax on pianos was reduced to $33\frac{1}{3}$ per cent. In 1951 – in which year Fred Saffell was President of the Piano Manufacturers' Association – the tax was taken off pianos altogether.

Thus it was that for six years after the war practically no new pianos were made for the home market, and the only pianos sold were second-hand and reconditioned. In addition, materials were in short supply. The appropriate woods for the bellies and cases, iron for the frames and wire for the strings took second place to materials being imported for more 'essential' industries. Labour, and particularly skilled labour, was also short. Experienced workmen had spent years in the services; no young apprentices had been learning their trade during the war years.

If there was any comfort to be drawn from this situation, it might have been found in the situation of the German piano trade, which was much worse. The Blüthner factory in Leipzig, for example, had three times been demolished by the Royal Air Force, and was having to start again (now in East Germany, under the Russian influence) from the beginning.

The pattern of home life in Britain was changing. Before 1939 only a few households in the country possessed a television set. The BBC started up its television service again in 1946. In the years of austerity television took hold comparatively slowly – not many families had money to spare to buy a set. But then in 1953 millions of Britons watched the Coronation of Queen Elizabeth, the first notable national event to be observed at such quarters in every corner of the country as it was actually happening. Two years later, Independent Television went on the air. By 1956, with the enticement of alternative programmes, the number of households in Britain with TV rose above 80 per cent. This proved a radical source of social change. The screen in the living-room that could provide instant entertainment and information at the turn of a switch captivated young and old.

Cinemas emptied and were turned into Bingo-halls. Pianos stood silent in a million front rooms. It was the end of the cheap piano that might once have been bought as a status-symbol. You had to have a 14-inch screen, and then a 19-inch screen, and then a 26-inch screen. Colour came later.

But the piano makers were not abashed. Sydney Zender, who had been making pianos since 1892 and had kept going during World War I by using iron for strings, had kept going during World War II by building up a successful business in the sale of reconditioned and second-hand pianos. He died in 1948. His son Ivan carried on the business. In 1953, undismayed by the pre-vailing economic conditions, he began to make pianos once more at the factory in Hackney. Within two years he was making 1000 a year, and in 1956 with production running at 2500 a year he expanded into a second factory next door.

Similar enterprise was being demonstrated by the dynamic and irrepressible Alfie Knight. He had the advantage that he had managed to continue making pianos throughout the war. He had always enjoyed travelling the world, making business contacts and building up licensing arrangements in North America, South Africa and Australia. He had been made a Kentucky Colonel and had been given the Freedom of the City of Santiago and made an Honorary Citizen. He was rare among piano makers in that he could play his own pianos to professional standards, and demon-strated them with flair and humour.

He believed that children should be able to read music as readily as words, and undertook many lecture tours of schools.

He could claim a flourishing export trade. Against all the pre-dictions that the piano would continue to decline in the battle with electronics, he believed that the piano trade would revive, and worked vigorously to make sure that it did. To provide his company with room for this expansion he moved out of central London in 1955 to a new factory of 50000 square feet in Loughton, Essex.

Music is something you can do and appreciate for the whole of a lifetime [said Alfred Knight, o.b.e.]. When parents give their children a musical education they are giving them the greatest gift possible. The playing of a musical instrument and appreciation of music is about the only thing left that can be done from nine to ninety.

There was one minor part of the keyboard instrument trade that was enjoying a resurgence of interest in those years. The attention and affection of the musical public had turned to pre-romantic music, particularly the music of the seventeenth and eighteenth centuries. The music of Johann Sebastian Bach enjoyed an unprecedented popularity; this is perhaps symbolized by the Baroque character of the organ designed for the Royal Festival Hall, London, in the 1950s.

The days when Broadwoods could write to a potential piano purchaser and say that harpsichords were out of fashion and virtually worthless were past. Genuine antique instruments were restored, and modern reproductions (such as those made by Arnold Dolmetsch and his family) valued.

At Robert Morley and Company in Lewisham, Douglas Morley had long loved these instruments and been humoured by his piano-making contemporaries for his interest in them. Now his son John Morley went to study harpsichord-making in Germany, and on his return the company turned over to making harpsichords, clavichords and spinets, and gave up making pianos. At about the same time the harp-making Morleys of Kensington retired. They had earned a high reputation for the restoration of antique instruments including pianos. John Morley had often spent time in the workshop and was interested in the historical fascination of the business: so the Morley workshop in Bromley became a haven where many ailing and ancient instruments, including some famous pianos, were brought back to playable condition. Some are to be found in the Colt Clavier

Collection, surely the most remarkable private collection of antique pianos in the world.

Another piano maker took an interest in harpsichords in 1959 when Whelpdale, Maxwell and Codd began to sell the instruments of the distinguished harpsichord maker William de Blaise.

Then in 1958, at a time when the piano trade was at a low ebb and had scarcely recovered from the war, came the battle of the piano action. There were by this time only three companies in the whole of Europe manufacturing piano actions (in effect, the working parts from the key to the hammer). The British piano industry had rationalized production so that all the manufacturers save two were using actions manufactured by central suppliers – either Herrburger Brooks, the American-owned company, or British Piano Actions.

In the late 1950s it transpired that the American company had bought the French manufacturer of piano actions and was now attempting to buy British Piano Actions – which would have meant that the whole industry, except for the two companies still making their own actions, would be dependent on a single supplier – virtually a world monopoly.

British Piano Actions was in a 'depressed area' – Llanelli, South Wales. The British Government was persuaded that to allow the company to close would mean widespread unemployment. Alfred Knight therefore formed a consortium of piano makers and suppliers round the world. This included Paling and Company Limited of Australia, Heintzmann and Company Limited of Canada, Pratt, Read and Company of America, the Bothner Polliack group of companies of South Africa, and Beale and Company of Australia, with Alfred Knight Limited of London.

Pratt, Read of America were the largest piano action manufacturers in the world, and they offered technical assistance.

The BPA factory at Llanelli was saved, with its 26000 square feet of factory space, and capability of making 400 piano actions a week, the majority being exported.

Subsequently the South African member of the consortium became Phil Morkel, controllers of Pianoforte Manufacturers of South Africa; and Beale and Company became the sole Australian member. This modest factory in South Wales now supplies the world with piano actions.

A New Confidence

There are about 5000 working parts in each piano. The character of every piano depends on the interrelation of three factors: men, materials, and machinery. All were changing, in the difficult postwar years, and it became clear to the British piano makers that they must associate more closely. They could be competitive without the cut-throat competition that had brought such desolation, with companies closing down, merging, and craftsmen being thrown out of work.

Sidney Hurren, as secretary of the Piano Manufacturers' Association, played a key part in this. As a young man he had worked for Brinsmeads. Subsequently he became head of the acoustic department of the London College of Furniture, and organized a block-release course within that department where apprentices from all the piano-making companies could learn their trade (inheriting the tradition of the former course at the Northern Polytechnic). Sidney Hurren was also a founder of the Institute of Musical Instrument Technology, and it was in his time at the Piano Manufacturers' Association that the annual Frankfurt Fair, an international forum of piano makers, was inaugurated.

Apprentices were not to be attracted into piano-making by financial rewards, though the pay improved over the years and there was no longer the insecurity of lay-offs each spring. But the trade found that young men were still growing up with an appreciation of craftsmanship, and of the satisfaction of making a musical instrument.

Materials too were changing. But some remained consistent. The wood of the soundboard, which provides the piano with its peculiar resonance, had still to be carefully chosen and matured.

The best soundboard wood – defying analysis to explain why – was still Romanian spruce, from those Balkan and Eastern European forests from which the classical violin makers of Cremona, the Amati, Guarneri and Stradivari families chose their wood. Sitka spruce from Canada has been found to have scarcely inferior quality.

The iron frame was now standard. Few wooden-framed uprights were produced after 1905, straight-stringing went out of use, and the conventional upright became the fully-iron-framed overstrung piano that even in the thirties had been considered a 'luxury' model.[1]

The casting of an iron piano frame is a difficult and skilled operation, since the shape is complex and the mix requires a high proportion of air to give the frame the necessary inert and rigid quality. Booth and Brooks of Norwich make the large frames for grands; upright frames are made by the Crown Foundry of Northampton, which has modernized its production to specialize in this trade.

An exception is Fred Saffell, whose business interests include a foundry which casts frames for Barratt and Robinson. That company is made further self-sufficient by manufacturing its own wrest-pins and actions. The Bentley Piano Company in Gloucestershire also manufactures its own actions, but there Douglas Grover imports wrest-pins from Japan, finding that the quality is more consistent and delivery dates better kept than he has found in Britain. Ivan Zender also felt it desirable to be self-sufficient and in 1965 bought the firm of W. G. Diggins, manufacturers of piano parts in Edmonton.

The takeover of British Piano Actions by an international consortium led by Alfred Knight led to a radical redesign of the standard piano action made by that company, introducing plastic

---

1. What happened to all the thousands of wooden-framed uprights? The *Guinness Book of Records* (1973) contains this entry:

'The record time for demolishing an upright piano and passing the entire wreckage through a circle 9 ins (22·8 cm.) in diameter is 2 min 26 sec by six men representing Ireland led by Johnny Leydon of Sligo, at Merton, Surrey, England on 7 Sept 1968. The Robin Hood Karate Club of Sherwood, Nottinghamshire smashed a piano with bare hands in 41 min 29 sec on 10 Mar 1973.'

It seems improbable that either piano had a full iron frame.

components in association with wood. At this time plastics still had a poor reputation, dating back to the early days in the thirties when the first objects made of primitive plastics tended to be brittle, and to break, crack or discolour. After the war the plastics industry expanded rapidly and the market was flooded with cheap and often highly coloured objects, mainly for the kitchen, some of which melted at a low temperature over heat. For a period, then, plastics tended to be associated with cut-price and shoddy goods: certainly no traditional craftsman would associate himself with them.

Alfred Knight recognized the great potential of these new materials, and their advantage to the piano trade not only as an alternative to wood in some uses, but as a better alternative because stronger and not liable to changes in humidity and temperature. He personally began a research programme to redesign the piano action using plastics.

He spent time making improved jacks and flanges by hand, and then in association with a plastics manufacturer prepared the moulds for these parts. He found that nylon impregnated with glass fibre and graphite ensured the necessary strength for the frictionless parts. It was found that the more burnished these plastic parts became, the better was the potential repetition in the action – so that today this part-plastic, part-wood action is capable of about 1000 repetitions a minute if correctly set up and adjusted. At this time Diakon sharps (black notes) were added, and subsequently the development of a non-staining white plastic that did not discolour was used for the keys in place of the traditional ivory, which had become rare and expensive and dis-coloured in use.

The criterion for this redesign was efficiency, and not solely or mainly economy. 'Where the wood did a better job, we still kept the wood; where the plastic did a better job, as in the jacks, we used plastic,' Alfred Knight explained. The outcome was an excellent action. Some other manufacturers waited to see how Alfred Knight succeeded when he marketed this action in his own pianos, before they adopted them for their own. Soon afterwards the Knight Piano Company won a top American prize for piano manufacture (Mr Knight, entirely through his own persistent ambassadorship, was one of the few British manufacturers to build up a substantial export market in the United States). The remainder of the trade was convinced, the composite plastic-and-wood action revived the fortunes of British Piano Actions in Llanelli and became a standard for the trade. At Barratt and Robinson, Fred Saffell recognized the disadvantage of trying to tune a piano when the tuning pins were placed at the back in the miniature layout and introduced an action in which the tuning pins were at the front of the piano just underneath the keyboard. He too was introducing modern materials, adding plastic bushing and a 'floating centre' (both invented by his colleague C. H. Wehlau) to withstand climatic extremes.

Alfred Knight went on investigating new materials and adapting them for the piano trade. In 1974 he perfected a fibre bush into which the tuning pin fitted. The new bush proved to have a holding purchase of 30000 lb, while the traditional wood bush had a tension of about 6 lb. The tuning pin could thus be held rigidly, and be guaranteed not to slip with changes in humidity or temperature.

The trade's wartime experience of heat-resisting glues, with later improvements, led to the general use of laminated wood for piano cases. In the nineteenth century Theodore Steinway had devised this method of perfecting the curving cases of his concert grands, but it was an expensive and time-consuming process for more modest instruments. Now it was generally used, with finishing veneers in a variety of woods for different markets.

Teak became the most popular finish for the British home market – oiled teak for the sophisticated South of England, polished for the North (and for New Zealand). Mahogany is the favourite finish in France and Germany; Switzerland prefers walnut. Though Scandinavia likes a 'natural wood' appearance, the rest of Europe has traditionally chosen a high gloss polish for pianos as for furniture. Ivan Zender noted that European furniture manufacturers were using polyesters to achieve a glass-like finish. He introduced polyester finishes to the British piano trade, and they were swiftly taken up.

The essentials of the piano were unchanged; but many of the materials were vastly different from anything the older piano makers had imagined. With actions from British Piano Actions or Herrburger Brooks, and other parts from suppliers such as

Fletcher and Newman, the British upright was a much more standardized instrument.

Factory methods also changed. Electronic machines were introduced to weld veneers using synthetic resins, to notch and drill the wrest-pin bridges – all with a precision that was previously impossible. Yet the strong element of human craftsmanship was not extinguished. Regulators were needed to set up the action accurately, stringers to fit the strings, tuners to perfect the complex harmonics that make up the piano tone. Despite all the modern innovations, it is on these skills that the quality of the piano rests.

There were a few more changes in the structure of the piano industry to come. When William Evans, C.B.E., retired in 1959, the Challen company ceased independent manufacture of pianos. The name went first to the Brasted Brothers; and when in 1970 they too ceased independent manufacture, the Challen piano went to Fred Saffell at Barratt and Robinson, while Kemble and Company continued to make the Eavestaff piano.

In 1963 George Rogers and Sons, one of the most successful of the Victorian piano-makers but subsequently in limbo, was bought by Ivan Zender and Herbert Lowry. With Herbert Lowry as director, the company set out to restore the firm's historic reputation with smaller uprights of traditional quality. Mr Lowry had been born in Berlin, and worked for his father's company, Steinberg, in that city. He left Hitler's Germany in 1936 and joined the piano trade in Britain, where he worked until 1940. He served with the British Army throughout the war in the Armoured Corps, and ironically was one of the first British soldiers into Berlin when it fell. Subsequently George Rogers and Sons incorporated another traditional name, Hopkinson, and became agents for the Steinberg piano.

In 1963 it seemed appropriate to emphasize the high standard of quality then attained by the British upright piano. As piano buyer for Harrods, Stanley Murdoch asked W. Danemann and Company to make 'the best upright piano in the world'. This piano was made in the Danemann factory at Northampton Street, Canonbury, that the company had occupied from its foundation in 1892. The project, named HS2, stimulated the whole company led by the directors Edgar and Tom Danemann, sons of the founder William Danemann.

William Danemann had trained as an architect and was a skilled and meticulous draughtsman (as well as a keen amateur photographer). His skill led him first to the design of piano cases; and later in 1892 to found his own piano-making company. His son Edgar, who with another son Tom has managed the company for many years, has spent his life working on tone production, through complex mathematical calculations, the exact measurement of the soundboard, the height and width of bridges, and the selection of the right type of timber.

Today Edgar Danemann may still be found from early in the morning in overalls working on the factory floor with his fellow craftsmen, who include some older workmen whose whole experience has been with the company, together with a leavening of youngsters learning the trade.

To them all the HS2 became the 'out of this world' piano. It was based on the classic and tried Danemann upright, but refined to a high degree by the use of the very best materials. The back is of Canadian silver spruce instead of the usual European softwood. The soundboard is of Romanian pine, grown at medium altitudes with the individual boards matched in texture, colour and evenness of grain. The ideal density is used of seventeen annual rings to the inch, and the graduated thickness of the finished board is from 10 mm in the treble to 8 mm in the bass. The bridges are carved by hand, a process requiring 176 separate carvings. The frame is of heavy duty iron, finished in bronze. The wires are from Scotland.

The case is of prime African mahogany, veneered with a crossing veneer of 1 mm mahogany which is again crossed with the final veneer of mahogany, French walnut or sappy walnut for an ebonized finish. All edges are veneered to match, and the normal six-week polishing period is doubled to three months.

Each key of the HS2 piano is covered in a continuous length of '16 cut' ivory, to avoid the usual key-join. The action is regulated and adjusted several times after heavy tests during the three months' settling period. A third or 'practice' pedal is fitted as standard, to reduce the volume for practising.

When the Danemann brothers resumed piano manufacture after the 1939–45 war they took a deliberate decision to concentrate on quality rather than the mass market. The HS2 piano is a tribute to that policy, as are the standard uprights produced by the company and also the grands from 4 ft 3 in. to 6 ft 8 in. and a full-scale Concert Grand of 9 ft. Danemann grands are to be found in twenty-seven British Embassies and High Commissioners' offices in all parts of the world. Several thousand solidly built Danemann school pianos are in London's schools, as a result of a series of tone-tests conducted on unmarked pianos by musicians for contracts apportioned by the London County Council and then the Greater London Council. It gave the Danemanns particular pleasure when in one such test their pianos were placed first, second and third.

Kemble and Company was still expanding. Michael Kemble had died in 1962, but the company was ably directed by his former partner Victor Jacobs aided by the Kemble sons Robert and Stanley, and the Jacobs son Denzil. In 1964 the company took over the famous names of John Brinsmead and Cramer and Company. The factory in Stoke Newington was becoming uncomfortably crowded, and the directors decided to look outside London. Emulating Alfred Knight, who had moved successfully to Essex in the previous decade, Kemble and Company chose a new factory at Bletchley, Buckinghamshire. It was a considerable challenge to move such an enterprise, and there was some doubt whether the Londoners who comprised the work-force would wish to leave their home town. In the event, 70 per cent of them chose to go to Bletchley, led by Miss Mabel Mack. Miss Mack had joined the company nearly fifty years earlier, and from being secretary to Victor Jacobs had become Company Secretary. Victor Jacobs was able to approve the change before his death in 1970.

Kembles found that the 'new town' situation was no hindrance in the recruitment of enthusiastic younger workers. The company also became agents for the Yamaha piano, being imported from Japan.

In Lewisham, Robert Morley and Company became agents for the Russian Estonia pianos, grands and uprights. This was partly because in 1969 the company had incorporated the family firm of harp makers, previously in Kensington; and while concert harps are no longer made in Britain, they are imported from the Russian company manufacturing them in Leningrad.

The British piano industry had always enjoyed a considerable export trade, and in the years immediately after the war had been obliged to live on it. But gradually more and more countries began to set up their own piano factories. Some of the British companies had licensing arrangements or were exporting pianos in knock-down form for assembly abroad (Knights had licensing arrangements in the United States, South Africa and Australia, and sent parts to Holland and Germany for assembly and distribution within the Common Market countries). But others felt acutely the tariff walls that grew up as a result of political changes. In 1961 South Africa's departure from the Commonwealth, and in 1962 the virtual closure of the New Zealand market (which had hitherto been supplied almost exclusively from Britain) meant that British manufacturers had to fight harder for outlets.

In 1968 the piano makers organized a British Piano Trade Mission. Eight leading manufacturers led by Denzil Jacobs of Kemble and Company (as immediate Past President of the Piano Manufacturers' Association) spent seven weeks touring the Far East and Australasia. They visited Hong Kong, Singapore, Bangkok, and Australia west to east. With Denzil Jacobs, the group consisted of Douglas Brasted (Brasted Bros. and W. G. Eavestaff and Sons), Jack Codd (Whelpdale, Maxwell and Codd), Richard Grover (the Bentley Piano Company), Robert Kemble (Kemble and Company), Douglas Morley (Robert Morley and Company), Geoffrey Newman (Fletcher and Newman), and Russell Taylor (Barratt and Robinson).

This adventurous tour produced a quantity of new orders that were to prove a healthy basis for the trade's expansion in future years.

It also proved to those who took part the advantages of friendly association. For the participants long remembered the conviviality of the trip as well as its commercial success, and they recall that as they were dealing with the same agents in each city, they devised a rota system so that each of them would have a chance to 'go in first'. In spite of the business rivalries between them, the mission was conducted in a thoroughly amicable spirit and concluded without any notable friction and in a mood of general optimism.

On the night of 6 May 1964 the Chappell store and offices at 50 New Bond Street, that home of British music for a century and a half, burnt down. The venerable Louis Dreyfus watched the flames sadly. He had bought the business in 1929, partly out of the profits from an acute investment in musical comedy – he had invested £200 in the *Chocolate Soldier*, the immensely popular musical made out of Bernard Shaw's *Arms and the Man*. He determined to rebuild the store, and though he did not live to see it completed (Louis Dreyfus died in 1966 at the age of eighty-nine, leaving a personal fortune of over £1 million), the Chappell Music Centre[1] opened in February 1967. It was designed by Michael Rosenauer, and an ornament of the front of the shop was a 40-foot long shining metal sculpture by Stephen Gilbert, the grandson of the sculptor of Eros, Alfred Gilbert.

It was a Music Centre for the latter half of the century. The front of the shop, open to the street, was given over to records; sheet music and pianos were to be found in smaller enclaves further within. The sounds to be heard spilling into Bond Street were more likely to be the Beatles than the Royal Philharmonic Orchestra.

For this was the decade of youth, when every other small group of youngsters met together, bought guitars, and set out to emulate the success of the four young men from Liverpool. Playing the guitar required skill, but many found they were prepared to practise when the prospect of fame and fortune beckoned.

But the Beatles were unusual for their period because Paul McCartney and John Lennon were composers; and their songs were tuneful and romantic enough to be taken up by greater singers. Paul McCartney was also a pianist, and in the Beatles' film *A Hard Day's Night* (1964) there was a rehearsal sequence in which a Knight piano was featured. With the speed at which fashions change in the youth cult, the pop world moved out and onward into the exploration of electronics in an orgy of amplification, radiophonics and Moog Synthesisers. The electronic keyboard came into vogue (Monington and Weston began to manufacture electronic organs). The new primitives favoured

1. The Chappell Company was purchased by the Philips Record Company of the United States in 1968 for a reported £17½ million.

primary colours and simple lines. Pop art became influential, hitting a peak in 1967, the year that colour television was first introduced in Britain (Zender produced pianos in glossy polyester finishes in white, yellow, red and orange, as well as black, and sold them in quantity).

But the conventional piano was still popular through the whole spectrum of music. It was one of the basic instruments of jazz, appreciated through the gramophone, radio and later television. There were the rags of Scott Joplin, the New Orleans jazz of 'Jelly Roll' Morton, the jazz pianos of Earl Hines, Teddy Wilson, Fats Waller and Oscar Peterson. There were the famous pianist-bandleaders Duke Ellington and Count Basie. Britain provided the American jazz world with two notable pianists, both blind – Alec Templeton, and the Battersea-born George Shearing.

A wide audience enjoyed the playing of Eileen Joyce, the Tasmanian pianist who made her home in England and delighted audiences by her custom of choosing a different dress to match each concerto. Cyril Smith and Phyllis Sellick became popular double-concerto pianists; and after Cyril Smith was paralysed in one hand by a stroke, several three-hand concertos were specially written for them. In London, Artur Rubinstein was a welcome visitor who packed concert-halls with his exquisite playing well into his eighties.

The audience was there, broadened and enlarged and made more knowledgeable and enthusiastic by the greater availability of good music through the media. But an increasing number of people, and particularly young people, became attracted enough to music to want to perform it.

In schools, music began to be taken more seriously. Learning to play a musical instrument had for years been an 'extra', to be submitted to, grudgingly and at extra cost outside normal school hours. Music lessons were often dreary recitals of tedious folksongs. The new vitality of school music was symbolised after 1948 by the National Youth Orchestra of Great Britain, founded by Dr Ruth Railton, which brought together the best young players to rehearse and then to give concerts to public acclaim.

Many other school orchestras were formed, notably the Leicestershire Schools Symphony Orchestra.

In 1963 Miss Fanny Watermann, the Leeds piano teacher, in association with the then Countess of Harewood (the former concert pianist Marion Stein, now Mrs Jeremy Thorpe) founded the Leeds International Pianoforte Competition, with the support of I. Jack Lyons. The competition was to be held in Leeds every three years, and offered to pianists under the age of thirty a first prize of £1000 and engagements at the Royal Festival Hall in London, the Edinburgh Festival and the Leeds Triennial Festival.

The first competition was chaired by Sir Arthur Bliss, Master of the Queen's Musick, and proved a triumphant success, rivalling in international significance the Van Cliburn contest in the United States and the Georges Enesco in Bucharest.[1]

The Leeds competition is now so highly regarded that in 1972 there were ninety-five competitors, and preliminary 'knock-out' competitions were held throughout Russia to establish the Russian entries.

Interest in classical piano in Britain has further been encouraged by the publicity given to two Britons who within a decade won the top piano prize in the world. In 1962 John Ogdon, who studied at the Royal Manchester College of Music, shared the Tschaikowsky Prize in Moscow with Vladimir Ashkenazy. In 1970 John Lill, a Leyton factory worker's son who studied at the Royal College of Music in London from the age of ten, shared the Tschaikowsky Prize with Vladimir Krainev.

None of them is known to be as idiosyncratic about pianos as the Canadian virtuoso Glenn Gould, who astonished the world on

1. The Leeds International Pianoforte Competition has been won by:
1963 1. Michael Roll (17), UK.
      2. Vladimir Krainev (19), USSR.
      3. Sebastian Risler (21), France.
1966 1. Rafael Orozco (20), Spain.
      2. Victoria Postnikova (22), USSR. and
        Semyon Kruchin (19), USSR.
      3. Aleksei Nasedkin (23), USSR.
      4. Jean Rodolphe Kars (19), Austria.
1969 1. Radu Lupu (23), Romania.
      2. Georges Pludermacher (25), France.
      3. Arthur Moreira-Lima (29), Brazil.
      4. Boris Petrushansky (20), USSR.
1972 1. Murray Perahia (25), USA.
      2. Craig Sheppard (24), USA.
      3. Eugene Inkjic (25), USA.

concert tours in the late fifties by his dramatic appearance on the concert platform. Winthrop Sergeant wrote in the *New Yorker*:

He gives the impression of a man subduing a piano by jujitsu. He staves it off with upraised feet, pummels it, feints with elaborate motions that seem designed to attract its attention, recoils from it as if it were a hot stove, beats time with one hand while playing with the other, and croons the music, inaudibly but very visibly, throughout the performance. But none of his physical flamboyance enters into what one hears.

Gould, possibly finding that the variations of piano touch and tone were more than he could bear, stopped playing in public early in the sixties and settled for making superlative recordings and an occasional television appearance.

Gould, it was reported, relied on an 1895 Chickering grand at his family's lakeside home by Lake Simcoe, a piano on which he had played from boyhood. Later he discovered a Steinway grand – in the Steinway showrooms in New York – that was marginally wider in keyboard construction than the norm (by three-eighths of an inch) and which had a 'tighter' and 'more puritan' feel than most pianos. Gould paid large sums of money to have this piano transported round the United States for his recitals. Then, as it was perceptibly becoming tired, it was rebuilt; and subsequently Gould found a German-built Steinway that suited him. It is perhaps the most remarkable pursuit of piano character recorded in history.[1]

The expansion of music in schools, concurrently with a substantial schools building programme and more Government investment in education, meant that education authorities in Britain were able to spend more money on pianos. In the forties and fifties education authorities had ordered second-hand pianos in quantity; from 1960 they began to commission school pianos to be built for them. The result was that a large market was created and manufacturers filled it; most piano makers produced school pianos, and considerable numbers were made for schools, colleges and universities. They were much better pianos than had previously been supplied, and were characterized by their solidity and reliability.

1. 'Glen Gould and "One-Seventy-Four" ', a profile by Joseph Roddy in the *New Yorker*, 14 May 1960.

Music began to explore new frontiers. Some composers found the romanticism of the nineteenth century basically negative. If Stravinsky, as an anti-romantic, was nevertheless prepared to experiment by writing for the player-piano, so Shoenberg also reacted against romanticism. But Bartók (in his Allegro Barbaro) was probably the first composer to use the piano as a percussive instrument, though using folksong as a base. It is probably significant that Bartók wrote a sonata for two pianos and percussion.

The most inventive composer for the piano in the twentieth century (and one of the most controversial) has been John Cage. Invited to write a ballet score for solo piano, he was frustrated in searching for '*chewns*', and chose to turn the piano into a percussive instrument. He added various foreign bodies – screws, indiarubbers, nails – and instructed the performer to pluck the strings and beat the case of the instrument, with or without the use of the sustaining pedal.

Cage argued that the physical construction of the piano was part of its musicality, as he argued also that the setting of the piano was similarly important. Cage devised a piece called 'Four Minutes, Thirty-Three Seconds', in which the pianist is required to sit at the closed keyboard for precisely that time, doing nothing. Cage explained that any sounds heard during that time were the 'music' – whether coughs, the rustling of paper, or passing aircraft. The part played by the piano in this was clearly minimal, other than as a nostalgic symbol, and some dared to doubt the musical relevance of the whole business.

But the piano meant something to John Cage, who wrote: 'The piano is yet an undiscovered instrument.'

The increase in popular awareness of music, whether classical or pop, and the continued popularity of piano music on record, radio and television, together with improved and widespread piano tuition in schools produced a greater demand for the instrument. An instance of this interest was the unpredicted popularity of a television panel game about music, 'Face the Music', hosted by the pianist Joseph Cooper and featuring the 'dummy keyboard' or practising keyboard.

Many people became bored with watching others playing. They yearned to learn how to play. A passive but receptive audience turned active, and the market for pianos began to increase. The depression of the forties and fifties was superseded by a steady increase in demand.

The number of piano makers in Britain had been reduced to scarcely more than a dozen. Only two or three were making grands any longer: but more uprights were being made than for many years, and of better quality. The demand was found not only in Britain, but throughout the world. Alfred Knight found himself buying American pianos to satisfy the requirements of his Australian agents, while the piano showrooms of Britain filled with imported pianos because the British workshops could not turn out pianos fast enough. In the mid-seventies the trade was producing 20000 pianos a year, and crying out for the skilled workmen to make more.

A company used to advertise its course with the legend: 'They laughed when I sat down to play . . .' More and more people wanted to sit down and play, and were prepared to go through the tedious and time-consuming process of learning.

The British piano makers found themselves faced with an extraordinary demand. They set out to make the pianos to satisfy it, providing the pianist, professional or amateur, with the 'instrument that can sing'.

Bibliography

ARMY AND NAVY STORES Catalogue for 1907 (David & Charles Reprints, 1969)

AYRE, Leslie *The Proms* (Leslie Frewin, 1968)

BRINSMEAD, Edgar *History of the Pianoforte* (Simkin Marshall, 1889)

CLOSSON, Ernest *History of the Piano* (ed. Robin Golding) (Paul Elek, 1974)

COLT, C. F. Catalogue of the Colt Clavier Collection (Bethersden, Kent)

COX, Dr J. E. *Musical Recollections of the Last Half-Century* (Tinsley Bros., 1872)

DENT, E. J. 'Early Victorian Music', article in *Early Victorian England*, Vol. 2 (OUP)

DOLGE, Alfred *Pianos and their Makers* (California, 1911; reprinted by Dover Books/Constable, London 1972)

FREEDLAND, Michael *Irving Berlin* (W. H. Allen, 1974)

GARDINER, William *Music and Friends*, 2 vols. (Longman, 1838)

Grove's Dictionary of Music and Musicians 5th Edn, Ed. Eric Blom (Macmillan & Co., London 1954)

HARDING, Dr Rosamond E. M. *The Piano-Forte, its History traced to the Great Exhibition of 1851* (Cambridge University Press, 1933)

HIPKINS, A. J. *A Description and History of the Pianoforte* (Novello, 1896)

HOLLAND, Frank W. *Introduction to the Collection at the National Musical Museum* (British Piano Museum Trust, Brentford)

HUEFFER, Francis *Half a Century of Music in England* (Chapman and Hall, 1889)

LAMBURN, Edward *A Short History of a Great House – Collard & Collard* (London, 1938)

LOCHHEAD, Marion *Young Victorians* (John Murray, 1959)

LOESSER, Arthur *Men, Women and Pianos, a Social History* (Gollancz, 1955)

MAIR, Carlene (Ed.) *The Chappell Story, 1811–1961* (Chappell, 1961)

MICHEL, N. E. *Old Pianos* (Rivera, California, 1954)

MOSCHELES, C. (Ed.)   *Life of Moscheles with Selections from his Diaries and Correspondence* (Hurst & Blackett, 1873)

NEWTON, Ivor   *At the Piano – Ivor Newton* (Hamish Hamilton, 1966)

PIGGOTT, Patrick   *The Life and Music of John Field 1782–1837* (Faber and Faber, 1973)

RUSSELL, Raymond   *The Harpsichord and Clavichord* (Faber & Faber, 2nd edn 1973)

RUSSELL, Raymond   *Victoria and Albert Museum Catalogue of Musical Instruments: Vol. 1, Keyboard Instruments* (HMSO, 1968)

SCHOLES, Percy   *The Oxford Companion to Music* (OUP)

STEINWAY, Theodore E.   *People and Pianos, a Century of Service to Music* (Steinway, New York, 1961)

SUMNER, W. L.   *The Pianoforte* (Macdonald, 1966)

SYDOW, Bronislaw Edward (Ed.)   *Selected Correspondence of Fryderyk Chopin* (Heinemann, 1962)

WALKER, Alan (Ed.)   *Franz Liszt, the Man and his Music* (Barrie and Jenkins, 1970)

WILSON, Michael I.   'The Case of the Victorian Piano' (article in *Victoria and Albert Museum Year Book*, 1972)

Discography

The Collection of Historic Instruments at the Victoria and Albert Museum: Vol. 1 *Early Keyboard Instruments*

> (including 'Queen Elizabeth's Virginals')
> ORYX Collectors Series 1600 Stereo

Vol. 2 *Early Pianos*
> (including a Zumpe square piano, a square by Longman & Broderip, a 'giraffe' piano, and a Robert Wornum grand of 1875)
> ORYX Collectors Series 1811 Stereo

The Virtuoso Piano: Herz, Godowsky, A. Rubinstein, Thalberg, Hummel and Paderewski, played by Earl Wild
VANGUARD VSL 11038

A Graf piano made in Vienna c. 1820: Piano Concerto No. 4 in G major, Op. 58 and Fantasia, Op. 77 (Beethoven), played by Paul Badura-Skoda with the Collegium aureum on original instruments.

BASF/HARMONIA MUNDI BAC 3002

A Fortepiano of Mozart's time: Piano Concertos No. 26 in D major ('Coronation') K.526 and No. 8 in C major, K.246 (Mozart), played by Jörg Demus with the Collegium aureum on original instruments.

BASF/HARMONIA MUNDI BAC 3003

A Fortepiano of Mozart's time: Piano Concertos No. 12 in A major, K.414 and No. 27 in B flat major, K.595 (Mozart), played by Jörg Demus with the Collegium aureum on original instruments.

BASF/HARMONIA MUNDI BAC 3066

Beethoven's 'last piano' by Conrad Graf, Vienna, c. 1825: Piano Sonata No. 30 in E major, Op. 109, Piano Sonata No. 24 in F sharp major, Op. 78 and Rondo in G major, Op. 51 No. 2 (Beethoven), played by Jörg Demus.

BASF/HARMONIA MUNDI BAC 3063

Index

Compiled by F. D. Buck

Abel, C. F., 60
Abel, Friedrich, 30
Academy of Antient Music, 60
Adam, Gerhard, 121
Addison, Robert, 101
Adelaide, Queen, 73
Aeolian Company, 127, 129, 140, 147
Aeolian Hall, 147
Age of Iron, 55
Aggio, George H., 101
'agraffe', 56, 88
Akerman, William H. H., 102
Albert and Jones, 131
Albert, Prince Consort, 94: Great
    Exhibition and, 98, 104
Albrechtsberger, Johann Georg, 45
Alexandra, Queen (Princess of Wales),
    119
All-British Music Exhibition, 137
Allied Music Traders of Scotland, 144
Allison, Arthur and Company, 134
Allison, Ralph, and Sons, 134, 148
Allison, Robert, 100
Alma Tadema, Sir Lawrence, 114
Amati violins, 109, 169
Ambridge, Henry and Son, 134
American Piano Company, 127
Ampico system, 127, 147
Anacreontic Society, 72
Anderson, Mrs, 83
Antient Concerts, 60, 63, 93
Arnault, Henri, Duke of Burgundy, 18
Artaria and Company, 45
'Artists' Rolls', 129
Arts and Crafts movement, 117
Arts Council, the, 120fn
Ashbee, C. R., 117, 118
Ashkenazy, Vladimir, 178
Aspull, George, 91
Associated Piano Company, 157:
    formed, 151
Astor, George, 38, 39
Astor, Johann Jacob, 38, 39

Babcock, Alpheus, 87
Bach, Carl Phillipp Emanuel, 26, 37
Bach, Johann Christian, 30
Bach, Johann Sebastian, 30, 37, 44

60, 68, 87, 93: piano demonstrated
    to, 26, 27: popularity of, 166
Backers, Americus, 27, 28, 31
Backhaus, Wilhelm, 129
Baker and Knight, 154
Bali, Baron, 47
Banger, 43
Banks, Master, 80
Banstall and Sons, 134
Barkers, John, 137
Barnard, Sir Andrew, 73
Barnes Company, 130, 144
Barnes music shop, 156
Barnett, Samuel and Decca Co., 151
Barrat and Robinson, 134, 147, 148,
    157, 161, 169, 171, 172, 175
Barry, E. M., 103
Barry, Sir Charles, 103
Bartók, Bela, 180
Basie, Count, 177
Bates, Mr, 34
Battenburg, Prince Louis of, 138fn
Beale and Company, 167
Beale, Frederick, 95
Beatles, the, 176
Bechstein (piano company), 138, 139, 158
Bechstein, Carl, 117, 120, 123
Bechstein Hall, 120
Beck, 56
Beckford, Peter, 40, 92: Clementi and,
    41: Clementi's father and, 40
Beckford, William, 40
Beethoven, Ludwig van, 37, 45, 48, 50,
    51, 61, 65, 70, 74, 81, 87, 91, 94, 105, 146
Behrend, Johann, 55
Bell, Alexander Graham, 105
Bennett, John, 92
Bennett, Sir William Sterndale, 92, 93,
    109
Bentley Piano Company, 136fn, 160,
    169, 175
Berger, Adam, 49, 56
Bergonzi violins, 109
Berlin, Irving, 84fn, 85fn
Berlioz, Hector, 104
Berry, Nathaniel, 134
Billington, Mrs, 64
Blaise, William de, 167
Bliss, Sir Arthur, 178

Blüthner, Ingbert, 154
Blüthner, Julius Ferdinand, 120
Blüthners, (piano makers), 121, 138, 139, 144, 145, 154, 158, 164
Boosey, John, 111, 148
Boosey, William, 107, 111
Booth and Brooks, 169
Bord, Antoine, 88
Bosendorfer Hall, 121
Bosendorfer, Ignaz, 121
Bosendorfer, Ludwig, 121
Bothner Polliack group, 167
Boyce, George Pryce, 115
Boyd Ltd merge with Brasted Brothers, 151
Braham, John, 74
Brahms, Johannes, 159
Brasted, Bert, 150
Brasted Brothers, 134, 140, 150, 151, 163, 172, 175
Brasted, Douglas, 175
Brasted, Gerald, 11
Brasted, Harry, 150
Brasted, H. F., 134
Brasted, Percy, 150, 151: discovers Lundholm miniature piano, 155
Brasted, R. A., 134
Bredt, Alice Verne, 142
Breitkopf and Hartel, 37, 47, 51
Bricker, Miss, 30
Brinsmead, John, 100, 174
Brinsmead, John, and Sons, 104, 109, 110, 122, 134, 144, 168
Brinsmead, John, and Sons (1921) Limited, 143
British Broadcasting Company, 146, 148
British Broadcasting Corporation, 158, 159
British Industries Fair (1935), 157
British Piano Actions, 151, 167, 169
British Piano Trade Mission, 175
British polar expedition, 111
British retailers and pianola challenge, 128
Broadhurst and Isherwood, 79
Broadhurst, Mr, 80
Broadwood, Barbara (*nee* Shudi), 30
Broadwood, Capt. Evelyn, 11, 154, 163
Broadwood, Henry, 115, 116, 118
Broadwood, Henry Fowler, 89
Broadwood, Henry John Shudi. 111
Broadwood, James Shudi, 52, 89, 153
Broadwood, John, 30, 31, 33, 35, 52, 53 54, 56, 59, 84, 88
Broadwood, John, and Sons, 31, 52, 54, 65, 82, 92, 95, 96, 103, 107, 108. 113, 117, 118, 122, 123, 129, 130, 133, 136, 145, 160, 163
Broadwood, Thomas, 52, 65
Broadwood White and Company, 135
Brock, Bernard, 134
Broderip, Francis, 38 (*see also* Longman)

Brodmann, Joseph, 121
Brooks, T. & H., 100
Brooks (*see* Booth)
Brown, Godfrey, 159
Browning, Robert, 106
Bruni, Antonio Bartolomeo, 55
Buckingham Palace, music making at, 85
Bull, John, 19
Bull, Ole, 87
Burghersh, Lord, 66
Burne-Jones, Edward, 115, 116, 118
Burney, Dr Charles, 19, 22, 90
Busoni, Ferruccio, 120, 129, 141
Byrd, William, 19

Cadby, C., 99, 100
Cage, John, 180
Capo Tasto bar, 88
'Case of the Victorian Piano, The', 114.*fn*
Cavallo, Signor, 33
Cave, Walter, 117
Challen and Son, 134, 138, 149, 153, 163, 172
Challen, Charles, H., 134
Challen, Frank, 138, 149
Chamber organ (*see* harpsichord)
Chappell and Company, 62, 65, 105, 111, 120, 148, 176*fn*
Chappell and Company Inc., 148
Chappell, Arthur, 105, 106
Chappell, Emily, 63, 66, 105
Chappell Music Centre, 176
Chappell music publishing, 148
Chappell Piano Company, 148, 149
Chappell, Samuel, 62, 63, 66, 105
Chappell, Thomas Patey, 66, 105. 106, 107, 111, 148
Chappell, William, 106
Charlotte, Queen, 30, 34
Chickering, Frank, 109
Chickering, Jonas, 88
Chiroplast, 67
Chopin, Fryderyk, 46, 83, 85, 87–8, 89–90, 96, 141
Cipriani, G. B., 69
Clavicytherium, 17
Clementi and Company, 43, 45, 50, 51
Clementi and Cramer, 63
Clementi, Caroline, 49
Clementi, Muzio, 37, 40, 41–2, 43, 44–46, 48, 49–52, 56, 59, 61, 62, 63, 65, 67, 68, 70, 75, 77, 78, 90, 92, 100, 107, 148
Codd, Jack, 11, 145, 154, 175
Colcutt, T. E., 120
Cole, Sir Henry, 99, 115, 152
Collard and Collard, 53*fn*, 96, 104, 123, 130, 134, 148
Collard brothers, 75, 77
Collard, Frederick William, 43, 52: Clementi writes to, on soundboards, 53: Clementi's confidence in, 46
Collard, Mrs, 49

Collard, William, 65, 75
Colles, H. C., 146
Collins, William, Sons and Co. Ltd, 132
Colt Clavier Collection, 166–7
Columbia Gramophone Company, 152
Cooper, Joseph, 180
Corri, Domenico, 61, 62
Corri, Dussek and Company, 63
Corri, Philip Anthony, 61, 62
Corri, Sophia, 61
Cortot, Alfred, 111, 142, 148
Couperin, François, 21
Coward, Noël, 148
Cox, Dr J. E., 64, 68, 69, 86
Cramer and Latour, 63
Cramer-Chappell business, 65, 131
Cramer J. B., and Company, 65, 134, 143, 144, 174
Cramer, Jean Baptist, 41, 42, 43, 51, 61, 62, 68, 69, 70, 71, 78, 80, 82, 86, 90
Cramer, Wilhelm, 41
Crapes, 144
Cremona, school, the, 109
Crisp, Samuel, 24
Cristofori, Bartolomeo, 22, 25, 26, 27, 29, 31, 64
Crotch, Dr William, 15, 16, 66
Crown Foundry, 169
Crystal Palace Orchestra, 133
Curzon, Clifford, 143, 148
Cutner, Solomon (*see* Solomon)
Czerny, Karl, 79

Damper(s), 25, 26, 54: bevel action for 102 (*see also* 'over damper')
damping, 18, 23, 25, 32: mechanics of, 23: pedals, 32, 33: pull-knobs, 32: system, 18
Dance, George, 62
Dance, William, 61, 62
Danemann, Edgar, 172, 173
Danemann, Tom, 172, 173
Danemann, William, 134, 172, 173
Danemann, W., and Company, 161, 172
Davies, 43
Davies, Sir Henry Walford, 146: Foundations of Music series, 158
Davies, Jack, 156
Debussy, Claude Achille, 127
Demidov, Prince, 46
Dewrance, John, 97
Diakon sharps, 170
Diary of a nobody, The, 130
Dibdin, Mr, 30
Dickens, Charles, 106, 107
Diggins, W. G., 169
Dimoline, Abraham, 101
Ditanklasis, 58
Dixon, Cecil, 159
Dohnanyi, Ernst von, 129
Dolge, Alfred, 121, 130, 134
Dolmetsch, Arnold, 166

domestic instrument, 83–95
Doré, Gustave, 104
Dow, Alexander, 132
Dow, John, 132
D'Oyly Carte Opera Company, 107
Dreyfus, Louis, 148, 176·
Dreyfus, Max, 148
Dulcken, Madame, 83
Duo-art system, 127
Dussek, Jan Ladislav, 35, 62

Eavestaff, W. E., 134, 150–1
Eavestaff, W. G., and Sons, 134, 150, 175
Edinburgh Festival, 142, 178
Edison, Thomas, 105
Edward VII (Prince of Wales), 108, 119
Electrelle, the, 128
Elizabeth I, 18, 19
Elizabeth II (Princess Elizabeth), 156, 164
Ellington, Duke, 177
Enesco, Georges, 178
Enever and Steedman, 100
English inventions, 122
ENSA, 142, 161
Erard brothers, 55, 56, 75, 76, 77, 78, 81, 82, 87, 88, 95, 99, 104, 132
Erard, Jean-Baptiste, 55
Erard, Pierre, 75, 77, 82
Erard, Pierre Orpheus, 102
Erard, Sebastian, 34–5, 55, 56, 57, 75, 77, 122, 132
Erloedy, Count, 44
escapement, 25
Etude for Pianola, 127
Evans, William, 149, 152, 153, 158, 159, 164, 172
Exhibited definition, 96–118

Factory methods, 31, 172
Farnaby, Giles, 19
Faulkner, Kate, 116
Faversear, 45, 47
Field, John, 'Russian Field', 41, 42, 43, 44, 45, 46, 49, 86
Field, Robert, 42
Fischer, Johann Christian, 30
Fleming, 20
Fletcher and Newman, 151, 172, 175
Floriani, Benedetto, 19
'Forte and Piano' (*see* piano)
Fournier, Pierre, 143
Fox, G. E., 114
Francescatti, Zinc, 143
Frankfurt, Fair, 168
Frederick, King of Prussia, 26, 28
Freedland, Michael, 85*fn*
French Revolution, 55
Friederici, C. E., 26, 57

Gamble, James, 115
Gardiner, William, 15, 16, 29, 34, 37, 44, 66, 67
Geib, John, 38
General Strike (1926), 145
George I, 145
George III, 30, 62
George IV, 57, 160
George V, 111, 142, 145, 157
George VI, 156
German competition, 119
Gilbert, Alfred, 176
Gilbert, Sir William, S., 107, 113, 138
Gilbert, Stephen, 176
Giordani, Tommaso, 42
'Giraffe', the, 58
Gladstone, Mary, 85
Gladstone, William, Ewart 85
Glinka, Michael Ivanovich, 46
Gluck, Cristoph Willibald, 31
Godowsky, Leopold, 129
Godoy, Don Manuel de, 35, 36
Goodman, E., 107, 138
Gosling, Mr, 155
Gould, Glenn, 178, 179, 179*fn*
Goulding and Company, 62
Gounod, Charles, 106
Graham, William, 115
Gravicembalo col piano e forte, 22, 24
Gray, Dr, 33
Gray Thomas,, 27, 31
Great Depression, the, 153
Great Exhibition, (1851) 97, 98, 99, 114
Great Piano Test, the, 159–60
Great Reform Bill (1832), 83, 92
'Great Universal Exposition' (1867), 104
Greig, Edvard, 127
Greiner, George Frederick, 99
Greville, Fulke, 24
Grossmith, George, 130
Grossmith, Weedon, 130
Grosvenor, Gallery, 108
Grotrian, Friedrich, 121: goes to Moscow, 121
Grotian-Steinweg, firm of, 121
Grover, Douglas W., 136, 145, 169
Grover, Richard, 11, 145, 175
Guarnerius violins, 109, 169
Guido of Arezzo, 17
Guildhall School of Music, 106: dispute over German pianos, 125
Guthrie, 118

H & P. Limited, 151
Halévy, Jacques François Fromental Elias, 83
Hallé, Sir Charles, 105, 106, 108
Hambourg, Mark, 143
Hammer, George, & Company, 151
Handel, George Frideric, 34, 51, 60, 61, 87, 94: tuning-fork, 63, 64
Hardman Peck Company, 157
Harewood, Countess of, 178

Harmer, Joseph, 102
Harp and Crown, the sign of, 38
harpsicord (chamber organ), 15, 16, 17, 20, 21, 22, 23, 28, 35, 37, 54, 155, 166, 167: action, 24: double-manual, 29: Kirckman, 38: limitations of, 21: Longman and Broderip, 38: makers of, 28: Shudi, 38: stop-controls, 32: superseded, 33: types of action, 18
Harpsicord and Clavichord, The, 259*fn*
Harrods, 137, 172
Hartel, 48 (*see also* Breitkopf)
Haward, Charles, 19, 20
Haward, John, 20
Hawards, the, 20
Hawkins, Isaac, 58
Hawkins, John, 96
Hawkins, John Isaac, 58
Haydn, Franz Joseph, 34, 41, 42, 44, 94
Healey. Mr 148
Heberstreit, Pantaleon, 21, 22, 25, 26
Heintzmann and Company, 167
Helmholtz, Hermann von, 97
Hely-Hutchinson, Victor, 159
Henry, VII 18
Henry VIII, 18
Henschel, Helen, 159
Hermitage, George, 144
Herrburger Brooks, 151, 152, 167, 171
Herz, Henri, 77, 86, 87 90, 104
Hess, Myra, 142
Hewitt, Daniel, 96
Hicks, Henry, 131
Hicks, Henry and Son, 131, 186, 144, 145, 152, 155, 163
Hicks, H. Tom, 11, 150, 163
Hicks, William Henry, 131
Hines, Earl, 177
His Masters Voice, 146
Hitchcock family, 20
Hitchcock, John, 20
Hitchcock, Thomas I, 20
Hitchcock, Thomas II, 20
Hoef, Van der, 58
Hoeke, 47
Holderness, Charles, 101
Hopkinson, J. and J., 103, 104, 122, 128 135, 144, 172
Hueffer, Francis, 80
Hughe , Arthur 79, 152
Hummel, Johann Nepomuk, 34, 38, 41, 46, 79, 81, 90
Hund, Frederick, and Son, 101
Hunsdean, Lord of, 19
Hunt, Richard, 100
Hurren, Sidney, 168
Hyde, 43

Ibach, Johannes, Adolf 121
Ibach Limited, 121, 123
Imperial Institute, 120
Industrial Revolution, 54, 83
Inkjic, Eugene, 178*fn*

Institute of Musical Instrument
Technology, 168
Ionides, Alexander, 116
Irving, Henry, 117
Isherwood, Mr, 80 (*see also* Broadhurst)

Jack(s), 18, 22, 23, 170: secondary, 23
Jackson, T. G., 116
Jacobs, Denzil, 11, 174, 175
Jacobs, Victor, 143, 194
Jenkins, William and Sons, 101
Joachim, Joseph, 106, 108
Johnson, Dr Samuel, 24
Jones, John Champion, 101
Jones, Peter, 117, 122
Jones (*see also* Albert)
Joplin, Scott, 128, 177
Joseph II, Emperor, 41
Joyce, Eileen, 177

Kabul, Emir of, 116
Kalkbrenner, Friedrich, 68, 69, 87, 88,
89
Kars, Jean Rodolphe, 178*fn*
Kastner Auto-piano Company, 147
Kastner, Maximilian, 147
Kemble and Company, 143, 152, 154,
157, 161, 172, 174, 175,
Kemble, Michael, 136, 143, 157, 174
Kemble, Robert, 157, 174, 175
Kemble, Stanley, 174
Kentner, Louis, 143
King Brothers, 152
King's Theatre, 63
Kirckman, Jacob, 20, 28, 29, 38
Kirkman, Joseph, 53
Kirkman, Joseph, and Son, 99
Klengel, 49
Knight, Alfred, 11, 137, 144, 154, 165,
166, 171
Knight, Alfred, Limited, 167, 175
Knight Piano Company, 154, 170
Koenig, 26
Kohler, Irene, 159
Krainev, Vladimir, 178, 178*fn*
Kreutzer, Conradin, 80
Kruchin, Semyon, 178*fn*
Krumpholtz, Madam, 42
Kunz, Charlie, 157

Lambert, F. B., 134
Lamond, Frederick, 108
Landor, Walter Savage, 85
Latour, Francis Tatton, 62
Lauska, 48
Lazare-Levy, 142
Leeds International Pianoforte
Competition, 178
Leicestershire Schools Symphony
Orchestra, 177
Lennon, John, 176
Leschetizsky, Theodor, 143
Lewis, Sir Anthony, 158, 159

Leydon, Johnny, 169*fn*
Lieber, Mons, 53
Lill, John, 178
Liszt, Franz, 46, 70, 78, 79, 80, 81, 82, 83
86, 87, 88, 90, 91, 95, 107, 110, 141
Litolff, Henry, 77
Littleton, Henry, 108
Loesser, Arthur, 55*fn*, 119*fn*
Logier, John Baptist, 67
London, centre of musical instrument
industry, 38
London College of Furniture, 168
London International Exhibition (1872),
136
London piano makers: location of,
130–1, 133
Longman and Broderip, 38, 41, 43, 56
Longman, James, 34, 38: publishes
Clementi's music, 41
Longson, (*see* Squire)
Longson and Waddington, 152
Loud, Lord, 58
Louis, Prince, 48
Louis XIV, 22
Louis XVI, 55
Lowry, Herbert, 172
Luft, George, and Son, 100
Lukey, 38
Lundholm, Messrs, 155
Lupu, Radu, 178*fn*
Lush, Ernest, 159
Lutyens, Edwin, 117, 118
Lyon, C. E. 'Clarrie', 144, 154
Lyons, Jack, 178
Lyrichord, 24

McCartney, Paul, 176
Mackenzie, Sir Alexander, 108
McTammany, John, 127
Mack, Mabel, 174
Maffei, Scipione, 22, 23, 24, 26
Malcolm and Company, 132
Malcolm, John, and Sons, 151, 152
manufacturing methods, 151
Mara, invention by, 103
March, Alexander, 70
Marconi, Guglielmo, 118
Margaret Rose, Princess, 156
Marie Louisa, Queen of Spain, 35, 36
Marklovsky, General, 46
Marshall, Sir Herbert, and Son, 160
Mary, Queen, 142, 145
Mary Queen of Scots, 19
Mason, Rev. William, 27
Massart, 81
Matthews, W., 103
Maxwell, W. M. Y., 138
Meadmore, J. 'Jimmy', 144
Mechanical Orguinette, 126
Medici, Prince Ferdinand dei, 22
Melotone accenting device, 128
Melville, Sir James, 19
Men Women and Pianos, 55*fn*

Mendelssohn, Felix, 70 86, 87, 89, 90, 91, 94, 159
Merrick, Frank, 159
Metzler, George, 100
Meyerbeer, Giacomo, 81
Ministrelle piano, 157
Moira, 120
Moiseiwitsch, Benno, 111, 143, 148
Monington and Weston, 135, 136, 145, 157, 176
Moog synthesisers, 176
Moore and Moore 134, 144
Moreira-Lima, Arthur, 178fn
Morkel, Phil, 167
Morley and Company, 131
Morley, Douglas, 11, 133, 150, 166, 185
Morley family, 110
Morley, Henry, 133
Morley, James, 133
Morley, John, 11, 166,
Morley, John Sebastian, 133
Morley, John S. P., 133
Morley, Joseph George, 133
Morley Phillips music shop, 133
Morley, Robert I, 133
Morley, Robert, II 133
Morley, Robert, and Company, 133, 166, 175: becomes agents for Russian pianos, 174: history of, 132-3
Morley, William, 133
Morris, William, 114, 116
Mortimer's Directory, 30
Morton, 'Jelly Roll', 177
Moscheles, Ignaz, 51, 67, 70, 71, 72, 74 75, 76, 77, 78, 80, 87, 90, 95
Mott, Isaac Henry Robert, 102
Mountbatten of Burma, Earl, 138fn
Mozart, Leopold, 32
Mozart, Wolfgang Amadeus, 18, 26, 32, 34, 37, 40, 41, 53, 87, 94, 142
Muller, Matthias, 58
multi-piano concerts, 87
Murdoch, James, 152
Murdoch, John Gloag, 132
Murdoch, Murdoch and Company, 131, 132, 152
Murdoch, Stanley, 11, 172
Music Trades Association, 138

NAAFI pianos, 161
Napoleon, 43, 55, 56
Napoleonic Wars, 43-4
Nares, Captain, 111
Nasedkin, Aleksei, 178fn
National Training School of Music, 106
National Youth Orchestra of Great Britain, 177
Nelson, Admiral Lord Horatio, 44, 53
Neubaur, Frederic, 30, 135
Newman, Geoffrey, 175
Newman, (*see also* Fletcher)
Newman, Robert, 111
Newton, Ivor, 130, 161

Normandy invasion, 161
Norris and Hyde, 84fn
Northern Polytechnic, 168
Novello Oratorio Choir, 108

Ogdon, John, 178
'One-Seventy-Four', 179fn
Orchestrelle Company, 128
organ, 25: chamber (*see* harpsichord): electronic, 176: Snetzler, 15: Wurlitzer, 153
Orozco, Rafael, 178fn
'over damper', 31
overstringing, 97, 122, 123, 163
'own name', system, 130

Pachmann, Vladimir von, 108, 111, 141, 143, 148
Paderwski, Ignace Jan, 111, 141, 148
Paganini, Nicolo, 95
Paling and Company, 167
Pantaleon, 22, 24, 25, 26
Pape, Jean Henri, 88
Pape, Johann Heinrich, 88
Paris Conservatoire, 66, 64, 68, 81
Paris Exhibition (1878), 112, 136
Paris Universal Exhibition, (1900), 118
Parry, Hubert, 85
Paul, Czar of Russia, 44
Paxton, Joseph, 99
Peachey, G., 103
Peck, Wilson, 156
pedal keys, 102
Pepys, Samuel, 19, 20
Perahia, Murray, 178fn
Perry, Comdr Matthew Calbraith, 113
Peterson, Oscar, 177
Petrushansky, Boris, 178fn
Phelps, Edmond, 54
Philadelphia Centennial, the, 104
'Philharmonic Pitch', 63, 64fn
Philharmonic Society, 51, 63, 64, 68, 69, 70, 74, 80, 82, 87, 91, 92, 93, 107
Philips Record Company, 176fn
piano and harpsichord combined, 13
pianoforte (*see* piano)
Pianoforte Manufacturers of South Africa, 167
Piano Galleries Ltd, 120fn
'Pianola', 126, 127 (*see also* piano, player)
piano legs, frills on, 114
Pianomaker, The, 122, 123, 124, 125, 126, 139
Piano Manufacturers Association, 150, 164, 168, 175
Piano Publicity Association, 11, 150
Pianos and Their Makers, 121
Piatti, 106
Pistonola, 129
Player Piano Group, 128fn
Plenius, Rutgerus, 24
Pleyel, Camille, 89

Pleyel Hall, 89
Pleyel, Ignaz, 44, 45, 51, 87, 88, 120
Pleyel, Salle, 89
Pleyel, Wolf and Company, 104
Pludermacher, Georges, 178fn
Pohlmann, Johannes (John), 15, 16, 27, 28, 29, 30, 31, 56
Portland, Lady, 72
Postnikova, Victoria, 178fn
post-war rationalization, 163–7
Potter, Philip Cipriani Hambly, 65, 69, 70, 78, 86, 90, 91, 92
Pratt, Read and Company, 167
Pre-Raphaelite Brotherhood, 115
price-cutting activites, 137
Promenade Concerts (Proms), 111, 148
Puccini, Giacomo, 113
Pugin, Augustus, 115
purchase tax, 164
Pythagoras, 17

Queen's Hall, 111, 141, 142, 143, 146, 148

Rachmaninov, Sergie Vassilievich, 127
radio, competition of, 146–7, 153
Radio Show (1935), 156, 158
Railton, Dr Ruth, 177
Ravel, Maurice, 127, 159
Reith, Lord John, 146, 158
Ries, Ferdinand, 65, 68: at Liszt's London debut, 78: Beethoven's student, 65, 70: letter from Beethoven, 65
Riley, Athelstan, 116
Rintoul, John, and Sons, 134
Risler, Sebastian, 178fn
Roberts (see Smyth)
Robinson (see Barratt)
Robson, Tracey, 154
Roddy, Joseph, 179fn
Rogers, George, 160
Rogers, George and Sons, 135, 144, 172
Rolfe, William, 100
Roll, Michael, 178fn
Rook, 79
Ronald, Sir Landon, 125, 125fn
Rosenaur, Michael, 176
Rossini, Gioacchino Antonio, 79
Rothschild, Madame de, 76
Royal Academy of Music, 66, 67, 69, 70, 90, 91, 92, 93, 143, 158fn
Royal Albert Hall, 106
Royal College of Music, 106, 178
Royal Festival Hall, 166, 178
Royal Manchester College of Music, 109, 178
Royal Opera House, Covent Garden, 61, 74, 79
Royal Philharmonic Orchestra, 176
Royal Philharmonic Society, 63fn

Royal Warrant Holders list, 139
Roylance, Mr, 79
Rubinstein, Artur, 93, 98, 177
Ruckers workshop, 20
Rushworth and Draper, 144
Ruskin, John, 114
Russell, Raymond, 29fn, 38
'Russian Field' (see Field John)
Ryley, Edward, 84

St James's Hall, 105, 106, 108
Sacred Harmonic Society, 94
Saffell, Frederick, 11, 147, 148, 171, 172: designs miniature piano, 157: frame casting and, 169: President of Piano Manufacturers Association, 164
Salomon, John Peter, 60, 63
Schiedmayer of Stuttgart. 121
Schnabel, Artur, 111, 148
Schoene, 53, 55
Scholes, Percy, 35
Schroeter, Cristoph Gottlieb, 25
Schubert, Franz, 85, 108
Schumann, Robert, 93, 106
Scott, Baillie, 117
Selfridges, 137
Sellick, Phyllis, 177
Sergeant, Winthrop, 179
Shaw, Bernard, 176
Shearing, George, 177
Sheppard, Craig, 178fn
Sheppard, H. V. 'Bert', 144, 154
Sheraton, Thomas, 35, 36, 52, 113
Shield, 80
Shoenberg, 180
Shudi, Barbara (see Broadwood)
Shudi, Burkat, 20, 28, 29, 30, 31, 38, 53
Shudi and Broadwood, 30
Silbermann, Gottfried, 25, 26, 27, 28, 29, 31, 32, 57
Silencer, 128
Sinclair, Herbert, 122, 126
Smart, Sir George, 51, 60, 63, 64, 79
Smith, Cyril, 177
Smith & Wellstood, 122
Smyth and Roberts, 102
Solomon, 111, 141–3, 148, 157
Southall, William, 99
Southwell, William, 58
Spencer, John, and Company, 132, 134
spinet (virginal), 18, 19, 20, 155, 166
Spinnetti, Giovanni, 18
Spohr, Louis, 45, 63
Spontini, Madame, 76
Squibb, Leonard, 11
Squire, A., 122
Squire and Longson, 144, 152, 153, 154
Squire, B., and Son, 143, 144
Squire, Frank, 143
Squire William, Jr, 134
Stavenhagen, 108

Stein Andreas, 26, 32, 64: pedals and, 32: weathering soundboards and, 53
Stein, Marion, 178
Steinberg, 172
Steinway, Albert, 97
Steinway and Sons, 97, 98, 104, 105, 119, 138, 154, 158
Steinway, C. F. Theodore, 97, 98, 120
Steinway, Charles, 97
Steinway family, 95
Steinway hall, 98
Steinway, Henry Jr, 97
Steinway, John H., 11, 162
Steinway, Theodore, 171
Steinway, William, 97, 98
Steinwig, Heinrich Englehard, 95, 97, 121
Sterling, Sir Louis, 152
Stodart, Robert, 31, 57
Stodart, William, 57, 77
Stodart, William, and Son, 95, 99
Stradivarius violins, 109, 169
Strauss, Richard, 120
Stravinsky, Igor, 127, 180
Streicher, Nanette, 64
striking, mechanics of, 23
Strohmenger and Sons, 148, 149
Strohmenger, John, 128, 134
Stroud Piano Company, 136
Sullivan, Sir Arthur S., 107, 113, 138
'Surrender Value Contract', 130
Symonds, Miss, 79, 80

Tabel, Hermann, 20: apprentices, 28, 29
Tallis, Thomas, 19
Tassie, James, 36
Taylor, Russell, 175
Templeton, Alec, 177
Tennyson, Lord Alfred, 110
Thalberg, Sigismond, 83, 86, 87, 90
Theatre Royal, Drury Lane, 61
Thorpe, Mrs Jeremy, 178
Tomkinson, 122
Triumph Auto Company, 147, 148
Tschaikowsky, Peter Ilyich, 142, 159
Tschaikowsky Prize, 178
Tschudi, Burkhardt, 28 (see also Shudi, Burkat)
Trinity College of Music, 106

Van Cliburn contest, 178
Vatek, 40
'Venetian swell', 28, 29, 30
Vestris, Madame, 74
Victoria, Queen, 71, 85, 94, 108, 119
Victorian testimonials, 109
Vienna Conservatoire, 66
Villeroi, Duchess de, 55
virginal (see spinet)
Voysey, 118

Votey, E. S., 126

Waddington (see Longson)
Wadkin, Messrs, 160
Wagner, Richard, 109, 110
Waller, Fats, 177
Waterhouse, Alfred, 116
Watermann, Fanny, 178
Watts, Bernard, 158
Watts, Terry, 158
Watts, William Shepherd, 136, 145, 157–8
Weber, Carl Maria, von 74, 79, 87
Wedgwood, Josiah, 36
Wehlau, C. H. 171
Wellesley, Arthur, Duke of Wellington, 53, 73
Wellington, Duke of (see Wellesley)
Wellstood (see Smith)
Welmar company, 154, 160
'Welmar' name coined, 144
Welte Company, 127
Weser company, 85fn
Westminster, Duke of, 117
Whelpdale and Maxwell, 144
Whelpdale, Arthur, 138, 145
Whelpdale, A. W., 144
Whelpdale, Maxwell and Codd, 154, 160, 167, 175
Whelpdale, W. J., 138
White and Hicks, 131
White, William Braid, 122, 127
Whiteleys, 137
Wigmore Hall, 120fn, 141
Wilkinson, George, 59
William, IV, 73
Wilson, Michael I., 114fn, 118fn
Wilson, Teddy, 177
Witton, Witton and Company, 135
Wood, Father, 24
Wood, Sir Henry, 143
Wooley, T., 102
Workers' Educational Association, 146
Wornum and Wilkinson, 59
Wornum, Robert, 59, 103, 122, 151: 'tape-check' upright action, 59
Wrest-plank, 32, 56: bridge, 88, 97
Wurlitzer, Mighty, 153

Xylophone, 21

Yamaha, Torakasu, 113
York, Sylvia, 11
Ysaÿe, Éugéne, 120

Zender, Henry and Company, 135, 169, 172, 177
Zender, Ivan, 165, polyesters and, 171
Zender, Sydney, 135, 140, 165
zither, 21
Zumpe, Johannes, 27, 28, 29, 30, 31, 53, 55, 130, 156